Sermons On The First Readings

Series II

Cycle A

Tony S. Everett
Schuyler Rhodes
Stan Purdum
David J. Kalas
Timothy J. Smith

CSS Publishing Company, Inc., Lima, Ohio

Scripture quotations are from the New Revised Standard Version of the Bible, copyright 1989 by the Division of Christian Education of the National Council of the Churches of Christ in the USA. Used by permission.

Scripture quotations marked (The Message) are from The Message by Eugene H. Peterson, copyright © 1993, 1994, 1995, 1996, 2000, 2001, 2002. Used by permission of NavPress Publishing Group. All rights reserved.

Scripture quotations marked (KJV) are from the King James Version of the Bible, in the public domain.

For more information about CSS Publishing Company resources, visit our website at www.csspub.com or email us at custserv@csspub.com or call (800) 241-4056.

Cover design by Barbara Spencer

ISSN: 1937-1446

ISBN-13: 978-0-7880-2451-1
ISBN-10: 0-7880-2451-5

PRINTED IN USA

Table Of Contents

Sermons For Sundays
After Pentecost (Last Third)
Forward March
by Timothy J. Smith

Sermons On The First Readings

For Sundays In
Advent, Christmas,
And Epiphany

Did You See That Gorilla?

Tony S. Everett

To Judy,
my best friend and life partner

and

To Lisa, Lori, and Dan
our children and now our colleagues
in serving all God's children

To Sanders, Everett, and Finn,
our grandchildren, who invite us to see
the promise through new eyes

Your love and support continually reveal
the gorilla who dances among us forever

Acknowledgments

Several people have provided insights and encouragement during the preparation of this material.

Thomas E. Ridenhour, professor of homiletics, has offered exegetical and hermeneutical focus during times of confusion. His advice, as always, has been clear and precise; proclaiming the good news in each text. His humor and friendship continue to reflect light in the midst of darkness.

Jo Ellen White, faculty secretary, has labored faithfully and patiently in typing and revising this manuscript.

Former parishioners have shared their own experiences of God's presence and guidance in the midst of devastating challenges. They have invited me to see God at work and to perceive God's gift of the promised new reality in their daily lives.

The entire community of Lutheran Theological Southern Seminary continually demonstrates what it looks like, really, to see and to discern God's presence in the midst of an often ambiguous and overwhelming wilderness.

Introduction

Have you ever noticed that when we find ourselves in the midst of difficult and challenging situations we tend to focus all of our thoughts and behavior on getting out of them as quickly and painlessly as possible? The more out of control we feel, the more desperately we concentrate all of our attention, energy, and effort to escaping the pain and returning back to the way our lives used to be.

Then, if nothing we try seems to work, we simply shut down in helpless, hopeless resignation. We murmur, complain, and blame everyone and everything for our misery. Our perception of reality narrows. We ruminate on the same topic of choice: our despair and adversity. We yearn longingly for the cherishable past when it seemed like "God was in heaven and all was right with our world."

When this happens, most of us simply cannot see the promise and possibilities that God has placed in our midst. We focus exclusively on either escaping the present or pining for the past.

This also describes the contexts of the Old Testament lessons for the season of Advent, Christmas, Epiphany, and Transfiguration. God's people were experiencing difficult and potentially devastating circumstances. The texts in Exodus, Leviticus, and Deuteronomy present the challenges of wandering in the wilderness between Egyptian slavery and occupying the promised land. Here, God was forming and shaping them as God's holy and faithful people. It was no simple task for a fearful and landless band of wanderers. It was easy to look for quick relief by worshiping pagan deities and forgetting the Lord's promise and instruction.

In the early Isaiah passages (chs. 2 through 9) and in Micah, the nation was either threatened or under attack by Assyria and the surrounding nations. Here, too, it was easy for God's people to

17

focus their thoughts and actions on any means that might result in some relief from fear.

Jeremiah and the later Isaiah lessons (chs. 40-63) describe either the circumstances of living as exiles in Babylon or the enormous rebuilding and renewing tasks the exiles faced when they returned to a Jerusalem in chaos. Here also, perceptions often were narrowed to hopelessness and helplessness. God's people looked for immediate success and happiness and could see only devastation and despair. They anticipated order and discipline and saw only chaos and confusion.

Within each lesson God proclaims new reality. God's message is intended to expand their (and our) perceptions, and to focus on the good news of God's continuing presence and guidance in the midst of the most difficult situations. This is the essence of the preaching task.

Recently, I discovered a research project that illustrates the challenges and the opportunities for expanding perceptions of individuals and congregations. Psychologists, Daniel Simons and Christopher Chabris, have discovered that when the human brain focuses on one particular task, a complete view of the whole situation is significantly inhibited, or even completely ignored. They call the phenomenon "inattentional blindness."[1]

To demonstrate this, Simons and Chabris placed one group of volunteers in a room. Half of them were dressed in dark clothing; the other half were dressed in white. Then the psychologists gave some basketballs to these volunteers with simple instructions: When the light above the door is turned on, pass the balls around for sixty seconds until the light goes off.

A second group of volunteers was given the task of counting the number of times members of group one passed basketballs. During the experiment, someone dressed in a gorilla costume entered the room where the basketballs were being passed. He danced around for eight seconds and then left.

When the experimental minute was concluded, volunteers in group two were asked if they had observed anything unusual during their counting task. One half of the volunteers said that they had seen the gorilla. The other volunteers not only did not see the gorilla, they accused the psychologists of deception by secretly requiring the "gorilla viewers" to lie. Even when the psychologists played the video tape of the experiment that clearly depicted the dancing gorilla, those same volunteers declared that the tape had been altered. For members of group two, there was, in fact, no gorilla. Why? Because they did not "see" it.

Simons and Chabris have repeated this experiment with more than 10,000 volunteers, with the same results. Inattentional blindness is the tendency for a person or group to focus on one perception of reality to the exclusion of the complete picture ... *even when a gorilla is dancing in the midst of us all.*

Dear readers, there is a gorilla dancing in our midst; the good news of God's continuing presence and guidance for us and for all God's people. We might not always perceive it. Nevertheless, the writers of our texts not only see it, they proclaim it. As you wrestle with these Old Testament lessons allow the Holy Spirit to expand your perception of reality so that you not only may see God's good news, you will also proclaim it with passion.

— Tony S. Everett

---

1. Daniel Simons and Christopher Chabris, *Perception*, Vol. 28 (1999), pp. 1059-1074. See also by the same authors, "Gorillas in Our Midst" at HYPERLINK http://viscog,beckman.vive.edu/djs lab.

Is It Time Yet?

A popular skit at church camps involves about a dozen folks lined up side-by-side, looking anxious and frustrated facing the audience. Each person rests a left elbow on the right shoulder of their neighbor. Then, from left to right, each member asks, "Is it time yet?" When the question arrives at the end of the line, the last person looks at his/her wristwatch and responds, "No." This reply is passed, one-by-one each with bored sighs, back to the first questioner. After a few moments, the same question is passed down the line (left elbows remaining on the right shoulders). The last person checks his/her watch and says, "Yes!" When the response again reaches the head of the line, the group lets out a loud and collective sigh. They then change position, now with right elbows leaning on the left shoulders of each neighbor.

There is no real change here at all. The group is still in the same old place with the same old anxious, frustrated expectations.

Indeed, many of us may be facing the coming days before Christmas with this very same perspective: anxious, frustrated, expecting little other than the same old hassles and problems; hoping for nothing more than perhaps a moment of relief from the stress of the Advent season.

Is it Advent already? That means that we have only four weeks to plan the "perfect" Christmas program; prepare the "perfect" family celebration; begin endless shopping excursions to purchase the "perfect" gifts; decorate the "perfect" tree; and our list of "to-do's" is endless, spinning out of control. We desperately seek happiness while simultaneously we anticipate the same old frustration. Our lives seem as cluttered and crowded as the traffic jams around shopping malls. We have learned that expecting perfection usually results in experiencing rejection.

Is it time yet? Is it time to break this cycle of wishing and wanting perfection? Let's look at our first scripture lesson.

Our text in Isaiah emerges from a time of high anxiety, impatience, discouragement, and despair for God's people. Powerful Assyria was gobbling up smaller nations and heading toward an inevitable clash with Israel. Political infighting and corruption was widespread. Many religious leaders had forsaken the teaching of the Lord and were promoting alliances with other nations against Assyria.

In the first chapter of Isaiah, God declares, "I reared children and brought them up, but they have rebelled against me. The ox knows its owner and the donkey its master's crib; but Israel does not know; my people do not understand" (Isaiah 1:2-3).

God's people simply did not see the reality of God's continuing presence and guidance. Is it time yet? For them it was only time for the "same old, same old thing"... no real change, no real hope, just a collective group sigh as they anticipated only more of the same misery. Isaiah describes this attitude in chapter 1, verse 5: "The whole head is sick, and the whole heart faint." In other words, the mind only perceives more desolation. The will to perceive God's presence and promise for the future is exhausted.

As hall of fame catcher, Yogi Barra, once remarked, "The future ain't what it used to be."

Perhaps many of us feel the same way as we consider our own life experiences on this first Sunday of Advent. The same turmoil exists in the Middle East as it did in Isaiah's time. We see political and moral corruption all around us. We witness broken families, economic hardship, and hypocritical religious practices ... and we watch helplessly, hoping only for a small bit of comfort and another shoulder to lean on while any joy always seems to pass us by.

Is it time yet? Is it time for a real word of promise, a real word of hope from the Lord?

The answer — the Advent answer — is a resounding "Yes!" Look again at our text. Here in verse 1, Isaiah *saw* the word of promise. God expands Isaiah's perception to see beyond the corruption and desolation a new reality — God's reality. God is turning their understanding upside down and inside out. Or, as the great jazz singer, Al Jolson, often remarked, "You ain't heard nothin' yet, folks!"

Isaiah then proceeds to unfold God's promised future for us and for all God's people. In Hebrew, the language of the Old Testament, God's word is not simply a concept or collection of letters. God's word is a *thing*, a *force*, a *power* that can be seen and experienced.

And this word, in the "days to come" is a sure and certain Advent promise from God, not just to Israel, not just to you and me, but to all God's people.

First, it is a promise of peace to all nations: "They shall beat their swords into plowshares, and their spears into pruning hooks; neither shall they learn war anymore" (Isaiah 2:4). How can this be? In Isaiah's time, tiny Israel was on the brink of annihilation. Throughout the following centuries, wars and rumors of war were a very real part of daily existence. Sadly, it is true today. And yet, "in the days to come," in God's time, with God's promise, peace will be a reality. Is it time yet?

Yes, indeed! And yet, in spite of the tumult of wars, God's Advent promise is being fulfilled in our midst. Christ, the Prince of Peace has come, is coming, and will come again! Isaiah proclaims, in the days to come, the Word of the Lord will come from Jerusalem (Isaiah 2:3). Friends, that Word, that force, that power *was* made flesh and dwelt among us (John 1:14). That Word, God's own Word of peace, suffered and died on a cross for you, for us, for all nations, in Jerusalem. God's Word rose again in Jerusalem. Through the Holy Spirit, God's Word reaches all nations. This is perfection ... God's perfect plan of salvation for us and for all people.

Is it time yet? We still yearn for a time and space that is free from the stress and anxiety of daily living. During this season of the year, family tensions, economic stress, and every day worries seem to grow even stronger occupying our existence. And yet, it is time ... God's time. Isaiah's "days to come" are here. In spite of our stress and worry, Christ has come! Christ is coming! Christ will come again!

So then, what does that mean for us? Advent is a time of remembering that Christ has come. Advent is also a time of preparation for the "days to come," the celebration of Christ's birth and the promise that Christ will come again. Isaiah invites the people of God to "come, let us walk in the light of the Lord!" (Isaiah 5). That invitation is also given to us, today.

Advent is a time to remember how God has been present and active in our experience; times when we were certain of Christ's presence and guidance.

At the end of each day, the parents of Thomas (age seven) and Stephen (age five) always ask them what they remember most about their daily activities. After a day of riding their body boards on high ocean waves, their mother asked, "Boys, what good time did God give you today? What do you remember most?" Stephen declared, "I was flying for joy over those waves!" Thomas proclaimed, "I learned to ride over the waves on my knees!"

They got it! In family gatherings, choir rehearsals, Sunday school classes and committee meetings this Advent, share with each other those times, even scary times, in your life when you "just knew" that the presence and guidance of Christ both placed you on your knees and lifted you up to fly for joy beyond the worries of the day. Christ has come! Christ is coming! Christ will come again! Walk in the light of the Lord!

Is it time yet? The stores and commercials and calendars remind us hourly of what yet needs to be "done" for the holidays. There's never enough time to complete every task and still find a little rest in the too few days to come.

It is time ... God's time ... and the time is here. The Word can be seen on the cross, in the waters of baptism, and in the bread and wine of holy communion. God has given us God's own shoulder to lean on. God has already given us loving arms to keep us flying for joy on our knees through and beyond whatever turmoil we are facing.

The days to come have begun! God's perfect plan of salvation is happening now! It is time to celebrate! Amen.

From "Uh-oh" To "Ah-hah!" — An Axe, A Stump, And A Shoot

One hot summer day, a young pastor decided to change the oil in his automobile for the very first time in his life. He had purchased five quarts of oil, a filter wrench, and a bucket in which to drain the used oil. He carefully and gently drove the car onto the shiny, yellow ramps and eased his way underneath his vehicle.

Unfortunately, lying there on his back, all he could see when he looked up was a confusing mass of hoses, wires, and unknown metal objects of various sizes and shapes. Uh-oh! "I'll never be able to get through this," he moaned aloud. "I can't even find the oil pan or the plug. This filter wrench doesn't look like any other wrench in my tool box. Everybody will laugh at me now."

Suddenly he heard a tiny voice exclaim, "I won't laugh at you, pastor. Let me show you something."

The startled pastor quickly looked around and saw five-year-old Melissa, his neighbor, crouching down beside him. "My daddy lets me help him work on his car. This is what he showed me," she remarked as she edged her way beside the pastor. She then pointed out the plug. She showed him how to place the filter wrench. Then, with wise confidence far beyond her age, remarked, "Now, you do it for yourself." And he did. Ah-hah!

In the midst of a mess, "a little child shall lead them" proclaims Isaiah (11:6). In the midst of a hopeless, chaotic mess, often of our own making, God provides a vision of what God's promised salvation looks like. For the pastor, that vision took the form of a wise little girl. For us, on this second Sunday of Advent, that vision of salvation looks like a manger, a baby, a cross, and an

25

empty tomb. Christ has come! Christ is coming! Christ will come again! Advent is a time to prepare for God's promised vision of a new reality; a time to prepare for the birth of the little child who leads us.

Our text in Isaiah 11:1-10 is a wonderful and poetic description of God's glorious vision of promise to a people trapped in the midst of a frightening, terrible mess. Political corruption and moral depravity were common. Religious leadership was weak, and business was conducted dishonestly. Pride and arrogance characterized a false belief that God would protect the people no matter how flagrantly they sinned against God. Elders and government dignitaries wrote laws to oppress the poor and needy (Isaiah 10:1-2). Prophets taught lies. The people were left in confusion (Isaiah 9:15-16). Uh-oh!

Even though the Lord stirred up the Arameans and Philistines to attack, God's people did not return to their faith (Isaiah 9:13 cf). "For wickedness burned like a fire ... and the people became like fuel for the fire" (Isaiah 9:18-19). Uh-oh!

Finally, mighty Assyria became the instrument of God's wrath against a disobedient and unfaithful people. "The club in their hands is my fury! Against a godless nation I send him ... to take spoil and seize plunder, and to tread them down like the mire of the streets" (Isaiah 10:5-6). Uh-oh! Now that's a mess all right!

Assyria, the club, the axe, was indeed lying at the root of the trees (Matthew 3:10), cutting and destroying forests; reducing the northern part of the nation to stumps, brush, and thorns.

Is the axe at the root of our trees? Our behavior? Our priorities? Our promises? In the midst of our incredibly crowded schedules during Advent, do we ever experience the feeling of impending doom ... that everything might come crashing down on us with no time to stop the chaos from destroying us?

Have you ever locked your keys in your car? In the act of slamming the door you see the key in the ignition but cannot stop in time. Uh-oh! Chaos! And you did it to yourself. We all do.

So then, where's the good news in all the doom and gloom? Where is God's promise? Where is the "ah-hah"?

First, in just one day, God will turn back the Assyrian armies before they can overcome Judah and Jerusalem, its capital city (Isaiah 10:17 and 34). It happened. God promised to destroy the controlling bondage of sin in our own lives and in the lives of all people. It happened ... Christ has come! Christ is coming! Christ will come again! Here is the Advent promise! Here is God's "ah-hah!"

Second, the Assyrian axe did leave a "stump" of God's people remaining. The "stump of Jesse," the father of King David (1 Samuel 16:1 cf). The kingship in David's line remained safe in Jerusalem. Although only a stump of the great tree, Israel, remained, God's covenant of faithfulness to God's people remained steadfast and secure. Indeed, fear was still tangible. Enemies still surrounded the people. Discouragement was still a common experience. Nevertheless, God was still a very real and guiding presence in their midst.

After the horrific devastation of the gulf coastline of Louisiana, Mississippi, and Alabama by Hurricane Katrina in the fall of 2005, residents were overwhelmed by the enormity of destruction. The task of rebuilding and reclaiming their lives often appeared futile to them and, in fact, to the entire nation. Nevertheless, examples of hope and renewal, through many acts of kindness, heroic self-giving, and incredible generosity, were demonstrated daily. One sign in particular reveals the energetic and vital faith of the survivors and volunteer aid workers. Hanging in the hallway of Christus Victor Lutheran Church in Ocean Springs, Mississippi, was a large poster proclaiming "Katrina was an act of nature. What we do here is an act of God." "Ah-hah!"

Destruction of the gulf region was immeasurable. Nevertheless, a "stump" of hope remained strong in this God-given vision of promise and encouragement.

Today, this second Sunday of Advent, God gives us "discouraged stumps" a vision of God's promised love as we view the cross, the altar, and see God's gathered people surrounding us. "Ah-hah!"

Third, from out of that stump of Jesse, Isaiah reminds us, will come a shoot, a king from the line of David. Do you begin to see the Advent promise here? Can you begin to see God's vision of a new reality taking shape? Just what, or better, just *who*, is this shoot, this branch? Is it the remainder of God's faithful people in Judah? Is it to be an unnamed future king of Judah? Scholars are uncertain regarding Isaiah's specific reference. Nevertheless, this new shoot is the vision of new life sprouting from a mutilated, devastated, and discovered people ... in the midst of a mess. Today we see, in these words of Isaiah, the vision of God's promised upside-down and inside-out reality in the person of Jesus Christ, whose birth we prepare to celebrate.

For Isaiah, this new king from David's line and his descendants will be bearers of the Spirit of God ... a spirit of wisdom and understanding, of counsel and might, of knowledge and the fear of the Lord (Isaiah 11:2). These are not simply qualities of character. The gift of God's Spirit is intended to result in practical actions. This new king will discern and do God's will. He will not be deceived by false claims of morality, contrary to the corrupt and unfaithful actions of previous leaders. He will act on behalf of the poor and weak in society (Isaiah 11:3-5). Do you catch a glimpse of Jesus here? Does this sound anything like the Sermon on the Mount in Matthew 5-7?

Look on in this text as Isaiah describes the new order — God's upside-down and inside-out order of the coming kingdom of this righteous branch. In the new creation, natural predators will live in peace with their usual victims: wolves and lambs, leopards and young goats, lions and calves, bears and cows, babies and poisonous snakes, will live together in peace (Isaiah 11:6-9). Now what kind of world is that? What kind of vision is that anyway? When is this ever going to happen? Aren't our lives, our communities, our very existence barely hanging on in the midst of one giant mess? Are we not living in the midst of so many "uh-ohs" that any "ah-hah" seems beyond the realm of possibility in the far distant future?

Indeed, at the beginning of both verses 10 and 11 Isaiah uses the phrase, "on that day." The Advent message, God's Advent message for us today, is "that day" has already dawned. The shoot from the stump of Jesse has grown into a mighty tree of life, a sign to all the nations that God's new creation has already begun with the birth of a little child who leads us into life in God's upside-down, inside-out new kingdom.

"Uh-ohs" still exist and seek to overwhelm us. But God has given us the everlasting and eternal "ah-hah!" in that little child, that mighty king, our Savior Jesus Christ.

Christ has come!

Christ is coming!

Christ will come again!

Ah-hah! Now that is good news! Amen.

The Holy Way

Our text centers on God's promised action in the wilderness. Have you ever seen photographs of the wilderness areas in the land of the Bible; for example today's Israel, Palestine, Syria, Iraq, Iran? The wilderness is a rocky, dry, and barren space. In the same day, temperatures may vary from a blazing 100 degrees Fahrenheit to nearly freezing. Food and water are scarce. Wild beasts and even bandits prowl around seeking to devour unsuspecting travelers. The wilderness can be a very scary and lonely space. It's easy to get lost there, far from home with no hope, no help, and no support in sight. In the wilderness spaces of our lives, one can feel abandoned even by God.

In today's lesson, the people of God have been living as exiles in Babylon approximately 500 miles from their homeland. The mighty Babylonian army, under King Nebuchadnezzar, had conquered Judah, shattered the city walls of Jerusalem, and left the Jerusalem temple in ruins. As was the custom in those days, conquering armies would relocate thousands of leading citizens in order to prevent any organized rebellion. The only way home was through this vast, frightening, and overwhelming wilderness. Perhaps even God had forgotten them. Their hands were weak, their knees had grown feeble, and their hearts had become fearful. There appeared to be no hope, no help, and no way to be restored and renewed.

You know, sometimes it may seem as if we are also living in a wilderness — a barren desert bereft of all hope for deliverance. Our families and friends don't understand our fears. Our world is in chaos. If anything can go wrong, it does. Even the little things of daily life become insurmountable obstacles for our fainting hearts and feeble knees.

One Advent season, while shopping in a crowded mall, I noticed a group of young people walking the corridors, cheerfully chanting, "Shop 'til you drop! Shop 'til you drop!" My immediate, though silent, response was the "Bah, humbug!" of Ebenezer Scrooge. Exhausted and frustrated with the "busy-ness" of this season, I wanted to crawl into bed and pull up the covers until January second. In our wilderness, there is never enough time, never enough money, never enough understanding, and never enough love. Our hands are weak. Our knees have grown feeble. Our hearts have become so fearful (Isaiah 35:3-4) that a way out seems truly impossible.

Where are those scary, wilderness spaces deep inside your souls? Where are those spaces in which your hands weaken, your knees won't support you anymore, and your courage just surrenders? What traps you in the prison of doubt and broken dreams? What blinds your eyes from seeing God's presence or stops your ears from hearing God's promise? What closes your mouth from proclaiming the joy of the coming Christ Child? (Isaiah 35:5-6).

Just like God's people in exile, we have our own wilderness space. We are exiled in our own, personal "bah-humbug" experience, and each one of us yearns for a way through it.

Today, God promises that way. It is God's holy way through the very wilderness space in our souls. "A highway shall be there and it shall be called the Holy Way ... it shall be for God's people: no traveler, not even fools, shall go astray" (Isaiah 35:8).

Now, pay attention to the fact that in our text God does not promise to obliterate the wilderness. God never promises a magical, science-fiction-like teleportation from Babylonian captivity to Jerusalem majesty without the people ever setting foot on any part of the 500 mile journey back home through the wilderness. Neither does God promise a magic elimination of our wilderness experience.

Instead, God's "Advent instead," promises a new way, a holy way right through the core of the wilderness itself. God does not eliminate the reality of the wilderness. Instead God promised a new, transformed, and holy way of living within and walking through the wilderness.

For Isaiah, this promised holy way would be a decisive event, a turning point in the history of God's people. Their current captivity in Babylon was similar to their bondage of servitude in Egypt. In our text, Isaiah describes a new exodus through a new wilderness. The Lord is about to establish a new and faithful kingship in the world. Again, God will do this not by eliminating any and all wilderness space, but by 1) changing the very wilderness itself, 2) changing the way God's people perceive the wilderness, and 3) transforming the way God's people behave in the wilderness.

First, God changes the wilderness. "Waters and streams shall nourish the dry land" (Isaiah 35:6 cf). "The burning sand shall become a pool and the thirsty ground springs of water" (Isaiah 35:7). "Wild beasts and predators will not be found there" (Isaiah 35:7, 9 cf). "Lions and other predatory beasts will not live in the wilderness anymore" (Isaiah 35:9 cf). "In the wilderness, the glory and majesty of the Lord will be revealed for all to see" (Isaiah 35:2 cf).

Wilderness exists for us and for all God's people. God does not take it away. Yet, God changes its sheer terror and desolation by entering. Scripture reminds us that God's presence and guidance are revealed in wilderness. God finds Moses "beyond the wilderness" and guides Moses into a mission of delivering the Jews from bondage in Egypt (Exodus 3). On the wilderness journey from Egypt to the promised land, God renews his promise of everlasting fidelity and reveals the Ten Commandments as guides for faithful keeping of that promise (Deuteronomy 5-6). When Queen Jezebel threatened Elijah's life, he fled a day's journey into the wilderness. Here, God met a fatigued and despairing Elijah and gave him a rekindled spirit and a renewed mission (1 Kings 19). It was the Spirit of God who led Jesus into the wilderness to be tested by the devil (Matthew 4:1-11). God was present in the wilderness of Roman-occupied Judea in the form of a baby, born to a young couple spending the night in a stable (Luke 2).

The Bible is filled with stories of how God changes the wilderness by being present within it. Remember that! Write it on your hearts! God does not eliminate wilderness from our lives. God *changes* those scary spaces by being present within them.

Second, God not only changes the wilderness spaces themselves, God opens blind eyes that just can't seem to see God's presence in those times of overwhelming fear, anxiety, confusion, and doubt. God opens ears so stopped up that they are deaf to God's word of promise and guidance (Isaiah 35:5). God empowers those who view themselves as trapped in their own wilderness; disabled by their own fears. God will increase their energy and send them leaping like a deer along God's holy way (Isaiah 35:6). To those whose voices can only speak pessimistic, contagious, doom and gloom about their own wilderness, God will give songs of joy (Isaiah 35:6).

Those chaotic and confusing spaces still exist. However, God changes the way we see and experience them; from hopeless and helpless, to potential and possibility; from exhaustion and despair, to renewed energy and anticipation.

Perhaps you have heard this story about a children's Sunday school Christmas pageant. At the climax of the event, the older children were portraying the scene at the manger with shepherds, angels, wise men, and assorted animals gathered around Mary, Joseph, and the baby Jesus. Each three- and four-year-old child was given a letter to hold high above their heads ... intending to spell out the meaning of the season — "Christmas Love." Unfortunately, little Matthew, who was to hold up the letter "M" ("Just like the letter in my name.") raised his card upside down. The "M" became a "W." Laughter began to spread throughout the audience. Matthew's teacher jumped to the stage and was starting to reverse Matthew's card when a voice from the back cried out, "Leave it like it is! Look what this spells now!" And everyone saw, with new eyes, how God was changing their vision of an embarrassing wilderness into a fresh and exciting Advent proclamation ... "Christ *was* love!" Indeed, Christ, was, is, and will continue to be God's promised holy way of love for us and for the world.

34

Look again with new eyes at your own wilderness spaces. Open your eyes to see God's presence and guidance on the holy journey of life.

3 Third, and finally, God's holy way includes changing behavior as we travel. Advent is part of that wilderness journey, a time of holy preparation for the coming Christ. In our text, Isaiah describes that preparation for the discouraged exiles and for us. "Strengthen the weak hands and make firm the feeble knees. Say to those who are of a fearful heart, be strong, do not fear! Here is your God ... He will come and save you" (Isaiah 35:3-4).

Well, that's easier said than done, right? Alone, yes; without God's promise to change the wilderness from burning sand to pools of water. Alone without God's promise to change the dry land to abundant streams and blossoming flowers. Impossible without God's promise of safety from prowling beasts and bandits; impossible without God's promise to change into rejoicing and singing the fearful, despairing way we see the wilderness. Isaiah writes in verse 8, "not even fools," like you and me perhaps, will go astray on God's holy way.

Of course, life is tough. Of course, wilderness spaces and places exist in the dark and dry spaces of our souls. Alone, our hands are weak; our knees feeble; and our hearts are fearful. We cannot do it alone.

But in Christ, God did, does, and promises to continue to be a guiding, loving presence in the wilderness. In Christ, God has promised to make your way a holy way. As you travel, remember God's refreshing splash of love in your baptism. Taste God's forgiving, transforming presence in the bread and wine of holy communion. Hear again, in the words of Isaiah, God's Advent promise to God's wilderness people, to you and to me! "Everlasting joy shall be upon their heads; they shall obtain joy and gladness, and sorrow and sighing shall flee away" (Isaiah 35:10).

That's good news! Splash in the promise! Taste it!

In Christ, we travel God's holy way through any wilderness journey! Christ has come! Christ is coming! Christ will come again! Amen.

Stop, Drop, Cover, And Roll!

Pastor Terry had planned what she anticipated would be an excellent children's message for the fourth Sunday of Advent. Using today's text, she intended to illustrate for the children and for the congregation the vital importance of paying attention to the signs of the coming Christ Child that God gives us. Her key verse was Isaiah 7:14a: "Therefore, the Lord himself will give you a sign." She had painstakingly constructed a "stop" sign, using red construction paper, a white marker, and a wooden dowel.

When the children gathered around her on the front of the chancel steps, Pastor Terry held up the sign and asked, "What is this?" And even the youngest of the children obligingly exclaimed, "A stop sign!" Pastor Terry thought to herself, "Oh, yes; it's going according to my plan."

She continued, "In your school the teacher always tells you what comes next after stop, right?" Well, Pastor Terry's carefully planned message was based on the expectation that the children's response would be "look and listen." Unfortunately, the children must have been attending a different nursery school, because, as one, they all loudly proclaimed, "Stop, drop, cover, and roll!"

"Let us pray," said Pastor Terry, still a bit startled by this abrupt change to her well-crafted message.

The point here is that we do not always get what we expect or even want from our carefully constructed plans for our children, our lives, our families, even for our congregations. We are not always in control. God is. Life is not about what *we* want and desire. Rather it is about what *God* wants and promises. Perhaps you have heard this statement before: "If you want to make God laugh, tell God your future plans." Pastor Terry and her congregation certainly experienced this lesson on that fourth Sunday in Advent.

In our Old Testament text, King Ahaz didn't even want to ask God for help with his plans. God invited Ahaz to "ask a sign of the Lord your God; let it be as deep as Sheol or high as heaven" (Isaiah 7:11). But Ahaz was in control, or so he imagined. He couldn't be bothered. He replied, "I will not ask, and I will not put the Lord to the test" (Isaiah 7:12). Hmmm ... if God invited you to ask for any sign of God's presence and guidance, even for a major miracle, your response would likely be to stop everything; drop to your knees; cover your face in humility, and roll with pleasure in God's glory! Amen! Bring it on Lord! Show me your sign!

Sadly, this wasn't for poor Ahaz. Let's look at his situation. Ahaz had been crowned King of Judah at the young age of twenty during the late eighth century before the birth of Christ. Surrounding nations of Aram, Ephraim, and Moab were threatening to conquer a Judah weakened by political infighting, religious turmoil, and social injustice. Huge and powerful Assyria, under Sennacherib and Tiglath-pileser III loomed on the horizon as a clear and present danger to the entire region. Wars and rumors of war were a daily part of life.

In the verse before today's lesson begins, the Lord warned Ahaz: "If you do not stand firm in faith, you shall not stand at all" (Isaiah 7:9). Ahaz stood firm on the quicksand of his own plans and efforts to keep power and control.

Early in chapter 7, Isaiah describes the first part of this meeting with Ahaz. Ahaz is at a water conduit on the highway to Fuller's field. He was inspecting Jerusalem's water supply in case of a long enemy siege. God had instructed Isaiah to bring his son, named Shear-Jashub, with him. Perhaps you already know that this name, Shear-Jashub, is translated "a remnant shall return" (Isaiah 7:3). Was the presence of Isaiah's son also a sign of God's promise to Ahaz? If so, Ahaz certainly did not or would not see it. Speaking the word of the Lord, Isaiah is even more specific: "Take heed, be quiet, do not fear, and do not let your heart be faint" because of the "smoldering stumps of firebrands ... who have plotted evil against you" (Isaiah 7:4-5). Speaking even more directly, the Lord God promises, "It shall not stand, and it shall not come to pass" (Isaiah 7:7).

Ahaz just wasn't able to give up control. He stood firm in his faith, all right; his faith in himself and his own need to be in control of events. In fact, he even allowed himself to be persuaded to seek aid from mighty Assyria. He did this by recognizing Assyrian supremacy over Judah *and* by paying enormous "protection" tribute to Assyria. Judah became a vassal state and Ahaz, a puppet of the Assyrian king.

No wonder Isaiah urged Ahaz to listen to the Lord! No wonder God continued to urge Ahaz to ask for a sign of God's presence and guidance.

Poor, wimpy, wishy-washy Ahaz the deal maker. He did whatever he could to keep power and maintain control. He even tried to "bow out" on God's promise of protection from a bunch of burned-out dolts who couldn't successfully attack an army of fleas.

There are lots of whimsical phrases in the English language that describe people like Ahaz, people who simply refuse to accept the obvious help that they desperately need. Maybe you know some of the following: 1) "His elevator doesn't quite make it to the top floor"; 2) "His porch light's on, but nobody's home"; 3) "He is a couple of fruit loops short of a bowl"; and 4) "His wheel is still spinning, but the gerbil fell off." My favorite is: "There's a sign on his bedroom mirror that states: 'Warning! Objects in mirror are dumber than they first appear.'"

Perhaps you can add even more Ahaz descriptions. Be careful, however, when it comes to recognizing and responding faithfully to many signs of God's promise and guidance. We can easily and often fit those same descriptions. The refusal of Ahaz to even ask God for a sign frustrates Isaiah, who responds; "Hear then, O house of David! It is too little for you to weary mortals that you weary my God also?" (Isaiah 7:13).

In spite of Ahaz' stubborn refusal, God persists and provides a sign that we all are ready to affirm and to celebrate. Look again at verse 14 in our text. "Therefore, the Lord himself will give you a sign. Look, the young woman is with child and shall bear a son, and shall name him Immanuel."

Now, that's a sign that can't be ignored. That's an offer from God that can't be refused: Immanuel ... God is with us, now. That is God's Advent promise! Christ has come! Christ is coming! Christ will come again!

Regardless of the destructive plans of Assyria and the surrounding nations, Isaiah proclaims that they will not prevail because of God's own "Immanuel plan." God is in control; not Ahaz. God's plan of salvation does not depend on stubborn Ahaz. Neither does it depend on us. God's "Immanuel plan" is to be with us and for us — forever.

Now, granted, it's often bewildering and confusing for us to recognize God's presence as Immanuel, and God's guidance as king and Lord of all. This is certainly true as we hear the news of tragedies throughout the world. In just one recent newscast, we heard of wars in Iraq, Afghanistan, and Lebanon; elevated terrorist threat levels; floods in the midwest; raging fires in the west; gang violence in our cities; and family violence in our community. And then, of course, our own family and personal stress levels are often elevated into the red zone the closer we get to Christmas day.

For God's people during the reign of Ahaz and for us today, this is a time of uncertainty, confusion, anger, and even fear. During this fourth week of Advent, the signs of the season can also bring us closer to one another and also closer to God. Advent is a specific season that draws us closer to the baby, the promised Immanuel, about to be born into a troubled and strife-torn world. Anxious families and fearful hearts are, indeed, part of our daily experience. However, friends, God's Advent is God's promised presence ... Immanuel — God with us.

World events and personal crises are daily reminders that we are not in control. Our best-laid plans and expectations may never come to pass, just like those of Pastor Terry. However, God's plan, "God's Immanuel plan" is sure and certain.

God surprised Pastor Terry, through the children, with some faithful ways for Immanuel living:

40

1. *Stop* all the "busy-ness" and pre-occupation with our own plans. Just stop it ... if even for five minutes.
2. *Drop* to your knees at the foot of Immanuel's manger. Remember, God *is* with us as you taste God's sign of promise in the bread and wine of holy communion and as you pass by the font of God's splash of belonging to God's people.
3. *Cover* your very souls with the "security blanket" of God's forever loving presence. And finally ...
4. *Roll* with joy and thanksgiving that God is in control, in the world and in your life. Roll with the contagious enthusiasm that God has given you. Sing the song of Immanuel, who was born into your life; who died for your life, and who rose again for your eternal salvation.

Christ has come! Christ is coming! Christ will come again!
Now *that's* a plan and a promise, for sure! Amen.

What About The Baby?

Brian had just received a major job promotion that required a 2,000-mile cross-country move during the Christmas season. As a dutiful father, Brian was very concerned about how this sudden move would affect his children, particularly his six-year-old son, Adam. When it was Adam's bedtime, Brian spent several minutes giving a carefully rehearsed presentation about the impending family relocation. He described the new city, their new house, and all the new friends Adam would meet at school. He even told Adam that he could play his favorite sport, baseball, every day of the year because of the warmer climate. Adam took it all in, silently. He did not pout. He did not cry. Adam was just silent. However, Brian could "see" the wheels turning in his young son's head. So, he asked, "Do you have any questions, Adam?" After a few agonizing (for Dad) seconds. Adam replied, "Just one question, Dad. Did you know that if you look a leprechaun right in the eyes he will steal your bag of gold?"

Good try, Dad. Adam will be fine. So will your baby daughter, Caroline, and your wife, Christy. Indeed, they were and they are. Their love for each other, the support of friends and family, and especially the love of God carried them through a challenging, anxiety-filled Christmas-time journey.

We might not get everything just right. We might not always understand everything. We might not even want to face the life challenges ahead, with our children and especially with the little child that still dwells within each one of us, but God understands. God is with us in every challenge. God gets it right every time.

This very night God gives a child to us and to the world. This very night God shows a love and joy that transcends all time and space; from cross-country moves to family separations; from hospitals to gravesides; from sorrow and grief to broken promises and shattered dreams; from oppressive terrors to depressive darkness. In the opening verse of our Old Testament lesson Isaiah declares; "The people who walked in darkness have seen a great light; those who lived in a land of deep darkness — on them light has shined" (Isaiah 9:2).

But what about the baby? Have no fear. This night, right here, right now, the baby is born. This night, right here, right now, the baby enters our world. This night, right here, right now, God enters the dark and empty spaces of our lives. This night, right here, right now, God places a baby, *the* baby, into the manger of our souls. Tonight, it's all about the baby, God's baby; God's Word becoming flesh and dwelling among us (John 1:14).

Rejoice in Isaiah's resounding proclamation: "For a child has been born for us, a son given to us" (Isaiah 9:6). For *us*, to *us*, ... wow! In Hebrew, the language of the Old Testament, Isaiah is using a marvelous play on words here to emphasize this gift of God. In Hebrew, the same word, *lanu*, is translated both as "for us" and "to us." Now, remember our Old Testament text in Isaiah 7:14 from last Sunday? Here, Isaiah also announces an impending kingdom changing birth! "Look, the young woman is with child and shall bear a son, and shall call him Immanuel." In Hebrew, *immanu* is translated "with us." *El* is translated as "God." But, what about the baby? Why bother with all this scholarly language stuff? This right here, right now, that baby has become *lanu immanu* or God's precious gift *for* us, *to* us, and *with* us forever. In the gospel words of the angel to the shepherds, "*To you* is born in the city of David, a Savior who is the Messiah [Christ], the Lord" (Luke 2:11).

When Christ was born, Judea was a conquered land, existing under the domination of the mighty Roman Empire. When Isaiah was announcing the birth of the Messiah, the powerful Assyrian army had devastated northern Israel and was laying siege to Judah. Military oppression, political unrest, and social injustice were part of daily existence. In both Isaiah's time and 700 years later during

44

the reign of the Roman Emperor Augustus (Luke 2:1) the outlook of God's people was filled with gloom and doom and darkness. Even in our time this very night, we hear news of wars and rumors of war; stories of economic injustice, racism, poverty, and violence. For us, too, at first glance, we see only gloom, doom, and darkness.

And yet, on the other hand, God gives light in the center of despair. But what about the baby? The baby was, is, and will always be the light that obliterates our darkness. That baby was, is, and will always be God's light, given *lanu immanu, for* us, *to* us, and *with* us always, even to the end of the age (Matthew 28:20).

In our text, Isaiah proclaims that in this baby, God will bring an end to military oppression. God promises to lift burdens, shatter the rod of violence, and use military boots and blood-stained garments as fuel for fire (Isaiah 9:4-5).

Using the language for the coronation of the new king, Isaiah presents the names by which the baby, the king, will be called: "Wonderful Counselor, Mighty God, Everlasting Father, Prince of Peace" (Isaiah 9:6). During this season, many of us have heard these words sung with power and praise in the "Halleluiah Chorus" of Handel's majestic choral work, *Messiah.*

So, what about the baby? Why is it so important to have just the right name for a baby? Well, as we all know, choosing the name is tough. Most of us have been involved in that process, and we know how difficult and confusing it can be. We consult countless books and online lists of popular names. We consider family names and biblical names. We try to avoid offending an overlooked family member. We try to avoid names that may rhyme with anything objectionable. The best names connect memory and hope, possibility and promise. Choosing names for a child is serious business. Indeed, the name we select is a major step in reflecting a child's identity and purpose in life.

Isaiah presents the ceremonial names for a king that certainly reaffirm God's promise and purpose. These names express God's intention for a renewal of spirit, a restoration of power, and a promise of eternal salvation. These names also connect with the yearning of God's people for a transformed identity and a renewed hope.

45

God's people were more than ready for a miracle. So are we! Get ready!

Keep your eyes on the manger, lying open in your family, in your community, and in your souls. Open the manger of your heart to receive the baby, the Christ Child. Get ready to see with new eyes the light of God that forever shines from the baby's face. Get ready to reflect the joy of the new baby, the joy given to God's named and claimed people everywhere. Get ready to show what it looks like to live in the promise of *lanu immanu*; the gift of God *for* us, *to* us, and *with* us.

Listen again to Isaiah's list of names for the child and pay attention to how they describe how the reign of that baby will turn our lives, our darkened world, upside down.

Wonderful Counselor — Here is wisdom that both listens to our heart hungers with understanding care and also shows us right and faithful paths through whatever valley of shadows that we may travel.

Mighty God — Here is the power we desperately want and need from the King of kings. Here is power, but not in terms of the world's expectations. Rather, this baby has power to forgive, to renew, and to transform exhausted, lost, and broken lives.

Everlasting Father — In this baby, God's promise endures forever. In this baby, God demonstrates resolute and unwavering commitment to be *lanu immanu*; *for* us, *to* us, and *with* us for eternity ... no matter what.

Prince of Peace — This baby, this king, born in this manger tonight, is a sure and certain promise of peace, in our hearts, in our families, and in our darkened world. Hear again, God's words of promise in tonight's lesson: "His authority shall grow continually, and there shall be endless peace ... He will establish and uphold it with justice and with righteousness from this time onward and forever more" (Isaiah 9:7).

It is incredibly difficult to recognize God's own words of promise in the midst of the hundreds of voices that constantly seek to distract and confuse us. Just think of the many conflicting voices you have heard these past few weeks that diverted your attention from the baby, or as folks say, "The reason for the season." Shop 'til you drop! Hurry, hurry, hurry! Do this, do that; run here, run there! There's never enough time and even less energy to pay attention to all the voices, sometimes even to God's voice of promise of hope and peace!

There's a story about a young student who had the habit of daydreaming during his high school physics class. One day, his teacher asked him, "Ralph, if you were in a perfect vacuum, would you be able to hear my voice?" Suddenly awakened, poor Ralph responded, "Well, it would depend if the vacuum was turned off or on."

Sometimes it really does seem as if our lives exist in an endless and perfect vacuum, with no escape whatsoever. Sometimes it seems that like Brian, we are so frightened by the Christmas journey that we are unable to hear the promise of God's Christmas gift, the baby given *lanu immanu*; *for* us, *to* us, and *with* us.

This night, we see the baby born and cradled into the manger of our darkened world. This night, breaking into the vacuum of our lives, we hear the voice of the Wonderful Counselor, Mighty God, Everlasting Father, Prince of Peace speaking directly for us, to us, and with us, as Jesus Christ proclaims, "This is my body, given *for* you! This is my blood, shed *for* you!"

There was no room at the inn for the baby. This night the baby, the Christ Child, makes room for you in his heart. Tonight, God gathers us and all God's children into his loving arms. Tonight God's voice, God's Word made flesh, declares to us, I love you. I will care for you. I will embrace you. I will forgive you. I will die for you.

That's the gospel truth!

Merry Christmas! Amen.

Restoration Frustration

Here we are gathered together a few days after Christmas. How did you celebrate the birthday of Jesus? How did everything go for you? For most folks, some empty spaces remain. Just like our pews this morning, where there are empty spaces that were filled on Christmas Eve, there may be post-Christmas empty spaces in our hearts. For most of us, Christmas preparations and celebrations rarely meet expectations. Not everything goes smoothly. Not every gathering is joyful. Not every program and worship service is as spiritually uplifting as we would have desired. Not every gift was given with grace-filled love. Not every gift was received with festive thanksgiving. Exchange desks in malls and department stores are in a frenzy of activity on December 26, perhaps their busiest day of the entire year. Finding a shopping mall parking space on December 26 is almost as frustrating as experiencing yet one more unmet Christmas expectation.

For many of us, our hopes for restored family and renewed energy have been extinguished with the Christmas candles ... again. For many of us, the presents we purchased with money we don't really have, were received with the same feeling we will have when the credit card bills arrive later this month. Folks who were lonely and forgotten before Christmas, feel even more lonely and forgotten on this first Sunday after Christmas. Persons barely existing on the margins of society before Christmas are even more marginalized today.

We often begin each Christmas season desperately seeking what can be called the "3-A's" of life: finding 1) acceptance,

2) affirmation, and 3) approval. Sadly, for many, the Christmas season ends with most of us feeling life's "3-P's": 1) pooped, 2) perplexed, and 3) pathetic. We then begin making New Year's resolutions on some variation of the theme, "never again!"

There's a story about three-year-old Mark, who had just learned to pray the Lord's Prayer. One evening, just after Christmas, his bedtime Lord's Prayer included the following petition: "Forgive us our Christmases as we forgive those who Christmas against us."

Well, Mark, maybe you are closer to our actual experience than we want to admit. Our annual expectations that the Christmas season itself will restore lasting meaning and joy to our lives inevitably results in a bitter disappointment: a restoration frustration.

Restoration frustration! That certainly describes the situation in our text in Isaiah today. Many of those who were living as captives in Babylonia had just returned from their fifty-year exile. Instead of returning to worship in a restored temple, they found the once-magnificent structure in the same demolished condition as when they were taken prisoner by King Nebuchadnezzar and his conquering army. Instead of being welcomed back into a just, moral, and familiar society, the returning exiles returned to a precarious, miserable, and alien context. Even though some traditional religious practices had been maintained, they were intermingled with superstitious and pagan rites.

This must have been a terrible disappointment for the returning exiles. After all, until they were deported, they and their families had once been the cream of Jewish political, intellectual, and religious leadership. Restoration anticipation quickly declined from restoration frustration into aggravation, desperation, and humiliation. Perhaps God was still punishing them; or worse, God had cancelled God's eternal covenant of salvation. A familiar lament for the exiles in Babylon also may illustrate their perspective upon returning home:

> Remember, O Lord, what has befallen us; look, and see our disgrace! Our inheritance has been turned over to strangers, our homes to aliens ... Mount Zion, which lies desolate; jackals prowl over it.
> — Lamentations 5:1-2, 18

So, what was your Christmas like? Did anyone "Christmas" against you? Did you "Christmas" against anyone? Did you return home after a long absence? Did anyone return to your home? Were you alone then and still alone today? What happened to your hopes for renewal and restoration? What is it like for you to experience restoration frustration? Where is God in all this? How do we find renewed energy and passionate faith?

Good questions! Isaiah proclaims God's response in today's lesson.

Restoration comes from God's action and not our own efforts. Restoration for the returning exiles, and for us, begins with remembering what God has done, is doing, and has promised to continue to do in our midst.

In these verses of our Old Testament lesson, God reminds the discouraged of God's continuing and loving presence. "Surely they are my people," says the Lord, "and he became their savior in all their distress" (Isaiah 63:8).

Surely we are God's people, named and claimed by God at baptism. In Jesus Christ, whose birth and resurrection we celebrate on this first Sunday after Christmas, God became our Savior in the midst of our own restoration frustration.

In this passage, God is showing us how to reclaim the vitality and energy that God has already given us. God is revealing to us a model for spiritual and communal renewal.

One afternoon, Thomas, age five, and Stephen, age three, were proudly showing their grandfather the see-saw that their daddy had constructed in the backyard. "Let's try it out," invited Grandfather. Thomas and Stephen sat on one end; Grandfather on the other. The boys' combined weight of 79 pounds was no match for Grandfather's heavy 185 pounds. His end crashed to the ground while the boys rocketed skyward with pupils dilated and tiny arms clinging desperately to the sides of the board. "Pa-Pa, you have to move to the center so we don't fall off!" exclaimed Thomas. "Yeah, move to the center so we can play," pleaded Stephen. Pa-Pa did. They played. Nobody fell off.

Move to the center so we can play ... what a concept for restoring frustrated relationships and exhausted spirits! Friends, the center, the very core of our existence is in the mighty acts of God in our past, our present, and in our future.

Hear again the words of Isaiah:

> *I will recount the gracious deeds of the Lord, the praise-worthy acts of the Lord, because of all that the Lord has done for us and the great favor to the house of Israel.* — Isaiah 63:7

This is both the *beginning* of restoration and the *end* of frustration and humiliation. All too often, especially just after Christmas, when congregations find themselves frustrated in accomplishing their mission, we hear leaders lament, "Ten percent of the people have been doing ninety percent of the work for too long, and we are exhausted!" These folks, even pastors and staff members, have become tired out, burned out, and ready to drop out. Once proud and vital mainline denominations find themselves dropping from mainline to side line, to flat line: bored, apathetic, and frustrated.

This happens with families, friendships, and communities, as well. Maybe it's happening to you. A danger here is to seek desperately for a quick fix, a gimmick or technique that would remedy the situation immediately. If only we had more members who would give more money. If only "they" would listen to us. If only "someone" would live up to their promises. If only they would show a little appreciation for all our hard work.

Do these laments sound familiar? They sure sound like the complaints of the returning exiles: If only those who remained in Jerusalem would have restored the temple. If only they would have kept God's law.

There was no "quick fix" for the returning captives. There is no quick fix for us either ... that is, without first returning to the center. Salvation comes as a result of God's presence and action, not by our own methods and techniques.

Restoration occurs through regular and specific recounting of the reality that God has and is revealing to us. As Isaiah states, "According to his mercy, according to the abundance of his steadfast love" (Isaiah 63:7).

Try this in your family and in your committee meetings and other parish groups. For the next few weeks, during a family gathering and before a parish group meeting, spend just a few minutes sharing an example of how each person has experienced God's presence in their lives. This might seem a bit awkward at first, yet you will be astonished by what happens when folks begin to "recount the gracious deeds and praiseworthy acts of the Lord" (Isaiah 63:7). Times of transition and tragedy, anxiety and sorrow will be the very times when folks describe how God's mercy and steadfast love has restored and supported them. Listen for powerful stories of renewal, particularly now during the Christmas season. Listen for what new power the baby, God's Word made flesh, brings to the dark spaces of living. Listen for how God's presence transforms even the most "pooped, perplexed, and pathetic" soul into a life that God proclaims as "accepted, affirmed, and approved."

Each time you receive the Lord's Supper, hear with restored joy, Jesus' own words: "This is my body, given for *you*. This is my blood, shed for *you*."

It is not just the pastor who proclaims these words. It is Jesus himself. It is not just a professional theologian or church leader who promises that recounting the glorious deeds of the Lord will end restoration and begin renewal. It is the Holy Spirit of God.

Listen again to the final verse of our text today.

> ... *It was no messenger or angel but his presence that saved them; in his love and in his pity he redeemed them; he lifted them up and carried them all the days of old.* — Isaiah 63:9

There may have been, in little Mark's prayer, a lot of "Christmasing" going on during the last few weeks. There may still be some remnants of restoration frustration that linger in your heart. In Christ, God's child, God has restored you and redeemed you. In Christ, God lifts you up and will carry you in his heart forever.

That's the gospel truth, for you, forever. Amen.

53

A Honeymoon At Church Camp: A Real Homecoming

Rachael and Wally first saw each other at church camp when they attended a January orientation meeting for new counselors. Just one look into one another's eyes was all it took for these high school seniors to realize that this might be the start of something wonderful. It was. Over the next four summers at camp, Rachael and Wally's infatuation blossomed into romance. They became engaged with plans to marry during the Christmas season following college graduation. Everyone was thrilled. Here was the perfect couple. Their pastors, families, and friends on the camp staff gave them the ideal (for Rachael and Wally, anyway) honeymoon — a free week in a secluded cabin on the grounds of the camp where they met and fell in love. The newlyweds were ecstatic and joyfully set off to begin their lifelong adventure.

Late one night, after they had fallen asleep, Rachael awakened to see Wally opening the cabin door. "Where are you going, sweetheart?" she inquired.

"I'm just going for a short walk outside," Wally replied. "Go back to sleep."

Rachael did fall asleep, but was startled by Wally's loud cries for help.

Fearing that Wally had been injured, Rachael grabbed a flashlight and rushed out of the cabin in search of her husband. When she finally found Wally, Rachael saw that he was moaning, but uninjured, and gazing into the darkness of the old farm well that was abandoned when the camp was constructed.

"What's the matter with you, Wally?" Rachael asked, with just a tiny bit of aggravation in her voice. "You're going to wake up the whole camp! I thought you were badly hurt. Now be quiet and come back to the cabin!"

"But I am hurt, sweetheart," Wally whimpered. "I can't go back yet. You see, I was here by the old farm well, remembering how this is the most romantic spot in the whole camp. Here is where I proposed to you. Here is the very spot where you agreed to be my Christmas bride. Here is where we pledged our eternal love!"

With her heart softening, but just a little, Rachael remained firm. "Come on, Wally. Let's go back to our cabin and go to sleep."

"But you don't understand, honey. When I was gazing into the well, my lucky fifty-cent coin fell down there," whined Wally. "This was the coin I held in my hand on the night we became engaged. This was the coin I held in my hand at our wedding when the pastor asked me, 'Will you, Wally, take this woman, Rachael, as your wife?' "

"That's nice, Wally," said Rachael, now shivering in the frosty night air. "The well was filled with dirt years ago. It's only a few feet to the bottom. Go down and get it. I'll hold the light for you."

Becoming more desperate now, Wally began to cry, "I can't go down there, my darling. I have claustrophobia. Besides, with all the weight lifting I do, my shoulders are too wide. I will get stuck. But you, oh, my beautiful svelte, sweetheart, can fit easily. Please would you do this for me?"

By now Rachael was not just aggravated, she was downright angry. "Wally, there's fifty years of muck and slime in that well. Who knows what sort of ugly things live down there? It's just fifty-cents. It's not worth it," replied Rachael. And she stomped back to the cabin and crawled into bed. Wally remained, sadly gazing helplessly down into the dark depths of a lost dream.

We will return to the honeymoon couple later. Now let's look at today's text in Jeremiah. More than a century before, Assyrian armies had conquered northern Israel and dispersed its inhabitants to the far reaches of the empire. Just a generation before, the Babylonian army had invaded Judah, the southern part of the nation. Jerusalem was laid waste. The temple of Solomon was in

56

ruins. City walls were only piles of rubble. Thousands of political and religious leaders were deported and living as exiles more than 500 miles from home.

Just like Wally at the old farm well, their situation appeared helpless and hopeless. Any possibility of returning to the way things were — and the way they ought to be — seemed beyond the realm of possibility. For the displaced and dispersed children of God, the way back was through a dangerous, dry, barren wilderness brimming with wild beasts and bandits just waiting to pounce on the vulnerable traveler. Just like Wally at the well, retrieving their dream seemed like a lost cause.

Or was it?

"For thus says the Lord," proclaims Jeremiah in the first verse of today's text. Please pay attention here. When Jeremiah uses this language, he means: "Listen up folks! The word of the Lord is coming next." Indeed, in the remaining verses, God declares that the despair of the lost is about to be turned upside down and inside out! Now they are scattered and shattered. Now they experience sorrow. Now they are weak and vulnerable. Now their wilderness is dry, barren, and dangerous. Then God promises that something new and wonderful will take place.

> *Then shall the young women rejoice in the dance, and the young men and the old shall be merry. I will turn their mourning into joy, I will comfort them, and give them gladness for sorrow.* — Jeremiah 33:13

Then, God will gather those dispersed by the Assyrians. Then God will bring forth the captives from Babylon (Jeremiah 31:8). Then God will return them all to their true home. Then God will fill the dry wilderness with brooks of water and make their journey swift and secure (Jeremiah 31:9 cf). Then God's scattered and scared people "shall be radiant over the goodness of the Lord" (Jeremiah 31:12).

This was God's promise to a shattered people 500 years before Christ was born. This is God's promise to us more than 2,000 years after that first Christmas.

Friends, for us, Jeremiah's "then" is "now." Now we are living in God's promise, fulfilled in the birth, death, and resurrection of Jesus, God's Word made flesh.

Note well here that God's promised restoration was not simply for the brave, courageous, and bold among God's people. God's promised renewal was not just for their leaders. Among those to be gathered were the weak and vulnerable, the lonely and forgotten, "the blind and the lame, those with child and those in labor" (Jeremiah 31:8). God will give them the joy, the power, and the legitimacy that they did not have on their own. Those whom the world has "devalued" God has valued. Those who are last to be loved will be first. God has, is, and will always turn upside down what the world considers to be worthy and important.

So, here we are, at the beginning of a new year, the second Sunday after the birth of our Savior; the second Sunday after celebrating God's promised miracle. Which of our dreams have been shattered? What New Year's resolutions have already been broken? What grief brings you to tears of loneliness? What painful situations leave you feeling helpless and vulnerable in our midst? Where are those dry spaces in your souls?

Remember Jeremiah's words, "Thus says the Lord!" In Christ, that means now! In Christ, God enters our dry and barren lives, promising that "their life shall become like a watered garden, and they shall never languish again" (Jeremiah 31:12).

Now, let's return to Rachael and Wally. Remember that we left them with Rachael having returned to sleep in the warmth of their honeymoon cabin. Wally sadly remained at the old, dry, farm well, mourning the loss of his lucky fifty-cent coin.

Once again, Wally's mournful moaning grew louder and louder. Once again, Rachael arose from sleep and came to Wally's side. Eagerly, Wally exclaimed, "You changed your mind. What a relief. I had given up hope. Are you going to go down there and get my/our lucky coin?"

"I told you before, Wally, it's just not worth it. Look at that dark, slimy mess down there," said Rachael, as she pointed her flashlight toward the bottom of the well.

Wally was crestfallen and started crying again.

58

With a heavy sigh, Rachael reached into the pocket of her housecoat and pulled out a fifty-dollar bill. Dropping it into the well, Rachael proclaimed, "Now it's well worth it!" And she climbed down into the old farm well.

Friends, this is precisely what God has done in Jesus Christ. In Christ, God entered the dark, murky, slimy mess of the world of our lives and made us worth it. In Christ, the Word, God's own self became flesh and dwelt among us. In Christ, God's "then" in Jeremiah has become our "now" and forever.

Now our life in Christ is and will always be "worth it." The bread we taste is Christ for us. The wine we drink is Christ for us. The water splashed in baptism is God's splash of new life. The proclaimed word at the pulpit and lectern become God's Word enfleshed and dwelling in our midst.

With Jeremiah, "Sing aloud with gladness" (Jeremiah 31:7) for God has indeed gathered us into God's very heart, forever. "Then" is "now" and forever. Amen.

The Epiphany Of Our Lord
Isaiah 60:1-6

The Porch Light's On

All of us have heard various short, sarcastic sayings that describe people and groups who seem to lack plain, old common sense. These folks appear to understand what's happening in their lives. However, when it comes to coping with reality, they just don't seem to get it. Here are some examples: "One brick short of a load." "Just one French fry short of a Happy Meal." "His elevator's stuck on the first floor." A good phrase that can describe many Christians celebrating Epiphany might be, "Their porch light's on, but nobody's home."

Christmas is over. Decorations are boxed up in the attic. Silent nights are once again filled with stress and anxiety. Joy *to* the world has become terror and violence *in* the world. Good Christian friends and families who were rejoicing during Christmas are back gossiping and quarreling today. Outside, our porch light is on, but inside there is little happiness at home. Isaiah states, "For darkness shall cover the earth and thick darkness the peoples" (Isaiah 60:2). You got that right, Isaiah!

Nevertheless, God's light pierces the darkest places. God's light shines with brilliance in our world of shadows. God's light is always at home in our families, in our community, and in our souls. No darkness can overcome it. In chapter 9, Isaiah declares:

> *The people who walked in darkness have seen a great*
> *light; those who lived in a land of deep darkness — on*
> *them light has shined.* — Isaiah 9:2

This day we celebrate the coming of that light, Jesus Christ, into our world. Together with Christians all over the earth, the Christ light has defeated the dark and chaotic nightmares of our souls. It often seems as if our lives are just one dark tunnel after another. We celebrate the light bursting through the tunnel, and it isn't the train of the tempter or the semi of Satan. That light is a baby in a manger; a guiding star of hope; a messiah on a cross; a folded shroud in an empty tomb. That light is the glory of God's own self.

In our text, Isaiah proclaims: "The glory of the Lord has risen upon you" (Isaiah 60:1). He continues that although darkness may seem to cover the earth, God promises that: "The Lord will arise upon you, and his glory will appear over you" (Isaiah 60:2).

For the past twenty centuries, Christians have celebrated Epiphany, the glorious good news that the light has already come, and it continues today.

Chapter 60 of Isaiah is filled with good news, first intended for those who had just returned to Jerusalem, after fifty years of captivity in far off Babylon. In their absence, nothing much had been done to rebuild the city or its temple. Even the moral, social, and religious practices had become perverse and polluted. The joy of the returning exiles quickly dissipated into despair. Their resolve quickly degenerated into a submissive fatigue and apathy.

Yet, God's resolve to reform them as God's faithful people remained powerful. God's resolve to bring goodness and well-being to them remained firm and unchanging. Through this band of returning refugees, God would make light shine as a glorious beacon, gathering the nations of the world to experience God's own glory. Through them, God's loving purpose would become a visible reality. A dimly burning wick would become a brilliant star in the heavens, beckoning the nations to experience God's glory.

In chapter 51, verse 18, Isaiah describes the disintegrative and leaderless situation of the children of Israel. "There is no one to guide her among all the children she has borne; there is no one to take her by the hand among all the children she has brought up." Indeed, their light had become nothing but a dimly burning wick.

God was acting to reverse reality for Israel. In former days, the people were subordinate and subservient to other nations. At first glance, it appeared as if they were still nothing more than tiny, dark, and insignificant blots among the powerful nations of the world. Their reality still looked like rejection and ruin. Their identity was shaped by their status, or lack of it, among the nations. Who shapes your present identity? How do you define yourself? Your family? Your community? Your congregation? How does this shape your future?

In our text, God promised a new and glorious identity to the downtrodden and discouraged people in Judah. God promised to reverse their identity from dark, distressed, and oppressed to light, ransomed, and redeemed.

This complete reversal was God's action; not theirs. This new identity as children of the light was given by God; not achieved by them. This new identity is also God's free gift to us through the light of the world, Jesus Christ. Our new, God-given identity is not given by others' perceptions. It is given by God in Jesus Christ.

Of course, it is not easy to see this guiding light every moment of our lives. It is often difficult to see anything but more darkness in our future.

There's a story about a man who had experienced a seven-year series of setbacks in business and in his love life. Every decision that he made, every relationship that he had, seemed to end in failure. One evening as he was walking home he saw a bright spotlight on the porch of a previously abandoned home. As he approached the house, he noticed that the light was illuminating a sign advertising the presence of a fortune-teller. "Fantastic futures forecast inside," he read. So, thinking that nothing else seemed to offer any hope, he walked through the door. The fortune-teller placed her hands on the crystal ball on the table between them. As she did so, a frown spread across her face as she predicted, "The next seven years will be just like the past seven ... filled with despair, unhappiness, and disappointment."

"Oh, no," said the young man. Still clinging to a tiny spark of hope, he asked timidly, "Then what?"

"You'll get used to it," responded the fortune-teller.

Her porch light was on, all right! But there was no hope in that home.

Left to their own efforts to rebuild the city walls and temple in Jerusalem, this also might describe the experience of God's children in our text. The hope of a glorious return from captivity had diminished into a dimly burning wick. Even that tiny spark of hope was nearly extinguished when they observed the enormous construction tasks and the lack of enthusiastic support from the people who had remained. It would be easy to simply give up and get used to it.

Maybe this happens to us as well. In difficult, dark, disappointing situations that assail us, we first follow any sort of light — gimmick — promise — that appears to offer a little bit of hope. We try anything that might suggest even a temporary relief from the stress and anxiety of life. Some of us spend a good portion of our income on unneeded material things. Some buy lottery tickets and risk their livelihood by gambling on card games and athletic contests. Others drink alcohol and take illegal drugs to blot out the pain. Some become trapped in shallow relationships that promise love and yield only more heartache. Still others grasp desperately to the latest fad of "feel good" philosophy that promises happiness and success but results only in more hopelessness and helplessness.

The porch light's on, but nobody is really at home.

Isaiah's message, God's Epiphany message, to all God's children, shines brightly tonight. The good news here is that God's true light of everlasting hope has already come into our midst. The light of Christ has arisen upon us. The glory of the Lord has appeared to us and shines upon us this very Epiphany day.

This is the light that led the wise men to the Bethlehem manger. This is the light that inspired them to bring gifts of gold and frankincense to God's baby, God's own Son. This is the light that "proclaims the praise of the Lord" to all the world, to you and me (Isaiah 60:6). This is the light that shines from the cross and ascends from the empty tomb.

So what? What can we do to overcome the darkness that is descending on our darkening world? Wrong question, folks! The right question — the Epiphany question — is what has God already done, is doing and has promised to continue doing to overcome that darkness?

64

And the answer — God's Epiphany answer — is, "Here is Jesus, my Son, my very self, my forever and promised light of love."

So what? So that "you shall see and be radiant; your heart shall thrill and rejoice" (Isaiah 60:5). So that in and through God's Epiphany light shining above and within you "nations shall come to your light and kings to the brightness of your dawn" (Isaiah 60:3). God's light shining above and within is contagious. That light that guides our journey through darkness will gather others along the way.

"Arise, shine; for your light has come," declares Isaiah (Isaiah 60:1). Here, now, tonight in this very space where we are all gathered, becomes God's holy space. Here, now, on this Epiphany day, the porch light is on. The light of the world is always at home here shining from the font of baptism; beckoning us to the table where Christ is serving the light of himself in bread and wine. God's Epiphany light glistens in the eyes of the people gathered. God's light of wisdom and power and understanding glows within the word of promise proclaimed here.

Arise, shine; our porch light is always on. Why? Because Christ is always home right here, right now, and forever. Amen.

Burned Beef

Jenny was employed as an emergency room nurse in a busy urban hospital. Often she worked many hours past the end of her shift, providing care to trauma victims and their families. Jenny was also a loving wife and mother, and an excellent cook. On the evening before starting her hectic work week, Jenny would prepare a huge pot of soup, a casserole, or stew; plentiful enough for her family to pop into the microwave or simmer on the stove in case she had to work overtime.

At 5:30 p.m. one evening, Jenny's husband, Terry, arrived home to an empty house and listened to Jenny's voice mail asking Terry to "warm up the beef stew that's in the casserole dish on the top shelf of the refrigerator. Keep the lid on to preserve the flavor."

Terry followed the directions perfectly ... or, so he thought. Placing the dish on the front burner of the stove, Terry turned on the heating dial and proceeded to make a salad. Then he began to read the paper as he waited for the boys to arrive home from soccer practice.

About thirty minutes later, his sons burst through the door, plopped down at the dinner table saying, "Okay, what did Mom make for dinner? Feed us. Hurry up, Dad! We are starving!"

Terry gingerly lifted the dish of beef stew from the stove. However, the glassware was not just warm, it was so hot that Terry quickly dropped the dish onto the wooden cupboard next to the stove. Carefully, he lifted the lid, and immediately the entire kitchen was engulfed with blue smoke. A terrible, burning stench filled their nostrils. Blackened chunks of beef adhered to the bottom of

67

the dish, securely fastened there by a glue-like paste that once was potatoes, carrots, and gravy.

By now the smoke alarm was blaring, and the boys were dashing through the house opening windows and doors as they went.

Naturally, in the middle of this chaos, headlights appeared in the driveway. Mom was home. Jenny was there and she looked tired and hungry.

Silently, Jenny walked through the opened front door, past her cowering men folk. Ignoring the billowing cloud of smoke, she shut off the ear-splitting blare of the alarm and turned on the ceiling fans and the exhaust fan above the stove. Lifting the cooling glassware dish of glop, Jenny pretended to be oblivious to the scorched wood on which it rested and placed it on the floor in front of Penny and Cookie, the family cat and dog. Naturally, they wouldn't eat it, either, and quickly scampered down the basement stairs. Then, Jenny slowly turned to face Terry.

"This can't be good," thought Terry as he feared the worst, knowing that he deserved whatever came next.

Looking into Terry's eyes, Jenny was unable to control herself any longer. She burst into laughter: long, loud, contagious laughter. Jenny grasped Terry's hands and said, "I just knew you'd do that! It's a good thing I didn't marry you for your money or for your cooking skills. Get in the car. Pizza's on me."

Jenny was well aware of her husband's tendency to mess up a meal. She chose him out of love. She gazed into his eyes, grasped his hands, and paid for the pizza. She married Terry because she loved him; not because he was often likely to "burn the beef."

God does it even better. In our Old Testament lesson, God announces to his beloved servant, "I have called you in righteousness. I have taken you by the hand and kept you" (Isaiah 42:6).

Friends, God has chosen us, even though in some fashion, like Terry, we all "burn the beef." Saint Paul writes, "There is no one who is righteous, not even one" (Romans 3:10). Paul recognized that he knew in his mind what actions God expected of him. However, he too, fell far short. By his own actions, Paul neither deserved nor earned God's promise of salvation. He writes: "I do not understand my own actions. For I do not do what I want, but I do the very thing that I hate" (Romans 7:15).

Paul has certainly described what Terry was experiencing as the smoke alarm was loudly reminding him of his helpless ineptitude. Paul has also described you and me. There is nothing we can do to even deserve the label "righteous" in the eyes of God. With Paul, we say, "Wretched man that I am! Who will rescue me from this body of death?" (Romans 7:24).

Again, Isaiah reminds us that God has chosen us in spite of our sin. It is the righteous God who has chosen to make us righteous. Listen again to God's promise in our text: "I am the Lord. [declares God — and we are not!] I have called you in righteousness. I have taken you by the hand and kept you" (Isaiah 42:6). Inscribe these words on your heart. Carry them deep inside your souls.

Now, why does God choose to do this? Why does our God choose us in spite of us? Read the next chapter in Isaiah and discover one of the most profound, grace-filled verses in the Bible. Why you? Why me? Why us? "Because you are precious in my sight, and honored, and I love you" (Isaiah 43:4).

Wow! Precious! Honored! Loved! Why? Just because God declares it!

Today we celebrate the baptism of our Lord. Today our lessons remind us of God's choice to name and claim and keep us as God's own children. Today we celebrate the prototype — the example of God's first choice ... Jesus Christ, God's own Son in whom he was well pleased. Let's look again at our text in Isaiah today. Keep in your mind God's choice of another messed up, fouled up, ready to give up group of sinful people. The people of Judah had messed up big time. They were worshiping false gods and cheating the poor. Their morals were terrible. Their politicians were corrupt.

As a consequence of their sin, God allowed the nation to be conquered by the Babylonian armies who destroyed the walls of Jerusalem and left the temple in ruins. Thousands of the most influential citizens were taken into exile. It was to these captives, 500 miles from home, that Isaiah's message of God's rescue was intended.

Instead of casting out the exiles for messing up, the Lord promised rescue and restoration. They were suffering for the pain of sin that they themselves had caused. God raised up a servant who would save them in spite of their sin. The Lord announces: "Here is my servant, whom I uphold, my chosen in whom my soul delights; I have put my spirit upon him; he will bring justice to the nations" (Isaiah 42:1).

Who was this servant? Some speculate that it was Isaiah himself. Others suggest that it might have been Cyrus, whose Persian nation was threatening Babylon. The fact is that no one really knows for sure. Today, most Christians see Jesus himself as the rescuing, saving, suffering, servant of God.

At his baptism, Jesus was reminded of God's choice. At the baptism of Jesus, God not only proclaimed that Jesus was God's beloved Son; God also revealed again that Jesus had become one with all people. At his baptism, Jesus became one with all sinners; all who messed up big time; all who are weak; all who are vulnerable; all who suffer pain and persecution.

At his death on the cross, Jesus, God's own suffering servant, made visible God's forever choice to declare us as God's own righteous children. At our own baptism, the risen Christ splashes us with God's word of rescue from the power of sin. At the Lord's table, Christ feeds us with a taste of that promise. As members of God's people, the Holy Spirit sends us, as servants to the suffering and the forgotten around us.

In the midst of a broken and fear-filled world, God sends us as servants of the promise, as light into a darkened world, to open blind eyes, and to rescue those who are imprisoned by the forces of sin and evil.

We cannot do this alone. We still "burn the beef." As Isaiah reminded us in chapter 42, verse 6, it is the Lord who takes us by the hand and keeps us, surrounding us with his love.

Billy and Johnny, four-year-old twins, wandered far from their daddy, who had taken them to a crowded beach. When they finally realized that they were lost, the boys just plopped down on the sand in tears. When their daddy couldn't find them, his heart sank.

He began to shout out their names, running everywhere in desperation. Finally, they saw each other and ran into the warmest, biggest hug of love ever. Hand-in-hand they returned to their place on the sand. As the boys' father told this story, he remarked, "I didn't feel really safe until they were holding my hands."

"Me, too, Daddy," said Billy.

"And me, Daddy," added Johnny.

And the Lord said: "I have called you in righteousness. I have taken you by the hand and kept you" (Isaiah 42:6).

People of God, you are chosen. By God you are baptized! God has kept you; is keeping you; and has promised to continue to keep you in his very own hands, even though we still "burn the beef," even though sin abounds and surrounds us in its prison. In Christ, God's own servant rescues us and sends us into the world. In the outstretched arms of the crucified Christ, God finds us and keeps us, embraced forever as God's own children! Gather at the Lord's table! Dinner's served! Amen.

Backseat Drivers:
Named, Claimed, Commissioned

When his oldest daughter, Nancy, was approaching her six-teenth birthday, Harold decided to teach her how to drive an automobile. After a brief orientation session in the family driveway, Nancy took the wheel and proceeded to drive — very cautiously — to the empty parish parking lot three blocks away. Harold couldn't help himself. He braced his feet firmly on the floor boards, both hands rigidly placed against the dashboard, with perspiration dripping from his brow, Harold began a rapid-fire critique of Nancy's driving.

"Use the brake! Put your foot on the brake right now! Okay, ease out onto the street. First put it in drive! Slow down! Watch out for that bicycle! Put your turn signal on. No, that's the wipers. Watch your speed."

This was just in the first block. After Nancy finally pulled into the parking lot to practice parallel parking, Harold finally lost control. "You just don't listen! Can't you do anything right? I can't believe you did that." On and on this went until Nancy, Harold's firstborn child, cherished daughter, burst into tears.

"I'll never be able to please you, Daddy," she cried as she got out of the car, slammed the door, and started to walk back home.

Suddenly, Harold recalled an inscription on the plaque that his high school metal shop class had made for his office: "I'm just a backseat driver in the tunnel of love." Harold was ashamed. During the first few weeks of that class, he had been far too quick to criticize and far too slow to praise. He would look over the

73

shoulders of each student, and find fault with each project. "Just like I did with Nancy," he thought.

After a few days of Harold's "backseat driving," the students rebelled and as a group, walked out, "just like Nancy did," Harold reminded himself. "I thought that I had learned my lesson." Then Harold rushed down the street to beg forgiveness and make a promise to enroll her in a driver training course the very next day.

Many of us can, no doubt, identify with Harold. What, at first, appears to be a simple task that would help someone we care about decidedly ends up as a total failure.

In today's Old Testament text, Isaiah presents the address of a servant called by God even before his birth. "The Lord called me before I was born, while I was in my mother's womb, he named me" (Isaiah 49:1).

Then the Lord gave the servant a specific task to accomplish: to bring the exiles back home and to gather again God's people who had been driven to far away lands by conquering armies (Isaiah 49:5). He was to be as focused as a polished arrow, hidden away in the Lord's quiver until it was time to act. Words of the servant would penetrate resistance like a sharp sword (Isaiah 49:2).

Now that's awesome — to be named, claimed, and commissioned by the Lord for a specific task. As God's servant, this should be easy. It might even be enjoyable to speak God's word with such clarity and precision that conquering armies would surrender their captives. Immediately, the captives themselves would return with rejoicing.

Harold also expected that it would be easy to teach his sixteen-year-old daughter how to drive. Poor Harold was quickly confronted with reality. So was God's servant, who complained to the Lord, "I have labored in vain, I have spent my strength for nothing and vanity" (Isaiah 49:4).

It's tough being a dad. It's tough being Dad's sixteen-year-old daughter. It's downright impossible to be a servant of God, particularly when we rely only upon our own efforts and perceptions.

Remember now, this text emerges from a time when everything seemed to be going wrong for God's people. The northern part of the nation had been conquered by Assyria more than a century ago. The people were scattered to distant nations. Judah, in the south, had been overrun by Babylon. The walls of Jerusalem were only rubble. The temple of the Lord was in ruins. Leaders of the nations were taken captive with little hope for return. Dreams disappeared. No wonder the servant's initial efforts were an exercise in futility. Just like Harold. Just like you and me. The servant's lament is also ours. "I have labored in vain. I have spent my strength for nothing and vanity" (Isaiah 49:4).

Friends, pay attention to the turning point in our text. The next two words in verse 4 are decisive for the complaining servant and for God's discouraged people. They are decisive words because they announce that God is about to transform our perception of reality from failure and futility to promise and possibility. With these two words God gets our attention. God is about to reverse our self-definition from weak, depressed, and exhausted to named, claimed, and commissioned. For the servant and for God's people, it's not all about us. It's all about God.

What are these two transforming words? They are, "Yet, surely." In the middle of the servant's exhausted complaining, he declares, "Yet, surely my cause is with the Lord, and my reward is with my God" (Isaiah 49:4).

Yet, surely, in his discouragement, Harold had a vision of God's renewal as he remembered the plaque given by his students. Yet, surely, in the midst of our own frequent failures and depleted energy, God gives us visions of renewal. Look around you right now. Look at the cross, the font, and the altar. See the scriptures opened. See God's gathered people around you. Yet, surely, right here, among us, God is naming, claiming, and commissioning us. Yet, surely, right here, God is reversing reality for all splashed and nourished sinner servants of the Lord. Yet, surely, with the servant, today we remember, both God's claim of us and God's commission to us.

Kathy dropped by her pastor's study one Saturday morning on her way to her last university class before graduation. Pastor noticed that Kathy's left arm was wrapped in a towel. In her right hand, Kathy held a straight razor. The towel dropped from her left arm revealing a long, open, bloody gash. Holding up the razor, with tears in her eyes, Kathy pleaded, "Convince me not to finish this."

With a gulp and a silent prayer, Pastor Michael said, "I don't know if I can, but let's take a memory walk first." Together they strolled through the church building, pausing to share stories of nursery school, confirmation classes, and youth group activities. Kathy recalled how her clinical depression kept coming back, reminding her how empty and meaningless her life had become. Even though she was on the dean's list, she felt stupid. Even though she had received a superior rating for her student teaching, she believed that she would be a disaster as an elementary school teacher. Even though her parents had chosen to adopt her while she was still in her birth mother's womb, Kathy could only see that she did not live up to their expectations. Just like God's servant in our text, Kathy believed: "I have labored in vain, I have spent my strength for nothing and vanity" (Isaiah 49:4).

"Come on, Kathy," urged Pastor Michael, "we have one more stop on our memory walk. Let's go into the sanctuary."

Together they stopped at the baptismal font. "Here is where your mother and father promised to introduce you to an enormous family who would support you always. Here is where God named and claimed you and chose you as a child in God's forever family," said Pastor Michael.

Kathy remained silent still clutching the towel around her arm. Yet she allowed the pastor to lead her down the center aisle toward the altar.

"Look at the cross, Kathy. Here is where Jesus suffered and died so that you might have life. Here is the altar where Jesus gave his own flesh and blood for you."

Kathy dropped to her knees and began sobbing uncontrollably.

After a few minutes, just when Pastor Michael was planning to call the emergency squad, Kathy stood up. Placing her bloodstained towel and straight razor on the altar, Kathy announced, "Okay, I remember. Let's go get some help now." And they did.

"Yet, surely," remembered the servant, "my cause is with the Lord" (Isaiah 49:4).

Surely, remembered Kathy, servant of God, there is still work to be done; a life to live, and a baptismal commission to fulfill.

At first the task of God's servant was limited to restoring the scattered children of Israel ... no simple job, but the servant knew that he was honored and strengthened by God to carry it out. "I am honored in the sight of the Lord and my God has become my strength" (Isaiah 49:5).

At first, the task of God's servant, Kathy, was to begin to heal and to graduate. At first, the task of God's servant, Harold, was to provide driving lessons for his daughter.

Each of these servants of God experienced failure and discouragement. What about us? What failures confront us? What dreams seem futile?

Yet, surely, just as the Lord refreshed the memory of God's servants with reminders of God's forever love, God reminds us, as well.

Not only did the servant in our text receive the necessary strength to complete his first mission, God expanded it. God said: "It is too light a thing that you should be my servant to raise up the tribes of Jacob and to restore the survivors of Israel; I will give you as a light to the nations, that my salvation may reach to the end of the earth" (Isaiah 49:6). Wow!

Not only did God's servant, Kathy, graduate with honors from college, she became Third Grade Teacher of the Year in her elementary school. Today she is principal of that school and serves as a youth advisor in her congregation. Wow!

Not only did God's servant, Harold, renew a relationship with his daughter, he now volunteers as part of a ministry team working with youthful gang members. Recently, some of these young people presented Harold with a cross, made from melted down pistols, knives, and chains. Wow!

These servants of God could not remain faithful to doing any of these things by their own efforts. They could only carry out their tasks in God's word to them, "... because of the Lord, who is faithful, the Holy One of Israel, who has chosen you" (Isaiah 49:7).

We are all, with Harold, backseat drivers in the tunnel of love. We all experience futility and failure. Yet, surely, God is the driver in the front seat, leading us to remember that, in Christ, God has named, claimed, and chosen us forever. Yet, surely, in Christ, God has commissioned us for mission. Wow! Now, servants of God, let's get moving! Amen.

No Room For Gloom

Baseball Hall of Fame catcher, Lawrence "Yogi" Berra, once remarked, "The future ain't what it used to be." Yogi might have been describing Isaiah's message in our text today.

On the one hand, things looked pretty bleak for God's people. A few years before that was written, the mighty Assyrian army under Tiglath-pileser III, had ravaged the land and absorbed the regions of Zebulon and Naphtali into one Assyrian Province (1 Kings 15:29).

After the Assyrians took over, many people had begun to worship pagan deities. Often, they were tempted to "consult the hosts and the familiar spirits that chirp and mutter" instead of the Lord (Isaiah 8:19).

"Surely," said the Lord, "those who speak like this will have no dawn ... but will see only distress and darkness, the gloom of anguish; and they will be thrust into thick darkness" (Isaiah 8:20, 22).

In today's text, Isaiah states: "In the former times he brought into contempt the Land of Zebulun and the land of Naphtali" (Isaiah 9:1).

On the one hand, this was a bitterly humiliated and devastated group. Their sin had brought the wrath of God upon them. For God's people, it was the worst of times.

On the one hand, many of us may be feeling the same way about our own situations in life. It may seem to us that if something bad could happen, it definitely will. We read in 1 Peter 5:8, "Your adversary the devil prowls around, looking for someone to devour." Sometimes it definitely feels like Satan is chomping on us! We experience so much pressure at work or in school that we are ready to explode. We are torn apart by the pangs of shame and guilt. We are humiliated by the hurtful words we have spoken in anger. We are devastated by the helpful things we have left undone. We stay awake at night awash in the pain of grief. We listen to absurd chirping and muttering of anyone and anything that promises an easy way out of our bondage.

On the one hand, we, like God's people in our text, are surrounded by thick, pessimistic, faithless darkness.

On the other hand, God's hand, the Lord never abandons God's children. God's future ain't as dark as it used to be or even seemed to be. In God's hand, the future is much better. When Yogi Berra was managing the New York Yankees during one of their rare losing seasons, he refused to let his players surrender to pessimism. "It ain't over 'til it's over," he frequently advised.

In former times, God's people in the seacoast provinces of Zebulun and Naphtali experienced only contempt and rejection. Their world was filled with darkness. Nevertheless, God's *promised* nevertheless, Isaiah proclaims: "In the latter time he [God] will make glorious the way of the sea, the land beyond the Jordan, Galilee" (Isaiah 9:1).

On the one hand, in former times, the people walked in deep darkness. On the other hand, in the latter time, God's people have seen a great light. On them, on us, a great light has shined (Isaiah 9:2). This, friends, was, is, and always will be God's action, not ours. In Christ, the latter days have already begun. During this Epiphany season, we celebrate the light that penetrates the thickest darkness that the universe can produce ... the darkness that seems to engulf our own hearts.

Indeed those "latter times" have already begun. During the season of Epiphany, we join God's people throughout the world in celebrating God's glorious light of Christ that penetrates the deepest, thickest darkness. The gospel of Matthew states that after John the Baptist was arrested by Herod, Jesus moved his home from Nazareth to Capernaum in the region of Zebulun and Naphtali.

This was the specific region of anguish and thick darkness Isaiah mentions in our Old Testament lesson (Matthew 4:12-16).

Through the Holy Spirit, the crucified and risen Christ makes his home with us. Through the action of the Holy Spirit the glorious light of the Christ penetrates and permeates each heart that is darkened by the shadows of gloom, grief, and death.

Pay careful attention to the very first sentence in today's lesson. Here is good news. Here is God's promise to the people of Zebulun and Naphtali and to us. "But there will be no gloom for those who were in anguish" (Isaiah 9:1). Look at the verbs here. The first verb is in the future tense ... "will be." In Christ, the future is now, today, and forever. As Yogi Berra, the manager, reminded his team, "The future ain't what it used to be." In Christ, *because* of Christ, the future is glorious now. The second verb, "were," is in the past tense. The residents of Zebulun "were" in anguish, living in the midst of contempt from other nations. In the past, in former times, gloom, doom, and scorn dominated their worldview. In former times, their darkness was too thick to penetrate on their own. Folks could see only that their sinful past would determine their future ... more of the same old misery. Yet, in the latter days, now this day, God promised a new and marvelous future, to them and to us.

It is so easy for us to become trapped in the misery of past sin; those things we have done, and those things we have left undone. Perhaps some of us here today are also living out our lives shaped only by the shame and guilt in our former days. Both our present and our future seem only to repeat our past. Truly, troubled actress, Tallulah Bankhead, once commented, "I'm as pure as the driven slush." We are in bondage to sin and are unable to free ourselves. We live each day trapped inside a slush-filled gloom room of our own making.

Emily was a captain of her high school soccer team and an excellent student. However, she had great difficulty accepting her own abilities. If her team lost, she would quickly point out the goal she missed or the pass she failed to make. If she made an "A" on an examination, Emily would focus only on the point or two that she failed to answer perfectly. After each "failure," Emily would arrive home in tears. She would run into her room, shut the door, close the blinds, and turn off all the lights, sitting alone for hours in what her parents labeled "Emily's gloom room."

Where is your "gloom room"? What is it like in there? What do you think about in there? Are your thoughts filled with anguish and self-contempt just like the people of Zebulun and Naphtali? Do you still allow the darkness and anguish of your former days to extinguish the light in your present and your future?

When he lost the election for prime minister after leading Great Britain to victory during World War II, it is said that Winston Churchill's wife attempted to comfort him by remarking, "Maybe this was a blessing in disguise."

Churchill gruffly responded, "If so, it's a pretty good disguise."

Living in the gloom room is living without hope, without promise, and without light. It is living with the heavy burdens that we are helpless to carry alone. In our text, God declares that oppressive and depressive gloom has already ended for the people of Zebulun and Naphtali and for us as well. "For the yoke of their burden, and the bar across their shoulders, the rod of their oppressor, you have broken" (Isaiah 9:4).

Upon them, God's glorious light has already shined (Isaiah 9:2). The Assyrian conquest was ending. God's glorious light had already illuminated their gloomy, pessimistic darkness. God, not the people, was the light source. God, not you, not me, is and will always be our light source. Look around and see that light source today. See how God's light shines from the baptismal waters. See the light shining from the bread and wine as God nourishes us to walk boldly in a darkened world. See how God's light shines from the cross, forever illuminating our own private gloom rooms. Look around and see and proclaim with the psalmist: "The Lord is my light and my salvation; whom shall I fear? The Lord is the stronghold of my life, of whom shall I be afraid?" (Psalm 27:1).

God's glorious light in Christ shines for all the Emilys who sit in the darkness of self-loathing. God's glorious light breaks through every disguise of shame and humiliation. God's glorious light transforms our dirty, sinful, slush into pure, white glistening snow.

Today God invites us to reflect that light of Christ to others. Let Christ's light shine through you to all who sit by themselves in their own personal gloom rooms.

No matter what evil occurs in the world or in our own lives, Christ has overcome it. No matter how often our inner voices shout, "Loser," in the light of Christ, God has already won the victory. In Christ, the future ain't what it used to be. The devil's darkness is defeated. The light of Christ shines forever. In Christ, there is no room for gloom!

Friends, that's the gospel truth. Amen.

What Were You Thinking?

Late one night, Pastor Bill was driving home after spending the past 23 hours in the hospital with his wife, celebrating the birth of their son. It had been a glorious day. His wife was peacefully resting. His extended family was ecstatic. His son was healthy. Surely God was in heaven and all was right with the world.

As he drove through the city streets, Pastor Bill began to think about all the plans he had to increase parish worship attendance and multiply its Sunday offerings. He reflected upon the recent workshop where he learned new techniques for congregational success. In his mind's eye, Pastor Bill began to visualize a brand-new sanctuary and family-life center for his people. As he was formulating a newspaper article commemorating this marvelous achievement — wham — Pastor Bill's car collided with the rear bumper of another automobile that had stopped at a red traffic signal.

Fortunately, no one was hurt. The pastor's car had only minor damage. Unfortunately, the other vehicle was a police car. Oops! Pastor Bill waited in silence while the gruff police officer meticulously filled out the necessary forms that would label him guilty. A few scruffy, disheveled folks emerged from alleys and shop doorways surrounding the pastor and officer offering themselves as witnesses to this terrible offense.

Finally, the officer completed her paperwork, handed it to Pastor Bill and said, "Appear in court next week. The judge will hand down your verdict."

After several days of explaining to family and parishioners why his car was dented and why his name (also their congregation) appeared in the newspaper police reports, Pastor Bill finally appeared before the judge.

"What were you thinking?" demanded the judge. "How could a man of your status in the community be so stupid that he crashes into a police car?"

With fear and trembling, Pastor Bill began to justify his actions. He explained about the birth of his son. He described in detail his growth plans for his congregation. "I guess I wasn't thinking, your Honor," replied Pastor Bill.

"Of course, you weren't, sir," responded the Judge. "Pay your fine on the way out. And by the way, as long as you're not thinking, don't even think about teaching your son how to drive."

Poor, humiliated, Pastor Bill. How many times do we also find ourselves so pre-occupied with our own dreams and desires that we forget what is going on around us? How many times do we neglect the needs of others while we strive to attain our own personal success and happiness? How many times do we forget and neglect the desperate concerns of those on the margins of society while focusing on our own status and lifestyle? Sadly, all too often for me and perhaps for you, too.

What are we thinking, anyway? Just like Pastor Bill, too often our thoughts and our actions demonstrate that we are thinking only about ourselves.

This certainly describes what Micah was observing in today's Old Testament lesson. Micah was a prophet of Israel during the time of Assyrian conquest approximately 730 years before the birth of Christ. He became appalled by the greed of wealthy nobles who exploited their peasant landholders. His anger grew as he watched corrupt rulers oppress the nation's citizens. He was furious with overconfident religious leaders who ignored the unrighteous acts going on unchecked around them. Maintaining their status was more important than proclaiming God's will. After all, God had chosen Israel, no matter what. God would prevent Assyria from harming Israel. All the religious professionals had to do was keep the temple coffers filled, offer enough animal sacrifices, and provide the "right kind" of worship.

Hmmm ... does that sound a bit like Pastor Bill's driving day-dream? Does that sound at all like our dreams for parish success and happiness? What was Israel thinking?

Our lesson today begins with God summoning Israel to court to explain just what exactly the people were thinking and doing. Here God is both judge and prosecutor. The nation of Israel is the defendant. The witnesses for the prosecution are the mountains and hills who are older than humankind. They know Israel's history and the righteousness of God.

In the first five verses, God presents the opening argument for the prosecution. "Hear, you mountains, the controversy of the Lord ... for the Lord has a controversy with his people, and he will contend with Israel" (Micah 6:2).

Israel had forgotten God's faithfulness of the past. The people had neglected their own faithful response to God's saving acts.

In his opening statement, God enters into evidence a review of his own saving deeds of commitment to the people. The Lord delivered them from Egyptian bondage and gave them powerful leaders (Micah 6:4). He foiled plots against them by the King of Moab and turned the curse of Balaam into a blessing (Micah 6:5). The Lord was with them as they camped at Shittim waiting to cross the Jordan River to possess their new land. The Lord did not abandon them after they entered the land and rested at Gilgal. The Lord did all these things, Micah declares, "... that you may know the saving acts of the Lord" (Micah 6:5).

What were they thinking? Didn't they know that God's faithful actions also required their own faithful response? Did they really think that God was some kind of magic genie who could be appeased by good and proper worship services, some holy oil, and the fragrant aroma of cooked meat? Did they really believe that they could get away with looking good on holy days and doing bad every other day? Did forgetting the Lord and neglecting the poor become commonplace for them? What were they thinking?

God expected, no *demanded* a response. "Rise, plead your case before the mountains; and let the hills hear your voice ... O my people, what have I done to you? In what have I wearied you? Answer me!" (Micah 6:1, 3).

Sometimes in our own, exhausting, stressful lives just showing up to worship is too much. Just keeping afloat in the storms of our own life is demanding enough. When we are able to attend worship, we want to experience some comfort. We want something that will make us happy. And now God expects even more! It seems like there's never enough time, never enough energy. What thing does God require now? It seems like nothing we do can please God.

Micah puts our complaints into the mouth of Israel, acting as its own defense attorney. Listen to the whining defiance inherent within Israel's response.

> *With what shall I come before the Lord ... shall I come before him with burnt offerings ... will the Lord be pleased with thousands of rams, with ten thousands of rivers of oil....*   — Micah 6:6-7

Poor Israel, they just didn't get it. They were still forgetting God's faithfulness. They were trying to appease God by "good and proper" worship. From their perspective, nothing they could offer was enough for the Lord.

Friends, there is the crucial insight of today's lesson. Truly, nothing Israel could do, nothing we can do, is enough to deserve God's love and guidance. Indeed, God wants no *thing from us.* God wants *us!* God reminds Israel, and you and me, that our daily way of life is our response to what God has already done for us.

C. J. had lived a hard, difficult life. He ran away from an abusive home at age thirteen and "traveled the rails," as he called it, for fifty years. Some called him a hobo and a bum. Others had even worse names for C. J.

After his right leg was severed by a moving boxcar, C. J. was placed in government housing next door to a beautiful church. Although he often stopped by to chat with the staff and members, he steadfastly refused to attend any worship service.

"I ain't a worshiping kind of guy," he would comment to everyone who invited him. "Besides, y'all wear them fancy clothes and drive them big cars and recite them high-falutin' words I can't even pronounce."

One day when a church elder offered to help him understand the worship service, C. J. began muttering to himself. The elder said, "I can't hear you, C. J., you'll have to speak louder."

Now screaming at the top of his voice, old disheveled, smelly, C. J. yelled: "I said, Mr. High and Mighty, 'What about them kids over next door? They don't belong to your church. They don't belong to nothin' except some gang! I don't see y'all trying to invite them! Show me *your* religion and maybe I'll show you mine! There's nothing good here anymore!' " And C. J., our modern day Micah, limped away.

And God said to Israel:

> *He has told you, O mortal, what is good, and what does*
> *the Lord require of you but to do justice, and to love*
> *kindness, and to walk humbly with your God?*
> — Micah 6:8

The prosecution rests. The case is airtight. Israel was guilty as charged. So was Pastor Bill. So were C. J.'s well-intentioned church friends — and so are we.

For the Lord, justice is daily living according to God's will and not our own comfort. Justice includes the weak, powerless, vulnerable, and exploited.

For the Lord, to love kindness means to live in deep communal relationship with the weak and the strong, the alien and the citizen. It means demonstrating that we are all bound together in the mercy of God.

For the Lord, walking humbly means to pay careful daily attention to every relationship that God has given us.

"But this is impossible," we complain. "We just cannot possibly do this." And that is true. Our text today begins and ends with God's actions, not Israel's; not even ours.

In and through God's saving act, Jesus Christ, the Lord, has cancelled the destructive power of sin for us and for the world. Through Christ, God had declared us "not guilty." God invites us not to merely remember the crucified and living Christ of the past. He invites us to demonstrate Christ's saving, amazing grace in the present. And that's not all: God promises to continue to save God's own weak, vulnerable, weary children in the future.

What were we thinking anyway?

Because of our sin, we were thinking only of ourselves — our wants — our happiness. Because of our sin we have not been mindful of the needs of others.

Now, here's the good news. Because of our sin, God gave his only son to die for us, to rise for us, to cancel the power of sin, forever. Because of God's once-and-for-all saving act, the Holy Spirit of God calls and sends us into the world as his missionaries to do justice, to love kindness, and to walk daily with our God.

It's not about what we are thinking; it's all about what God has done, is doing, and has promised to continue to do — save and send. Amen.

What Did The Turkey Say?
(Or Contentious Communities)

Here is a story that has been told for many years. Some of you may have heard it.

Jenny had been living alone since her husband died several years earlier. One particular evening, Pastor Alice had scheduled a visit to Jenny's home. Jenny still had a parrot that was her husband's pride and joy. Knowing that the parrot was prone to repeat the profanity it heard form her husband's retired Navy buddies, Jenny cautioned the parrot to be silent during the pastor's visit.

"I promise you, that if you start cursing and swearing when Pastor Alice is here, I will put you in the freezer until she leaves," warned Jenny.

"Okay, okay, I'll be quiet; I'll be good, I promise," pledged the parrot.

Pastor Alice did not even sit down before the parrot began spewing forth foul language.

With a loud sigh, Jenny grabbed the parrot and tossed it into the freezer beside the frozen turkey she was saving for Thanksgiving dinner.

Meanwhile, Pastor Alice stayed much longer than Jenny expected. When the pastor finally left, Jenny rushed to the freezer to free the parrot. When she grasped the parrot, Jenny asked, "Have you learned your lesson now?" The shivering parrot stuttered, "Y-y-yess. B-b-but I have j-j-just one q-q-question. What did that t-t-turkey say?"

There's a lesson here, somewhere, for us and for all God's people. It's not about the turkey, it's about the parrot. It's about hypocrisy; promising one thing and doing the opposite; it's about hypocrisy; putting on an outward appearance of goodness as if we were just as righteous on the inside. Like the parrot, we are all guilty.

What do you think the most common accusation of church members might be? You are absolutely correct if you guessed "hypocrisy."

This hypocritical attitude and behavior is not new for God's people. Isaiah addresses it in our Old Testament text. Just before our lesson begins, God accuses the people of being contentious and rebellious in their actions while putting on a good, religious front with their words.

> *Announce to my people their rebellion, to the house of Jacob their sins. Yet day after day they seek me ... as if they were a nation that practiced righteousness and did not forsake the ordinance of their God.*
> — Isaiah 58:1-2

Let's look at what was happening here, approximately 500 years before the birth of Christ. The religious and political leaders of Judah had been living in exile in Babylon, taken as captives by the conquering army of King Nebuchadnezzar. Jerusalem was a defeated city. Its temple destroyed; its walls crumbled. The exiles had lost all hope of returning.

Perhaps many of them remembered that Isaiah also declared God's promise of deliverance, a new exodus. "Comfort, O comfort my people, says your God, speak tenderly to Jerusalem and cry to her that she has served her term, that her penalty is paid ..." (Isaiah 40:1-2).

They would return home at last! Thanks be to God! Praise the Lord! Just like Moses led the people from Egyptian bondage, so would God lead them out of Babylonian captivity. Soon, God's promise would come true. "Then the glory of the Lord shall be revealed, and all people shall see it together ..." (Isaiah 40:5).

Then the exiles arrived back home. They were really surprised by what they found. Rubble was everywhere. Nobody had even tried to rebuild the temple, let alone the city walls. Worse yet, no one seemed to care! How could these wretched people live in this mess for fifty years and not do anything at all to improve things? If anything, the city was in worse shape now than when the exiles were carted off to Babylon.

Now, remember the returning people had been the "crème dé lá crème" of society. They, or their parents and grandparents, had been cream of the crop, the top of the heap. They were wealthy nobles and landowners in Judah before the exile. Since they were forbidden to own property in Babylon, many became bankers, and business people in one of the world's most powerful empires.

It was this group of "haves" who expected to be welcomed home by a rejoicing city of "have nots" as they marched triumphantly through the streets of Jerusalem. *Not!* Instead the exiles returned to rubble, rubble, toil, and trouble.

They observed new people in leadership positions; new people occupying their vineyards and farms; new people living in their old houses.

So, they tried everything from appeals to guilt and duty to new organizational structures and planning models. Nothing seemed to arouse the "wretched ones" to change the present state of affairs.

Finally, they became even more rigid and demanding in their practices. This would surely show God how serious they were. This would surely convince the lazy among them to begin their rebuilding task. They put on sackcloth and smeared their bodies with ashes. They practiced fasting with strict intensity.

Sadly, the returning "haves" still maintained a wide breach between themselves and the "have nots," the rich and the poor, the powerful and the weak. In their own minds, the returning exiles were still the heroes. Those who remained in Jerusalem were still the chumps.

Just like the parrot, the exiles, in those days, were demonstrating the depths of hypocrisy. Just like the parrot, we, too, have become examples of what hypocrisy looks like. We, too, see a breach between rich and poor, powerful and vulnerable, haves and have nots. It's easy for us to speak and act as if God favors us "heroes" just a little bit more than those "chumps" who never darken the church doors. After all, we keep the fast by our worship and committees and offerings. They do not, and they probably don't even care.

Listen to Isaiah's denunciation of these hypocritical attitudes and religious practices:

> *Look, you serve your own interest on your fast day, and*
> *oppress all your workers. Look, you fast only to quar-*
> *rel and to fight ... Such fasting as you do today will not*
> *make your voice heard on high. Is such the fast that I*
> *choose ... is it to bow down the head like a bulrush?*
> — Isaiah 58:3-5

We, too, stand accused. We, too, speak holy words and perform holy actions during worship. Then, in the parking lots and emails and living rooms we resume the contentious quarrels of Christians throughout history. Christians fight, and make no mistake about it, we fight dirty — even, and often especially — among ourselves. It is a rare congregation that has not experienced the bitter divisiveness of a church conflict.

So then, where is our hope? Where is God's promise? Why doesn't God just thrust us into the freezer before popping us into an eternal oven? Why didn't God just obliterate the returning exiles for their hypocritical, sinful behavior?

God's answer is simple. God chose to deliver his children from the bondage of Egypt and Babylon. God named them and claimed them as his own people. God made them his precious and honored people.

In the waters of baptism, God has named and claimed us as his own children. In the bread and wine of the Lord's Supper, God nourishes and sustains us with the living presence of God's own Son.

Because the returning exiles were God's precious children, God could expect them to show his gifts to others. In Christ, God has gathered us hypocrites into his arms; God gives us the ability to show his gifts to others, and he expects that from us.

Today's text is intended to be received and demonstrated by God's delivered, splashed, and nourished people.

Here is another story ... an airline was having trouble with large flocks of shore birds on runways near the ocean. Frequently the roar of incoming engines would startle the birds and they would fly up, only to crash into and often shatter the windshields of the approaching planes.

After many failed experiments, the company engineers developed a formula for windshields that would both keep the windshields intact as well as causing no harm to the birds. They tested this by using turkeys that were the same size and weight as the shore birds. The engineers then placed a turkey into an air cannon and fired it at a windshield. They repeated this over and over with no harm to either the turkey or the windshield. Success!

Another airline was experiencing the same problem and requested the formula and the method for testing. Unfortunately, when these engineers tested their new windshields, the glass didn't just shatter, the turkey landed in the pilot's seat.

These engineers complained angrily that they had been deliberately given the wrong formula, and demanded an explanation.

"Send us your formula and testing methods!" demanded the original chief engineer.

After reading through the failed method, the chief engineer responded with this brief reply: "First thaw the turkey!"

Friends in Jesus Christ, God has already thawed us frozen turkeys. Because of God's forever love, the exiles could stop their hypocritical, frozen fasting and show others what it looks like to be God's children.

The fast that God chooses looks like this:

> ... *share your bread with the hungry, and bring the home-*
> *less poor into your house; when you see the naked, to*
> *cover them and not to hide yourself from your own kin.*
> — Isaiah 58:7

The exiles could do this because God had chosen them as his own children. They could stop finger pointing and evil speaking (Isaiah 58:9) because God had redeemed them.

They could not do this by their own religious fasts and rites. Neither can we. Because God had redeemed us frozen turkeys, God therefore, sends us to show others what it looks like to be thawed, named, and claimed by the Lord.

Listen to God's promise to the returning exiles and to us:

> *... Then your light shall rise in the darkness and your gloom be like the noonday. The Lord will guide you continually ... and you shall be like a watered garden, like a spring of water, whose waters never fail.*
> — Isaiah 58:10-11

This is the Lord's promise to us hypocritical parrots and frozen turkeys. In Christ, God's promised "then" has become God's thawing embrace "now and forever."

Because God has named us his people, therefore let us show we belong to him. Amen.

Aprons Or Bibs

Potluck dinners are wonderful! We enjoy marvelous fellowship, contagious laughter, and the comfort of being in a place where everybody knows your name. And, oh yes, the food! Tempting aromas fill us with anticipation of the glorious feast to come. Gazing and grazing at the buffet table is one of the true joys of parish life. The major challenge at a parish potluck is that the vast array of tasty choices always exceeds our ability to sample each selection!

There is always more than enough to pile our plates with culinary delicacies; not just once, but twice, or even three times. There is always more than enough leftovers, too, so that each one of us can take home still another meal to pop into the microwave.

One congregation even provides bibs for grazers and aprons for its servers.

Today's Old Testament lesson addresses the issue of choice in the religious life of God's people. Here, Moses' task has been completed. He had led God's people out of Egyptian bondage through the wilderness. The promised land was in sight. Their instruction in faith was complete. God's "buffet table" was visible just across the Jordan River. The people were ready to don their bibs. They were eager to stop gazing and begin grazing. They were ready to change their identity from "losers" to "choosers."

However, their choice was not as simple as deciding whether to select meatloaf or fried chicken. Their choice was truly a matter of life and death. "... I have set before you life and death, blessings and curses. Choose life so that you and your descendants may live" (Deuteronomy 30:19).

Now that's a powerful choice and an even more powerful promise! It should also be pretty easy, a "no-brainer," right? Who among us would choose curses over blessing not just for ourselves but for our entire families for generations to come? Who among us in their right minds would choose death over life? Naturally, we would choose life and blessings every time. After all, we shape our future by the choices we make in the present.

Let's go back to God's people in our text. Their history up to this point certainly was not filled with good life choices. They often turned away from the Lord and worshiped other gods. They were often unjust and unfair in their treatment of the poor and vulnerable. They often ignored and even openly opposed the leadership of Moses. They often experienced bitter quarreling and dissention within their midst ... just like roots "sprouting poisonous and bitter growth" (Deuteronomy 29:18).

Choosing life and blessing was not as easy as it looked for God's people then. It is at least as difficult for us today, especially during troubled and frightening times. When the storms and challenges of life are crashing upon us from every direction, it's almost impossible to make any decision at all except to stop the immediate pain and eliminate the overwhelming fear. We will choose any port to ride out the storm in safety.

When giving directions to his home, retired New York Yankees catcher, Yogi Berra, explained, "When you come to a fork in the road, take it."

Which fork leads home? Which port is safe? How do we know for sure? How can we really know what choosing life and blessing looks like?

In our lesson, Moses was wrapping up his final address to God's children. Here, Moses reviewed their tumultuous forty-year wilderness journey and summarized faithful living as God's people in the promised land. "... loving the Lord your God, walking in his ways, and observing his commandments, decrees and ordinances ... obeying him and holding fast to him ..." (Deuteronomy 30:16, 20). Choosing life was to be demonstrated by faithful worship, purity of lifestyle, fair treatment of the weak and vulnerable, faithful leadership, and the honoring of all creation. (Actually, chapters 1-30 of Deuteronomy describe this in some detail!)

Even with these specific directions, God's people would often miss the mark completely. Left to their own efforts they would deserve not life and blessings, but death and curses. In the very next chapter of Deuteronomy, the Lord tells Moses that after Moses dies, the people will begin to worship pagan gods in their midst and will forsake God by breaking the covenant they made. "... they have eaten their fill and grown fat, they will turn to other gods ... despising me and breaking my covenant" (Deuteronomy 31:20).

Left on our own, we cannot follow the clear direction of God's teachings and decrees. Left on our own, life can be just one curse after another. Then we die. Left on our own, in the middle of life's cursed troubles, we gaze at folks who seem to have it all together. We long to graze at their buffet table of happiness and security. If only we could just understand the step-by-step directions to success and joy.

A doctoral student who was living in another state forwarded a dissertation proposal for her major professor to critique. She enclosed a self-addressed, stamped envelope for his convenience. After making suggestions on the proposal, the professor placed it back inside the envelope. Across the flap he noticed a tape on which the following clear directions were painted in large capital letters "Press it. Seal it." So he pressed it, but it would not seal. Again and again, the professor followed the directions explicitly. He pressed and he pressed, but still the envelope did not seal. He then began to pound and then to stomp on the flap with the same failed results.

Finally, the faculty secretary heard the uproar in the mail room and rushed in to see what was happening. With a twinkle in her eyes and a smile that she could not fully disguise, she took the envelope from the helpless and befuddled professor and said, "Watch and learn."

She then grasped one corner of the tape and peeled it away from the envelope flap. She then pressed it, sealed it, dropped it into the mail slot, and returned to her duties.

"Oh," said the professor.

No matter how clear the directions, God's people, you and I, cannot follow them alone. No matter what seems to be a clear-cut choice, God's people always seem to gaze and graze at the wrong buffet table, and we need enormous bibs to catch the overflow from our sinful choices.

The good news here is that God has already made the first choice. Through his covenant with Abraham, God chose these people to become his own. Through Moses, God chose to deliver his people from bondage and to form them in faithful living as they journeyed through the wilderness to arrive at the edge of the land God had chosen for them. God kept his covenantal promise to them often in spite of them.

God had already made the crucial choice of life and blessings for them. Because God had chosen them, God gave them the ability to choose life and the clear directions for living as God's people. And, with those directions, God intended for them to be ready to exchange their grazing bibs for serving aprons.

In Jesus Christ, God has continued to choose us as his own children. In Christ, the living Word of God, God promises, "The word is very near to you; it is in your mouth and in your heart for you to observe" (Deuteronomy 30:14; see also Romans 10:8).

What does that choice look like? God's choice looks like the Word made flesh in a Bethlehem manger. It looks like the water mingled with that Word in baptism. God's choice looks like the Word broken and poured out for us in holy communion. God's choice looks like a cross and an empty tomb.

Jane was in hospice care, suffering from the effects of a massive stroke that would soon end her life. During her last few days, Jane was unable to move or to speak; yet the gleam in her eyes and a "yahoo" when a visitor entered the room let folks know that she was fully aware of her surroundings. Finally, it appeared to all that Jane had slipped into a coma. The pastor was called. Family and friends were gathered at her bedside. Together they shared "Jane stories." The room was filled with laughter and tears. It was time to share the meal Jesus served to his disciples in that upper room long ago. Clustered around Jane's bed, the small group of family and friends heard the familiar and life giving words: "This is my body, given for you. This is my blood, shed for you." And suddenly, from Jane's bed, they heard, "Yahoo!"

At the very moment, God's choice of Jane and of each of those gathered around her became visible. In that one exclamation, "Yahoo," Jane removed her grazing bib and put on her serving apron ... for the pastor and for all God's gathered people.

At that very moment, God demonstrated what our text looks like in this life and the next: "I have set before you life and death, blessings and curses. Choose life so that you and your descendants may live" (Deuteronomy 30:19).

Jesus Christ, host at the buffet table, serves God's chosen children. Because God had chosen her to serve, even in her most fragile hour, Jane was able to serve others with a foretaste of the buffet that would come very soon. Thanks be to God for Jane. Thanks be to God for giving us bibs for receiving and aprons for serving. Yahoo! Amen.

Epiphany 7
Ordinary Time 7
Leviticus 19:1-2, 9-18

The Hungry Monkey

During a meeting of the parish stewardship committee, members viewed a thirty-second video clip taken in the monkey house of a local zoo. The zookeeper placed some "monkey delicacies" (banana bits, lettuce, and others) into a plastic container with a very tiny opening. Then she put the bottle on a table and left the room. Soon, one of the monkeys slowly approached the container, reached carefully inside, and grasped a large handful of treats. Unfortunately, with its fist full of food, the monkey was unable to remove its hand from the container. The monkey would first shake the container; then vigorously pound it on the table. This happened time after time, monkey after monkey. After a training session, the monkeys learned that the only way they could get their hands free was to let go of the food. The only way they could receive any food was to dump the contents of the bottle on the table, in the middle of the other hungry monkeys who were observing. The only way for a monkey to taste the gourmet food was to share it with others.

There's a lesson here for all of us; a lesson that is clearly demonstrated in our text in Leviticus. Moses addressed the people in the wilderness, describing God's will for faithful and holy sharing. Pay attention here — the key to unlock meaning in this text is who God is and not what we do. We see this in God's first words to the people. "... You shall be holy, for I the Lord your God am holy" (Leviticus 19:2).

The gathered congregation of Israel can be holy because God is holy ... not because of what they do. They can do holy things ... sharing with the poor and weak, loving their neighbor, living at peace within their families — because God is holy and they are already God's holy people. Because they are God's holy people, they can unclench greedy fists that grasp all of God's blessings for themselves and share their abundance with others.

Because God has made us his holy people through our baptism into Christ Jesus, therefore, we can also do holy things. Holy, ethical behavior is not only a consequence of God's love for us; it is an authentic demonstration of God's love for us and for all creation. Holy behavior becomes holy witness, not to ourselves, but to the holy and loving God of the universe.

At noon one Thanksgiving day, six-year-old Felicia was helping a large group of church folks who were serving dinner at a local shelter for homeless families. When Felicia placed a still-steaming dinner roll on his plate, one of the men asked why she was there and not at home on Thanksgiving.

Wise beyond her years, Felicia declared, "My granddaddy says that Thanksgiving day should be a holy day for everybody, and we should make sure to show it! Now keep moving. Somebody else needs a roll!"

Now, that's what holiness looks like. Thanks, Felicia. Holy deeds might actually speak at least as loudly as holy words. Keep moving, someone else needs a roll. That almost sounds like a mission statement, doesn't it?

God made us holy in order that God's holy love is made visible to others.

The writer of 1 Peter states it like this: "... you are a chosen race, a royal priesthood, a holy nation, God's own people, in order that you may proclaim the mighty acts of him who called you out of darkness into his marvelous light" (1 Peter 2:9).

In the Sermon on the Mount, Jesus charges his followers: "... let your light shine before others, so that they may see your good works and give glory to your Father in heaven" (Matthew 5:16).

You see, it's not about what we do, or even fail to do; it's about what God has done, is doing, and has promised to continue to do. God declared that the congregation of Israel shall be holy because God is holy. God had declared God's people to be a holy nation because God made them holy through the gift of his own Son. Jesus calls upon Christians to let our light shine before others because, through him, we have been given God's own holy light.

Now, what does holy living look like in our Leviticus text? When we look at Leviticus 19:9-18, it's important to remember a lesson from cultural anthropologists ... a technical term that describes people who study ancient civilizations. These folks examine what the laws and teachings of a society *prohibit* in order to develop a picture of what people were actually doing. In other words, they first examine the "don'ts" before they could describe a reason for the "do's."

Think about the "don'ts" in our society, our schools, our workplace, our families, or even our congregations. Don't break the speed limit. Don't talk in class. Don't play computer games during working hours. Don't throw your dirty clothes on the floor. Don't park your car in the preacher's space. Each "don't" describes actual behavior or it would not be prohibited. You can think of many more examples.

As you read our text, watch for what behaviors were actually happening among God's people. Owners of farms and vineyards were harvesting all of their crops, reaping to the very edges of [their] field (Leviticus 19:9). They would strip [their] vineyards bare gathering even the fallen grapes for themselves (Leviticus 19:10).

Others were guilty of stealing, dealing falsely, speaking lies, and using God's name to justify phony promises in order to defraud others (Leviticus 19:11-12). Some were holding back wages from laborers who had expected to be paid at the end of each day's work. Still others took advantage of the deaf and blind (Leviticus 19:13-14). Injustice, slander, family grudges, and favoritism were common place (Leviticus 19:15-18).

Doesn't this sound a lot like the monkeys with their fists filled with food and trapped inside the plastic container? Doesn't this also reflect what we see in our society, even among Christians today? What does our own plastic container look like? What do we grasp so tightly in our clenched fists that prevents us from holy living?

105

Holy living is summarized in our text: "... You shall love your neighbor as yourself ..." (Leviticus 19:18). Here are some examples of open handed, holy living from today's lesson:

1. Sharing your food supply with the poor and the alien (Leviticus 19:10).
2. Speaking the truth and dealing fairly with all persons regardless of their social status (Leviticus 19:11-16).
3. Making peace with friends, and family members with whom you hold a grudge (Leviticus 19:17-18).

In our text, the neighbor is not simply a peer, or one who shares our lifestyle and value system. The neighbor includes those who are shunned by society — those on the margins — those whom we are likely to forget.

When we show partiality to certain groups, when we carry longstanding grudges and prejudice, we not only wound others, we also wound our own souls. Everyone is wounded, not just the intended objects of our private grudges and selfishness. When we keep our fists tightly clenched around God's gifts, no one, not even ourselves, can share God's blessings. How we relate to all God's children does reveal a measure of faithfulness to God.

Holy living is really tough! Loving our neighbor as ourselves is next to impossible! That is, if we think we can do this alone. Look at the text again. God says that indeed holy lives are possible. Why? "... For I the Lord your God am holy" (Leviticus 19:2). It's not about our actions. It's about God's promised love.

Note well that in each section where God describes the "don'ts" and prescribes the "do's" God declares "I am the Lord" (Leviticus 19:10, 12, 14, 16, 18). Five times we read God's saving declaration. Five times, God proclaims that because God is the Lord (and we are not), therefore, God's chosen children are able to live holy lives.

Because God has made us his children through baptism into Christ, we are able to unclench our fists and release God's gifts to others. Because God's own Son died for us and for all people, with Felicia, we are able to see others who also "need a roll."

D. T. Niles, retired bishop of South India, once defined evangelism as "one beggar showing another beggar where the bread is." Friends, the bread is here in our midst, on the altar. The bread is the body of Christ, "given for you," and for all God's monkeys. Here God nourishes his children and opens our hands to release this bread for the entire world.

Let's keep moving. Somebody else needs a roll. Amen.

Losers, Weepers

All of us have experienced the pain of loss in many different forms. We have lost wallets or purses; keys or address books; tools or toys. Some of us have even lost our automobiles in crowded parking lots.

Have you ever watched young children participating in their first organized athletic competition? Winning brings loud cheers and high fives. Losing brings jeers and tears.

Losing hurts. It can be devastating to lose even what seems to be a trivial object or a meaningless game. Losing can often shape the way we understand ourselves, our families, our very lives. The way in which we learn to cope with even a small loss in childhood greatly affects how we cope with any major loss that follows ... such as a job loss, a broken relationship, an illness, or even the death of a loved one. It is so very easy to label ourselves and others as "losers." Most of us have seen or experienced the taunts of others, who pretend to whine, and display the "L" for loser sign with thumb and forefinger on their hands. Losers, weepers!

Losing hurts. Losers do weep. Left on our own, we can easily live as if we were lifelong, hopeless, and helpless losers.

In our text, Isaiah addresses a bunch of losers. A few years before, their nation, Judah, had lost a war with Babylon. The strong, protecting walls of Jerusalem were now in rubble. Hope of safety was lost and long gone. Their glorious worship center lay in ruins. The promised spiritual security of the temple was lost. In fact, these folks had also lost their homes, their citizenship, and their social standing. Even worse, they had lost their homeland and were now living as captives in Babylon, more than 500 miles to the north. They were losers in every sense of the term. It seemed as if even God had abandoned them. Losers! Weepers!

Their losing cry of hopelessness is found in these words: "But Zion said, 'the Lord has forsaken me, my Lord has forgotten me' " (Isaiah 49:14).

Perhaps this is the cry of many of us now. We have experienced so many losses in our lives that we have begun to think of ourselves only as losers. We look at life through "L-shaped" lenses. If anything bad can happen it does, and if something bad hasn't happened yet, it will. We expect to lose and we begin to shape our identity with the "L" clearly marked on our foreheads and deeply embedded in our souls. Losers! Weepers! Even if, by chance, something good does happen, we are certain that it will soon be taken away ... lost again! What else is new for us losers and weepers?

It's interesting to see that the exiles' forgotten loser lament in Isaiah 49:14 comes in the middle of the Lord's declaration of deliverance, favor, and victory in our text. Our lesson begins with this promise: "Thus says the Lord; in a time of favor I have answered you on a day of salvation I have helped you" (Isaiah 49:8).

The Lord promised a safe deliverance from captivity; nourishing and protecting them on their homeward journey (Isaiah 49:9-12). The Lord proclaimed a time of praise and rejoicing.

> *Sing for joy, O heavens and exult, O Earth; break forth, O mountains, into singing! For the Lord had comforted his people, and will have compassion on his suffering ones.* — Isaiah 49:13

Did you notice the past tense of many verbs in this text so far? God has answered, has helped, has kept (Isaiah 49:8-9), and has comforted (Isaiah 49:13). Sadly, the losers-weepers didn't get it, yet. In the very next verse (v. 14), the whining complaint of the loser prevailed. They still saw themselves as helpless and hopeless, forgotten by the Lord. They seemed to be unwilling and unable to understand and accept what God had already done to change their perspective from loser to victor. If they could not see God's past actions for them — answering, helping, saving, comforting — it would be very difficult for them to see God acting in their present situation. It would be nearly impossible for them to believe God's promises in the future. Losers! Weepers! Hopeless, helpless, forsaken, forgotten losers — all of them — all of us.

However, even if we view life through the eyes of a forgotten loser, God does not forget us. Here is the good news, friends. Pay attention to God's reply to Zion's complaint: "Can a woman forget her nursing child, or show no compassion to the child of her womb?" (Isaiah 49:15).

Did you hear how the Lord persists with faithfulness and love in spite of the pessimistic doubts of the people? Do you know that God is patient with our own suspicious "buts" and "what ifs"?

Listen to one of the most wonderful promises God gives in all of scripture: "See, I have inscribed you on the palms of my hands" (Isaiah 49:16). With these words the Lord reveals a deep, intimate, personal love for his people. No longer will they see themselves as forgotten and forsaken. God has inscribed (perhaps tattooed?) the image of Jerusalem on his own hands. Note well, that God did not say that he had the name "Zion" on his hands. God had engraved the image of the *whole* people, represented by the holy city of Jerusalem on his hands. This would be similar to a lover having a picture of his beloved tattooed on each hand. The image of the *whole* people cannot be mistaken. That is permanent attachment! That is God's forever, invincible love!

With outstretched arms and hands, God embraced the exiles, those who remained in devastated Jerusalem and those who had been scattered throughout the known world. With outstretched arms and open hands, God gathered them and declared, "Finders, keepers! You are mine forever!"

With outstretched arms and open hands, pierced by nails fastening him to the cross, Jesus Christ demonstrated that forever love for you and the world. The marks of those nails bear the permanent image of God's love for you, for us, for the world. In Christ, God has also inscribed us on the palms of his hands. That's good news, friends! We may be "losers, weepers" if left alone, but in Christ, God proclaims, us to be, "Finders, keepers, forever!"

And that's not all! God finds, keeps, and then sends us on mission trips into the world. In our text, God declares to his servant people! "... I have kept you and given you as a covenant to the people ..." (Isaiah 49:8).

Because God finds and keeps them, therefore, these "losers and weepers" are able to assert themselves in specific acts of witness and rebuilding, "saying to the prisoners, 'Come out,' to those who are in darkness, 'Show yourselves' " (Isaiah 49:9).

Because God, in Christ, has found and kept us, therefore, we "losers and weepers" are sent to touch the lives of those who are trapped in the darkness of despair, rejection, and violence. Because Christ has inscribed us on the palms of his hands, therefore, we "losers and weepers" are sent to rebuild hearts and souls that lay in ruins, just like the walls of Jerusalem long ago.

God proclaims to the exiles and to us that he sees the brokenness around us and within us, and gives us power to do something about it. "... your walls are continually before me. Your builders outdo your destroyers" (Isaiah 49:16-17).

Alone, we are helpless and hopeless. Alone, we are like the walls of Jerusalem after the Babylonian conquest: broken and fragmented, rubble and ruins. Alone, we are losers.

However, on the cross, God has transformed us from losers to victors. Remember, that sign of the letter "L" made by thumb and pointing finger on our foreheads?

Let's try an experiment. Make the letter "L" in the center of a blank sheet of paper. Be sure to leave lots of room in all four margins. Now turn the paper around, so that the top and bottom edges of your "L" are reversed. You are now looking at an upside-down "L." Extend the vertical line of the "L" an inch or two upward, past the horizontal line. Finally, extend the horizontal line of the original "L" an inch or two beyond the vertical line. Do you see what happened to your first "L" for loser? The image is now a cross ... God's forever promise of forgiveness, mercy, and steadfast love. In Christ, God has turned losers into victors. In Christ, God has turned the world's reality upside down. With the crucifixion of Christ, God has turned the mark of the "L" into a permanent inscription of victorious love.

At baptism, God marks both our foreheads and our souls with this triumphant cross of victory.

At the Lord's Supper, Christ feeds us with outstretched palms "inscribed" with wounds that proclaim, "For you."

Losers, weepers no more, we are children of God. The victorious arms of Christ exclaim, "Finders, keepers!"

That's the gospel truth! Amen.

I Don't Do Windows

For months, members of the parish property team had been having difficulty finding volunteers to clean the many windows of the new education building. No one signed up to do this when the annual "time and talent" sheets were distributed the previous fall. No one responded to the requests for volunteers placed in bulletins and newsletters. No one answered their "fuss and beg" pleas for help during Sunday morning announcements.

Finally, committee members decided to make individual and personal pleas to parishioners. After all, it was getting close to Easter and the windows had never been cleaned. The dust and dirt on the inside of the windows made it nearly impossible to see outside. The grime on the outside was a poor witness to the community.

Sadly, each potential volunteer contacted by committee members gave the same reply: "I don't do windows!"

You can't really blame them. Cleaning windows is a very tedious, time-consuming task. You clean the grime outside, and then see dust and handprints on the inside. So, you clean the inside and notice all the streaks and missed spots on the outside. You try soap and water, spray cleaners and chamois, even vinegar and newspapers. Nothing seems to work. Streaks and smudges and scratches abound; even when you use one of those expensive squeegees.

Well, members of the property committee finally had to clean the windows themselves. When Easter Sunday arrived, each property committee member greeted parishioners by saying: "Christ is risen! Don't look too closely at the windows; we did our best."

Each property committee member was painfully aware of exactly which windows she or he had cleaned. Each member was painfully aware of her or his own streaks and missed spots.

Like the property committee, each one of us is seeking a better way to clean the windows of our lives, inside and outside. We have become painfully aware that we need help and guidance. We can't do it alone. We might get the outside clean in the eyes of others, but the inside is still blotted by sin. We need help. We can't do this alone.

This describes the situation of God's people in today's Old Testament text. Here they are wandering in the wilderness for many years. Looking back, they remembered that God had delivered them from bondage in Egypt. That was wonderful! Looking forward, they could catch a glimpse of the new land that God had promised to them and to their descendants. That was glorious!

However, if they looked inside, they would also see the streaks and stain of sin still visible in their wilderness journey. There was that incident with the golden calf, remember that? Moses was on Mount Sinai receiving God's covenant with the people, which was written on two stone tablets. The people were so anxious and impatient that they induced Aaron, Moses' brother, to make them an idol of gold to worship. When God saw this, he told Moses: "... I have seen this people, how stiff-necked they are. Now let me alone, so that my wrath may burn hot against them, and I may consume them ..." (Exodus 32:9-10).

When Moses rushed down the mountain to see the calf and the dancing people for himself: "Moses' anger burned hot, and he threw the tablets from his hands and broke them at the foot of the mountain" (Exodus 32:19b).

In the wilderness journey, even God's called leaders are stained with sin, both outside and inside. It's hard to journey faithfully in the wilderness of the present. We remember wonderful times in the past and yearn for glorious times in a promised future. However, a closer look through the windows of the past also reveals shameful streaks and guilty grime. The future appears only as a wishful, wistful dream.

Certainly many of us have experienced the same frustration. The property committee certainly did. It's hard to be in the wilderness, remembering the past comforts and longing for the future promise. It's hard to feel alone experiencing the stained, streaked wilderness of the present. Moses said this well as he complained to God: "I am not able to carry all this people alone, for they are too heavy for me" (Numbers 11:14).

Have we not said these very words, when we have asked for volunteer help and heard only "I don't do windows!"?

Now we get to the core of our text in Deuteronomy. Here God describes faithful living in the wilderness. Israel is existing on the boundary between Egyptian bondage and the promised new land; between blessing and curse; life and death (Deuteronomy 11:26-28). Indeed, the past experience of God's deliverance was exciting. The vision of a new land of their very own was terrific. Yet, wandering endlessly in the present anxious wilderness brought constant frustration and fears. How long must they wander? We know the journey lasted forty years, but they did not. In fact, in Hebrew, "forty" is also an adjective that is translated as "many." With no specific end date in sight, it's no wonder that this band of God's people murmured, complained, and rebelled.

Life in our present wilderness, between God's deliverance from the stain of sin at our baptism and God's promise of eternal life is filled with frustration, failure, and stress. It's hard to live in the perilous and rapidly changing wilderness of an uncertain present. It's hard to live with only wishes and wants for a better future. It's easy to grasp any new idea or self-help method that promises to help us cope with a stressful present and an uncertain future. The Lord knows that. Just before our text begins, God warns Israel: "Take care, or you will be seduced into turning away, serving other gods and worshiping them" (Deuteronomy 11:16).

Hanging on the wall of one pastor's study is a framed cartoon of a man with a rope around his neck, standing on a tall stack of self-help books. He had tried the advice in each book and found only emptiness, futility, and failure.

In the wilderness of the present, God does not abandon us. God persists with passion. It is in the wilderness of the present that

God forms us as a community, immune to the seductive temptations that bombard us from all sides. In the wilderness of the present, God cleanses us from the stain of sin on the inside. In the wilderness of the present, God shows us how to see clearly the reminders of his love in the past. In the wilderness of the present, God shows us how to live faithfully so that a blurry and uncertain future is transformed into a focused, promised reality. That's good news!

Look again at our text. God had already claimed Israel as his own people; had already rescued them from slavery; had already given them an irrevocable promise of a new land. Because God was with them in their present wilderness, they were able to live as God's people, cleansed, both inside and outside. Therefore, on the inside, God says, "You shall put these words of mine in your heart and soul ..." (Deuteronomy 11:18).

Because God was with them in the past, and continued to be in the present, and promised to be with them in the future, therefore, Israel could do this. God did not and would not abandon them.

The "heart" here refers to the will, the intentional focus of God's people. Here is a clear, *proactive* purpose, for faithful wilderness living. It is not a reactive response to window cleaning problems of present living.

The "soul" here refers to all of one's life and experience. It is not some wispy, ghost-like substance that flutters away at death. In Hebrew thought, the soul is our total identity: both *who* we are, and *whose* we are. A danger in the present wilderness living was for Israel and for us is to ignore the "whose" we are. This inevitably results in reliance on more self-help strategies and a surrender to the seductive temptations of the currently popular "gods" that promise immediate success and satisfaction.

On the outside, God designated specific, clear signs that would both remind Israel of God's past deliverance and of God's continuing presence and guidance.

> You shall bind them [God's teachings] as a sign on your hand, and fix them as an emblem on your forehead ... Write them on the doorposts of your house and on your gates. — Deuteronomy 11:18b-20

Now, these were very specific signs. They were small hollow cubes. Inside each one were three tiny scrolls from sacred scripture, including today's text (Deuteronomy 11:13-21; Deuteronomy 6:4-9; Exodus 13:1-10). Here God's promise was clear every day. God's teachings were available every day. God's directions for faithful living were present every day. God's love and mercy were visible, every day.

What are some everyday, inside and outside, reminders of God's promise and presence that are clearly visible to us on our wilderness journey? God has given us many — thank God! There is the water of baptism that is visible and tangible every time we wash our faces. Here is a sign that God has claimed us as his people and names us as God's own children, both inside and out. The water, together with God's Word, Jesus Christ, has cleaned the windows of our souls, inside and outside.

Then there is the cross, in our sanctuaries, on our jewelry, even on many of the doors in our homes. Look closely at some of the wooden doors in your house today. Here are visible reminders of Christ who gave his life and rose again to make visible God's new and promised reality.

Look at the altar. It is here that God's new reality shatters our present wilderness each time we receive the body and blood of Christ and hear his words, "Given and shed for you."

Look around and see God's people gathered in worship and in Sunday school classes. They hear God's word proclaimed and taught. Look at the many faithful acts of kindness given by God's people to the weak and vulnerable and suffering ones.

Here are clear and visible reminders of God's presence and guidance in our present wilderness. Perhaps you can think of others.

The Lord urged Israel, and invites us to remember *who* and *whose* we are every day. Pass the promises to others, every day. "Teach them to your children, talking about them when you are at home and when you are away, when you lie down and when you rise" (Deuteronomy 11:19).

We might not "do windows" very well. We always seem to leave streaks and stains inside and outside. The good news is that Jesus Christ does windows perfectly. Through Jesus Christ, God's promise to Israel in the wilderness is a present and clear and unstained reality today. In Christ, the inside grime of our souls is cleansed, forever. Because of Christ, the outside stain of sinful behavior can also reflect God's abounding and steadfast love and mercy.

God does windows! Thank God! Amen.

The Transfiguration Of Our Lord
(Last Sunday After Epiphany)
Exodus 24:12-18

Forty Days And Forever

Here's a story that many church members have been telling for a while.

Two seminary professors entered a local fast-food restaurant loudly chanting, "For-ty days! For-ty days!" Then they were joined by three more. Then five more gathered at their table, all chanting, "For-ty days! For-ty days!" Soon, the uproar had disrupted the entire restaurant and the manager came over to ask the professors to keep the noise down.

"What's all the chanting about anyway?" asked the manager. "You are disturbing everybody." Still shouting, the professors began pointing vigorously at the center of their table. Here the manager saw a fully assembled and framed child's puzzle depicting the face of Winnie-the-Pooh.

Becoming annoyed, the manager said, "So? What's the big deal about this puzzle?"

Finally, as the chanting subsided, a senior faculty member explained. "Everyone thinks that seminary professors have no common sense and are out of touch with the real world. We grew tired of being ridiculed, so we decided to set the record straight. Our entire faculty got together and purchased this puzzle. We put it together, working as a team among the community of believers."

"Uh huh," replied the manager, as she began to look around for something, anything, that required her attention. "So, what's the big deal about *this* puzzle?"

"Just look at the side of this puzzle box," exclaimed another professor. "It clearly and precisely bears the inscription '2-4 years.' We assembled it in only forty days!"

The chanting bedlam resumed. "For-ty days! For-ty days!"

And the manager bowed her head and silently prayed, "Lord, give me strength," as she swiftly darted behind the counter.

Can you see the core issue of the professors here? They were too concerned with other's opinions about them. What others thought about them began to dominate their behavior and ultimately resulted in even more foolish, ridiculous actions.

It has been said before that many Christians have been raised with eleven (not ten) commandments. The eleventh commandment was the question ... "What will people think about you?"

You see, the real issue here, for those foolish faculty members and for us, is "What does God think about you?" It's not about us; it is about God.

Today, Transfiguration Sunday, celebrates what God thinks about us and what God does among us in forming us as God's people. Indeed, it is not simply a matter of what God has thought and has done. The transfiguration also declares what God is thinking and doing among us, and promises to continue thinking and doing among us in the future.

Let's look at our Old Testament lesson for Transfiguration Sunday.

The text immediately follows a gathering of elders near Mount Sinai, the holy mountain of God. Here Moses and the elders celebrated God's presence and guidance. Here they pledged to obey God's instruction.

Our text begins with an articulation of three crucial aspects of God's forming and guiding presence in the lives of God's people: God invites, God's people wait, God gives.

> *The Lord said to Moses, "Come up to me on the mountain, and wait there, and I will give you the tablets of stone, with the law and the commandments which I have written for their instruction."* — Exodus 24:12

First, God invited Moses to meet him on the holy mountain of Sinai. Here in this place the glory of the Lord would be revealed in all its power and intensity. Here in this place the presence of God would illumine the identity and clarify the mission of God's people. Here, on this mountaintop, at the invitation of God, Moses was invited to experience the highest of "spiritual highs."

Two thousand years later, Jesus invited the inner circle of his disciples to a mountaintop where they, too, experienced the transfiguring glory of God and a powerful affirmation of their identity as part of God's holy people.

Wouldn't it be wonderful if we could live our lives on one everlasting spiritual high? Wouldn't it be marvelous if every day was mountaintop day? One life-long glorious, happy time of joy and wonder would be just fine, thank you.

God *does* invite us to a special space where God does show us his glory and reveals to us his eternal love and forgiveness. God *does* think about us with an abundance of steadfast love and mercy, and that holy space, obviously, can be anywhere, because we know God is everywhere.

However, the children of Israel knew from past experience (Exodus 3) that God's presence would definitely be revealed on this mountain at this time. In the same way, we know that God reveals his presence and guidance wherever God's people are gathered for worship. Here beneath the cross, in front of the altar, beside the baptismal waters, in the midst of God's people, God reveals his presence to us. Here in the proclaimed word we hear what God has done, is doing, and promises to continue to do among us and for us. Here God invites us to be formed and "transfigured" into a new identity as God's own people. Here could be a spiritual mountaintop high for us, just as it was for Moses and for the disciples.

However, we don't always get it. We don't always feel it. Nor should we expect to. It's not about us; it's about God!

Little Jasmine was preparing for her first worship anthem as a member of the cherub choir, a group of three-year-old angels in her congregation. Many times, the choir director had the children practice walking to the chancel steps from their seats beside their parents. "When all the people sit down, you leave your parents in the pew and come up here. Then we'll sing 'Jesus Loves Me' so loudly that people can hear us out in the parking lot." The anthem was a joy to behold! At the proper time in the service, eleven cherubs, including Jasmine, made a glorious noise to the Lord.

The next Sunday, "when all the people sat down," Jasmine still remembered her instructions from the previous Sunday. She calmly walked to the chancel steps, and, all by herself, began to sing "Jesus Loves Me." Jasmine's daddy knew that his daughter's impromptu solo was not in the bulletin, and he rushed to her "rescue." Scooping up his little girl in his arms, Daddy started jogging toward the nursery, with Jasmine loudly pleading to the congregation, "Somebody help me!"

Maybe Daddy didn't get it. Maybe Daddy was too worried about what people would think ... about his daughter and about him.

Jasmine's solo is a good example of the second point in our lesson. God's people wait. What is faithful waiting anyway? Again, let's look at the text. After God invited Moses and Joshua to ascend Mount Sinai, Moses instructed the elders: "Wait here for us, until we come to you again; for Aaron and Hur are with you; whoever has a dispute may go to them" (Exodus 24:14).

Faithful waiting for God's people does not mean sitting on our thumbs and doing nothing. It means hearing God's word and obeying God's teachings. In fact, Moses urged the people to do just that in the verses just prior to today's lesson (Exodus 24:7-8).

Even though Jasmine's solo was not in the bulletin, she did proclaim God's love both in word and in deed. She sang God's praise in the past (the week before) and she was proclaiming God's love in the present. Her spontaneous declaration of God's love would also permeate the soul of that congregation in the future. On that day, Jasmine's faithful waiting became a transfiguring moment for everyone.

Note that Aaron and Hur were designated by Moses to serve as leaders of the people as they waited faithfully for Moses' return. They were charged with insuring that God's words would be proclaimed and God's instructions would be obeyed. Perhaps you also recall that it was Aaron and Hur who held Moses' tired arms high in order to bring victory in a battle with Amalek (Exodus 17:10-12). Aaron, Moses' brother, was responsible for faithful worship and proclaiming God's words. Hur, possibly Moses' brother-in-law, was responsible for faithful obedience to God's teachings. Together, they were to insure faithful waiting ... to make sure that the people *got* it even if they did not always *feel* it ... to make certain that faithful waiting was all about God, and not all about them.

Jasmine did that, too. Faithful waiting includes everyone in God's family — brothers and brothers-in-law, sisters and aunts, moms and dads, grandparents and cousins — all of God's baptized family. When we just don't get it, when we are too exhausted or pre-occupied to feel it, God gives strength and courage to press on faithfully.

So, God invites. God's people wait. Most important here is the third point of our text: God gives.

In today's lesson, when Moses ascended the mountain, "the glory of the Lord settled on Mount Sinai" (Exodus 24:16). Moses and the elders assembled below. They knew for a fact that God was truly present there and yet the mountaintop was shrouded by a covering of clouds for six days.

Nevertheless, they were well aware that the real presence of God was specific and real on that mountain. Why? Because God said so. God invited Moses to see it. God gave the onlookers a glimpse of his presence. "Now, the appearance of the glory of the Lord was like a devouring fire on the top of the mountain in the sight of the people of Israel" (Exodus 24:17).

God gives us glimpses of his awesome presence. As he penetrates our cloudy perceptions, God reveals his radiant transfiguring presence to us in the waters of baptism. God's words to us echo his words to Jesus, "You are my beloved child." These words embraced Jasmine at her baptism. These words clear the clouds that cover our very souls today.

Today, Transfiguration Sunday, God invites us, with Moses, to "enter the cloud" enveloping God's presence. Today, God gives us a taste of his abiding love at the altar. Today, here in this place, God shows us his radiant glory as we see with the disciples, the shining wonder of God's beloved Son. God is indeed giving us a mountaintop spiritual high.

Nevertheless, we will not always get it or feel it. Just like the professors with the puzzle, we will expend enormous energy in futile and ridiculous feel-good tasks.

Today, Transfiguration Sunday, mountaintop Sunday, God sends us with the disciples, back down into the valley of waiting. God did not abandon Jesus or the disciples as they began their journey to the cross. God does not and will not abandon us. God gives us many "Jasmines" who surprise us with the wonder of God's presence. Best of all, God gives us his beloved Son, Jesus Christ, who invites us to journey with him during the forty days of Lent and forever. Now that's glory! That's good news! Amen.

Sermons On The First Readings

For Sundays In
Lent And Easter

Words Of Hope And Clarity

Schuyler Rhodes

These words are dedicated
to
Daniel Berrigan, SJ

Foreword

Wake Up! Power Up!

Peter Drucker once wrote, "Every few hundred years in Western history, there occurs a sharp transition. Within a few short decades, society rearranges itself — its worldview, its basic values, its social and political structure, its arts, its key institutions. Fifty years later there is a new world, and the people born then cannot imagine the world in which their grandparents lived and into which their own parents were born. We are currently living through just such a transformation."

In "Words Of Hope And Clarity," Schuyler Rhodes contends that this new world invites the church on a journey of self-examination with the potential of resurrection. A resurrection that is not possible without the declarations from Jesus, "... it is finished ..." and "... into thy hands I commend my spirit...." In this provocative group of sermons, Rhodes sounds the alarm for the church to wake up from its sleep, display the courage to give up its worldly ways, and surrender once again to God. Yes, its time to sacrifice our "golden cows" and surrender to no other gods but God. These sermons challenge Christians in a courageous Lenten journey with audacious questions. Are we to affect or reflect the world? How will we sing the Lord's song in the midst of such challenging transitions and ongoing rearrangements? Can we live the gospel with authenticity and integrity?

These sermons display the confluence of Rhodes' unique style of holding together the evangelical and prophetic voices. The substance of this style is embedded in the fact that he is challenging the Christian community to move beyond seeking common ground. Rhodes is opening the door for the Christian community to rediscover a moral higher ground, and reclaim her prophetic place in the public square. Hence, in a world enveloped by cynicism, narcissism, and prejudice, the Christian community is called to live the great commission with clarity in identity and purpose. In a society driven by individualism, consumerism, and materialism, the Christian community is compelled to live out the great commandment through authentic acts of making visible God's beloved community. In a culture that thrives on militarism, neo-colonialism, and neo-imperialism, the Christian community must be provoked by the great requirement to "do justice, love mercy, and walk humbly with God."

As the politics of fear and the ideology of apartheid spread its manifestation globally "Words Of Hope And Clarity" joins with the apostle Paul in sounding the trumpet to the Christian community, " 'Sleeper, awake! Rise from the dead, and Christ will shine on you.' Be careful then how you live, not as unwise people but as wise, making the most of the time, because the days are evil. So do not be foolish, but understand what the will of the Lord is" (Ephesians 5:14-15).

The words of hope and clarity emanating from this body of writing contends that for the Christian community to thrive during these times of ongoing transitions, nominal membership must be replaced by vital discipleship. To be a vital Christian community during these times of massive rearrangements, spiritual lethargy must be replaced with spiritual maturity.

The "Words Of Hope And Clarity" are that this is the season for ecclesial and personal conversion. It is *kairos* time for renewed faith formation and congregational transformation. The whole earth eagerly awaits the manifestation of the children of God to facilitate incarnation with authenticity. All of creation waits with eager anticipation for the resurrection of the church of Jesus with integrity. For Rhodes, such a movement of incarnation has nothing to do with our human vocabulary or articulation — such a resurrection revolution must be powered up by the Holy Spirit. Paul explains it as follows to the Church at Corinth, "My speech and my proclamation were not with plausible words of wisdom, but with a demonstration of the Spirit and of power, so that your faith might rest not on human wisdom but on the power of God" (1 Corinthians 2:4-5).

In the turbulent 1960s, the sensational soul singing group, Harold Melvin and the BlueNotes captured our dilemma and opportunity with the song, "Wake Up Everybody." Just like they sounded the alarm then, Rhodes is sounding the alarm today. For Rhodes, the Christian community can no longer sleep behind its stained-glass windows. For such a time as this the Christian community needs to wake up and get up! Now is the time for the Christian community to power up and go up! We have been in bed far too long with religion that has become spiritually moribund. Now is the anointed time for us to power up and become the Christian community in new and upgraded ways. If our imagination has failed in the type of world our grandparents and parents were born into, then "Words Of Hope And Clarity" can reload our imagination and fuel us into being the Christian community for the world into which our children and grandchildren are born. To this extent, Schuyler Rhodes invites us to step up and step out in being effective witnesses by receiving again the power of the Holy Spirit.

— Reverend Kelvin Sauls

Introduction

Taking a long look in the mirror is not an easy task, unless of course, one is a narcissist. A narcissist can gaze admiringly for hours, tweaking a smile this way or moving a strand of hair that way. But as we all know, the gaze of the narcissist is, at best, a focus upon the most trivial of details. The image suffices. The image satisfies. In such a reflective reality, substance and authenticity do not have much currency. Indeed, they are suspect.

Narcissism is one of the primary hallmarks of the culture in which our church finds itself today. It is a culture of self-absorbed, alienated individuals who have little, if any, understanding of what it means to live in community. Instead the drive for self-fulfillment and self-realization underscores peoples' waking hours. Each person, each individual wanders through their days soaking up the pervasive messages of the culture. "You have to take care of yourself first." "You better get what you want before someone else gets it." "Use this product or no one will like you." "Don't worry about that person. He's responsible for himself. You need to worry about you!" Under the weight of such myopic selfishness, we watch the fabric of the social contracts fray and the image of mutual caring and accountability fade from sight.

In such a world, the mutuality and selfless love of Christian community becomes an island in a tumultuous ocean, and it's members a truly remnant people.

This is why church folk are called to gaze into the mirror with more depth and critical clarity than most others. For us, there is more than image, more than a tweak of the smile. What do we see when we look therein? Who are we looking at exactly? What have we become? Where are we going? Is there, in fact, a "we" that has any coherent vision or sense of direction?

133

If there is to be an authentic church in the North American culture of the twenty-first century, it must be a community that understands itself as distinct and different from the culture around it. And one of the key factors in the self-identity of a Christian community is the preached word of God.

Few sermons can speak to everyone. There are, of course, notable exceptions in Reverend Martin Luther King Jr. and others. But most sermons are tailored for a community living in a specific time and place and facing particular struggles and challenges. So it is with humility that I offer the conviction that many, if not all, Christians living in twenty-first-century America face the challenge of being clear and authentic in their faith while wading through the rising torrent of post-modern culture.

These sermons are tailored to speak to a people in search of that clarity and authenticity. They strive to move through the rhythms of a holy season, calling the hearers to new levels of commitment and higher expectations of themselves and the churches in which they worship and serve.

The hope, of course, is that in some small way these offerings will lead us to the mirror for more than a cursory glance. What we see may be what we get. But it doesn't need to stay that way. Change can and must happen. Transformation isn't just a buzzword filtering down from so called church growth experts. It is the gospel call to us and to all who follow the teachings of Jesus.

The desire is for a church that is quickened by the passion of revival and deepened by the awesome reality of the cross. The vision is of a church standing with clarity and wonder on that island of hope in the raging waters of our world.

Special thanks go to the members of the Christian community at Temple United Methodist Church, with whom I journey as pastor in these days. Their willingness to step out of the culture trap and into faith is a powerful thing indeed. Their openness and palpable sense of joy spreads God's word far more effectively than a thousand of my sermons. God bless you all!

— Schuyler Rhodes

Ash Wednesday
Joel 2:1-2, 12-17

Sleeping Through The Alarm

I might as well get this off my chest. I have an abiding dislike for alarm clocks. Truth be told, more than a few of them have met an untimely demise as they have flown across the room after daring to interrupt my sleep. It's true. There is nothing quite so grating, so unpleasant as the electronic wheezing that emerges from the clock by my bedside every morning at 6 a.m. It doesn't matter if I'm dreaming or not. I could even be laying there half awake and thinking about getting up a little early. Sometimes I am already sitting on the edge of the bed rubbing my eyes and thinking of the day's schedule when it goes off. No matter what state of sleeping or waking I am in, alarms set me on edge. They raise the hairs on the back of my neck and hurl me into the day with a kind of graceless beginning.

I have often thought that a great technological advancement might be some kind of robot alarm that could gently reach out and say, "Hey there, it's time to get up." It would then wait a few moments before gently reminding me again, this time placing a nice cup of coffee on the nightstand. "Here's your coffee." What a pleasant way to start the day. But in my case, such gentleness wouldn't really work. I'd nod to the robot, roll over, and go back to sleep. That's why the clock radio doesn't really work for me. It's just too nice. A little Mozart in the morning doesn't wake me, it merely accompanies me as I continue to sleep.

I guess I have to just deal with the fact that I need the sound of the trumpet blowing. I need the alarm telling me that it's time to get up and get going. It's time to make the coffee and the family

135

breakfast. It's time to begin the day. Sleep, as wonderful as it is, needs to give way to the rest of life's demands. I don't much like it, but I have to wake up or all kinds of bad things could happen.

If I don't wake up, my children won't get a nourishing breakfast before school. If I don't wake up, the dog doesn't get walked. If I don't wake up, I miss meetings, hospital and home visits, and a host of other responsibilities that come with pastoral ministry. I don't much like the alarm, and there are days when I don't like waking up, but I know that it needs to happen. You just can't sleep your life away. In fact, if you do sleep your life away, can you actually call it life?

As I think about my own life and the need to be awakened so that I can take care of business, I can't help thinking about the church, and it's long and deep sleep. Like me, I think the church is a deep sleeper. Walk in the room, call it by name, and it will not awaken. Tap it on the shoulder and shake it gently. It continues to snore. In fact, I wonder if the church is in the process of sleeping its life away? What do you think?

The prophet Joel brings this call sharply into focus for us.

Good old Joel seems clear. The people are sound asleep and he is calling for the alarm to sound. Forget the gentle clock radio music. Don't even think about some annoying buzzer just beyond reach. Scripture calls us here to a true alarm. "Blow the trumpet!" Can you imagine someone standing next to your bed while you are sound asleep and putting a trumpet to your ear? This is what I call an alarm.

We are not being awakened, however, merely to take care of business as usual. We are not being jolted from our quiescent snoozing just for the fun of it. We are being called out because the "day of the Lord" is upon us. For the original readers of this text, this was a call for a whole nation to awaken from the slumber of its sinfulness and to enter into repentance. A call to everyone, even the writer. The old, the children, even those still breast-feeding are called. Even newlyweds are called from their bedchambers. This is not a mere waking from an afternoon nap. This is a true alarm — a wake up call to face the fact that the people have traveled far from where God calls them to be. Is it possible that such a call comes to us as we enter this season of penitence? Is there a trumpet blowing in our land that we need to hear? Could we be in a similar bind as the people of Israel seem to be in this passage? Are there changes we need to make?

I'm going to go out on a limb here and say a loud, emphatic, "Yes."

The temptation in this literature is to go to the historic value of the work and to look at what it meant to the people of Israel. Certainly this is the good academic work that needs to be studied, but the prophet's voice is not merely an ancient and dusty word to a bygone people. If this were so, all we would have here would be an old story that might not even be worth the telling. As it is, though, the prophet's voice echoes down the centuries to you and to me, shaking us from our own dazed slumber and calling us to repentance. More than that, we are called away from our religiosity to a true change of heart.

I know you're sitting there thinking, "I'm not such a bad person. I'm good. I go to work, take care of my family, and I try to do the right thing. Why do you have to be so judgmental? I need the sermon to make me feel good, not bad. Get it together, pastor, and give us a word that puts a smile on our faces!"

A smile will come. But first we really do need to heed the prophet's voice.

This passage from Joel isn't about personal piety. It's not about individual morals, it's about the character and behavior of a people. The word here has to do with the fact that God is not mocked (Galatians 6:7), and that while we may slip blithely — even unconsciously — away from God's calling to us, God does notice. God does care. Judgment, it turns out, is real. This prophetic call comes to *us* to repent as a people — as a church — as a nation. In the wake of this call we need to stop what we're doing. We need to pause and pay attention in a confessional, truth-telling kind of way. Let us, in this season, learn how to rend our hearts and look past the carefully constructed numbness of our lives. Forget, for a moment, any impulses toward defensiveness. Let go of the temptation to retreat into ideology or rigid orthodoxy. Dispel the smog of our

137

own narrowly held points of view and pose the questions that beg the asking.

What things are we doing that we need to stop doing? If we lift the veil of our own unconsciousness, the answers are right there, waiting, yearning for us to embrace them. How are we, as the church, called to repentance? In what ways do we carry on that are not faithful to who God has called us to be in Jesus Christ? What walls have we built? Who have we kept out? What actions do we take, what rules do we enforce that make a mockery of what Jesus did for us on the cross? Does our church act and look like the kingdom of God that we hear about in the parables of Jesus? When we describe the reality that God calls us to build and give our lives to, does it sound like our church? If not, what do we need to do? All of these are hard questions, to be sure. But friends, our salvation waits in the answers.

Let us look not only to our church, but to our nation, as well. As we enter another year of a war that seems to have no end, is there something that calls for repentance? As we hear the language of fear and retribution, does our faith have a response? Is there a change in national behavior that God might have in mind for us? And in the midst of this national malaise, where is our voice? What words of truth, hope, healing, and peace are we offering as more and more people fall to unspeakable suffering and death? Do we speak and live the words of Jesus about loving our enemies?

As billions are spent on war while millions go without health care, what is the priority to which God is calling us? As schools crumble and education falters while there is plenty of money for weapons and destruction, what do we hear from the voice of the holy? We are the wealthiest people on the planet. As starvation and disease stalk the earth, are we called to offer solutions? As the very environment that supports life is unraveling because of us, how are we called to behave?

Though the sound is unpleasant, and the waking is no fun, I want to suggest that both our nation and our church have need of an alarm clock, or maybe as Joel suggests, a trumpet placed right in our ear. It is time for us to awaken from the slumber of our lives, and what better time to rise from the beds of our collective numbness than in this Lenten time that comes upon us? What better time to "rend our hearts" with words of truth than this day of ashes?

A first reaction of some who hear this may be one of defensiveness. That's understandable. Confession is a difficult thing. Besides, most people resent being awakened from a deep sleep. It's hard to shake the sleep from our eyes; it's difficult to center our attention on what is really happening in our churches and in our world. But make no mistake, the alarm is being sounded, and we are being called, all of us.

The day of the Lord is indeed at hand. In fact, I'd go a little further than the prophet and suggest that God's judgment upon us is not something fixed and far off; something we can ignore until a later time. I would submit that God's judgment comes all at once with God's love and God's grace. It's what you might call a package deal. And if we can find the courage to tell the truth to ourselves about who we are and what it is we are truly doing, then we might find the tender taste of God's mercy as we turn in our hearts to healing and hope; as we stand up for what we know to be good and right. We might experience a new birth and a new beginning, as church and nation, if we open our eyes and our hearts to what is truly going on and how we are playing a role in it.

It's Ash Wednesday, and the suggestion, the call, to us is ultimately a call to authenticity in our faith. Let us take these days and weeks ahead as a time to examine what we're doing, how we're doing it, and especially let us look at what results come from our actions. Let us do this as ones awakened from a deep sleep so that we might attend to the business at hand. God's business. God's work. Amen.

Putting The Genie
Back In The Bottle ...

When our twins were quite young — infants really — I remember a scene that played out on our living room floor. My son, ever the gregarious and energetic one had managed one afternoon to yank the leg off our old studio piano. He was sitting there gleefully pounding it on the carpet while his twin sister egged him on, shouting, "Go, Aaron, go!" In defense of my daughter, it needs to be said that the boy didn't require any encouragement. Furthermore, it didn't occur to either their mother or myself that we needed to lay down the law about tearing the leg off the piano. Nonetheless, there they were, in the Garden of Eden, reaching for the fruit.

Another time we had stayed up with the children watching the ice skating championships. It was fun seeing the artistry and beauty of the skating, and a nice evening was had by all. The next day, though, my wife and I were upstairs cleaning when we became aware of a kind of frightening silence down in the dining room. We tiptoed down the stairs and there they were. They had found a gallon bottle of vegetable oil and poured it out on the hardwood floor where they were now gliding along playing ice skating. They looked up at our shocked faces and said, "Look, Mom! Look, Dad! We're skating!"

Innocence really is wonderful. These children had no idea of wrong or right. They only knew hunger, sleepiness, discomfort, and of course, curiosity. The delight for them was in the seeking of experience. That look that would come across their faces when they tasted something new or had a surprising new experience is a look that is emblazoned in my mind. I will remember it always.

But alas, the days of innocence are few and children grow to a place where they must learn about good and evil, about consequences of actions, and ultimately the truth about things like Santa and political parties.

We see this journey out of innocence in the story of Adam and Eve, as well, don't we? Loss of innocence is mourned, almost universally. And the consequences of its loss are large, if unavoidable. I don't know how many of us can remember, or even imagine, what it might feel like to not have any knowledge of good or evil? Part of the beauty of the stories of my children come, not because of the acts themselves, but because they were utterly clueless that these things — done by an adult — would have been quite unacceptable.

Can you imagine what it would be like to be pure and innocent? It reminds me of the first time I traveled to another country. I was, quite literally, a babe in the woods. I had no idea about the realities of the culture, and only the barest grasp of the language. I was, for all intents and purposes, an innocent. After a few weeks of social gaffs and being laughed at politely behind my back, I began to pick up the cues and to learn about the expectations and realities of the country I was visiting.

To me, the story of Adam and Eve is a mourning story. It mourns the loss of innocence for us all and speaks to a deep yearning in each of us for some kind of return to Eden and its ways. Why else would we be so charmed by the antics of children?

But alas, the genie is out of the bottle for us.

Child-like innocence, while precious in a child, doesn't work for us once we are grown. We can cast all the forlorn backward glances we like, but the truth is as Paul writes. "When I was a child I spoke like a child, I thought like a child, I reasoned like a child; when I became an adult, I put an end to childish ways" (1 Corinthians 13:11). No matter what we might wish for, the truth is that we do know the difference between good and evil. We do know what is right and what is wrong, and we are called to plant our standard with the good and the right. It is on that ground that we are called to live and have our being.

Of course, there is a world out there that slides, with Pontius Pilate, into the dangerous waters of relativism. "What is truth?"

Pilate asks, as he grills Jesus, as though truth takes a break when challenged. Others get into the act as the challenges come to us, tempting us in ways not dissimilar to the serpent. You've heard them before. "Well, who's to say what's right and wrong?" Or, "That's just your opinion. Who died and made you God?"

Let me say this one more time. In spite of the smog thrown up by others, we do know what is right and what is wrong. We do know the difference between good and evil. We know it from our personal experiences. We know it from holy scripture. We know it because God gave us the good sense to recognize it, and we know it because we have a deep wellspring of tradition that teaches us about this. If we pay attention to life and people around us, we know that it hurts when you get hit. Hitting, therefore, might just be wrong. We know, too, from our traditions and scripture that hurting others is not what God would have us do, and this is just the beginning.

We know it's wrong to steal. Whether it's the burglar taking your stereo or the giant corporation stealing billions from the people, it's wrong. And though it is virtually epidemic in our culture, we know that lying is wrong. Whether it is a slight untruth on your job application or the lies told by governments to cover their misdeeds, we know that it is wrong. The list extends to oppressing workers, to violating God's good creation, and on and on. And again, we know.

We also know what is good. We know what it feels like to help someone who needs our assistance. We know what it's like to feed someone who is hungry, and we know what it is like to lift up someone who is downtrodden. We know what it's like to offer good things for our children — indeed for all the children. These are good things, and we well know it.

Yes, we all long for a time of innocence remembered in ancient biblical texts like this one. But the genie is indeed out of the bottle. Blame the loss of innocence on whomever you wish. Whether it was the fruit, the serpent, Eve, or even hapless Adam, it doesn't much matter. We have been given the knowledge of good and evil, right and wrong. God stands with us today calling us to choose the good and the right. God walks with us today, double daring us to risk it all if need be to stand for what is just and right.

It is as the writer puts it in Deuteronomy. "I have set before you life and death, blessing and curses. Choose life so that you and your descendants may live ..." (Deuteronomy 30:19b). The choices that we are making virtually every minute are before us in so many ways today. As we step together into this Lenten time, let us use this knowledge that we have and let us choose the things that make for abundant life.

Let us choose healing in our relationships. Let us choose to assume the good in others. Let us choose to stand for the weak and vulnerable. Let us choose to be people who follow God's ways in all things, and sisters and brothers, let us do so — not looking back wistfully at lost innocence, but gazing forward, "forgetting what lies behind and straining forward to what lies ahead, I press on toward the goal for the prize of the heavenly call of God in Christ Jesus" (Philippians 3:13-14). Amen.

Being A Blessing

Have you ever been blessed by someone? By this I mean has someone ever stopped, placed a hand on you, and declared a blessing on you in some enterprise or undertaking? I know that in the life of our church, we often pause to lay hands on sisters and brothers who are about to take leave of the community. Sometimes they are leaving on mission trips. Sometimes they may be moving away to a new job or opportunity. Other times they may just need a blessing as they encounter struggles on their journey.

Sometimes, of course, blessing happens in different ways. My father-in-law, who was quite ill when my wife and I were engaged, gave his blessing to our marriage. Some years back, when I left on a lengthy trip to Central America, my father gave me the gift of an expensive pocketknife, something I carry with me to this day. This was his way of giving me his blessing.

In this context, "blessing" means approval, but it means more than that. In Hebrew, the word is *berakah*, and it has to do with the declaration or the public announcement of blessings. When someone leaves and says, "God bless you," this is *berakah*.

Blessings such as this have a long history in our tradition. Throughout scripture, God offers such blessings in manifold ways and in numerous circumstances. Similarly, God receives such blessings from those who follow God.

It is this declared blessing that God bestows upon Abram as he calls him away from everything he knows into a new land. It is a blessing that is both approval and promise, and something further. The blessing of God on Abram doesn't just stop with Abram. This blessing has consequence. It has reach. It extends beyond the original declaration. This blessing has purpose. God says, "... I will bless you and make your name great so that you will be a blessing" (Genesis 12:2).

God's purpose, then, in making a great nation out of Abram's lineage, and in making Abram's name great, is so that he himself will become a blessing. This is heady stuff. And it leads me to ask if the blessings that each of us receive from God have that self same purpose. Do you think that the blessings you have received have been given you so that you might use those blessings in order to become a blessing to others? What a thought. If this is so, we might be able to engender an epidemic of blessing. Each blessing we receive, from material wealth, to children, to the gifts and talents we have, each one is given so that we might, in turn, bless others.

In our congregation, we have a doctor who has been blessed with the gift of healing. This one man, in turn, has taken his blessing and turned it into an annual medical mission to the Philippines, where he and a team of doctors treat thousands of people over a period of a few weeks. He got the blessing of a medical training and a good job as a doctor and, in turn, he has used that blessing to bless others with the gift of healing. How might you use the gifts, the blessings, you have been given to be a blessing for others?

I can't help but wonder how many of us are even aware of the many blessings we have been given. Life gets crazy, challenging, difficult, and sometimes it is beyond painful. But even on the worst of days we still stand in a downpour of blessings. How often do we accept the blessings of God without taking that next step of becoming a blessing ourselves? Have we even considered that step?

We dare not forget about the nations that have been blessed by God. What of the nations whose names have been made great? Their greatness, their blessings have a purpose! There is a purpose for those nations themselves to be a blessing.

Almost every day I see a bumper sticker somewhere that says, "God bless America!" When you stop to think about it, it's an odd statement. It almost feels like a demand, rather than a request or a prayerful hope. Indeed, the phrase overlooks the inescapable truth

146

that God has blessed America in a million different ways: prosperity greater than any nation in history, natural beauty, abundant resources, and a wonderful, caring citizenry. Think about it. We don't need to ask or implore at all. Just look around and see the manifold ways in which our nation has been blessed. As we count up these blessings, we need to ask the same question of the nation that we ask of ourselves. In what way is our nation a blessing to others?

Certainly we can look to things like the Peace Corps or AmeriCorps, where Americans volunteer to offer their skills and training to others. After World War II, the US became a blessing as it used its wealth to rebuild much of the devastation from the war. But let us be honest here, there are also ways that our greatness is used to exploit. There are ways that we strive to horde and keep our wealth to ourselves. As a nation with only a fraction of the world's population, we use a huge percentage of the world's resources. Is that a blessing to the world? As global warming threatens, we need to be aware that it is our nation that sends the most greenhouse gases into the atmosphere. Are we being a blessing?

Yes, in many ways we are being a blessing. But we can do better. As individuals and as a nation we can do much better at responding to God's call to be a blessing to the world. Perhaps you're wondering exactly how we might do this? Perhaps the first step is to enumerate, to count our blessings. As individuals, how are we blessed? Can we make a list? After each blessing, perhaps we might note how we are using that blessing to be a blessing to others. What of our church? Shall we discuss blessings showered upon the church? Property? Combined talents of our members? Wealth? Spiritual gifts and graces? Let us make a list here, as well.

As we look to God's call and promise to Abram, we have to imagine that this same call comes to us. We have been blessed so that we can be a blessing. The possibilities are virtually endless and the future spreads before us, beckoning, calling, daring us to step up to the plate with our sisters and brothers as we work to become the blessings that we have received. Let us renew our hope. Let us claim this day as a new beginning, and let us be a blessing to one another, to our community, and to our world.

In Jesus' name. Amen.

Why Did You Bring Us Out Of Egypt?

I am a baby boomer. I am part of that generation that emerged following World War II. Yes, we're the ones who will soon be clogging the social security system. We're the ones who climbed to adulthood during the 1960s. We grooved to the Beatles and rocked to the Rolling Stones. We got political and protested a war, and many of us — many more than ever before — went to college. We were the ones who were going to change the world. Well, so much for good intentions. Some things, though, did change during those times.

Perhaps the most significant thing that shifted during those years was the way people trusted their leaders. Prior to the '60s, or more precisely, prior to the Vietnam War and Watergate, there was a deep and abiding trust in those who were our leaders. I can recall my parents and grandparents reflecting that trust and doing their duty as they served in all manner of civic services. From the military to volunteer fire fighters to helping out at schools and summer camps, people did their part for the greater good. For the most part, they did that because of this trust.

That trust unraveled in the wake of the 1960s. For good or ill, the generations that have lined up since then lack trust in government, in civic organizations, in church, and beyond. Check with any group that depends upon volunteer labor. Look at the scores of organizations and groups that have receded and even disappeared as the folk who have matured over the last fifty years have turned and walked away.

We don't much like our leaders. Whether it's presidents, congress, governors, mayors, or even pastors ... we just don't trust them anymore. We are the perfect reflection of the people of Israel as they are described in this passage from Exodus. If we follow anyone, we do it grumbling every step of the way. Leaders are to be mistrusted and their motives are to be questioned. Indeed, some folk make it their business to be certain that no leaders can rise up to move the people. Anyone who tries to step into roles of leadership becomes a target, and if that person has any skeletons in his or her closet, they will be revealed.

The truth is that we whine a lot. We complain endlessly and are strikingly similar to the Israelites as they shook their fists at Moses and shouted, "Why did you bring us out of Egypt, anyway? Did you lead us out here so we would die of thirst?" No one is suggesting that blind, unquestioning trust is a good thing. Indeed, a healthy skepticism can save us from those who do not, in fact, have our best interests at heart. Neither can it be argued that everyone who tries to assume leadership is worthy of it. We need, both in government and in the church, to examine those who would lead us in order to determine their fitness. But once this is done, we need to offer up a little bit of trust. We need to be willing to accept leadership.

The current climate in our culture makes this acceptance difficult at best. Cynicism and mistrust permeate our lives these days and erode the mortar that holds us together as community. Who can blame Moses for running to God in frustration and fear? He lays it out with painful clarity before God. In fact, he "cries out" to the Lord, "What shall I do with this people? They are almost ready to stone me." God, of course, leads Moses and the people to the place where the water springs from the rock and things calm down for the present.

It seems we have much in common with this Exodus people. Not only do we whine and complain and fail to trust in our leaders, we are also — like them — wandering in the wilderness. Our wilderness, though, is not the Sinai desert. Our thirst does not come from a lack of water, nor our hunger from too little food.

The wilderness in which we wander these days is one of our own making.

It is a frightening landscape in which we find ourselves etched and carved by this epidemic of cynicism and doubt; this pervasive mood of mistrust and fear. The thirst from which we suffer is one caused by a runaway sense of individualism and narcissism. We are bombarded with messages that tell us we must meet our own needs before meeting the needs of others. From the news, to television, to film, and back again we hear and see the story of the rugged individualist who trusts no one and does whatever it takes to get what he wants or thinks he needs.

Our spirits are parched by the lack of community and the trust that makes such joinings possible. We hunger for a vision and a direction, and yet are unable to move because we are unable to trust.

What happens, we ask, if we trust someone and they betray us? What happens if we love someone and they hurt us? What happens if we follow a leader and that leader turns out to be leading us where we cannot go? What happens then?

Let me say this.

If you trust, your trust is certain — sooner or later — to be betrayed. But life without trust is far more desolate than any pain of betrayal. If you love, the person you love *will* wound and hurt you sooner or later. Humans are imperfect. But the beauty and wonder of love far outweighs any pain that comes from love's wounding. All those who step into leadership are also human and imperfect.

Take Moses as our example! He was wanted for murder, a questionable character under even the best circumstances. Martin Luther King Jr., it has been learned, was less than perfect in his life. But still, it is clear that he was a man of God sent to lead God's people out of the sin of racism. Indeed, look at the people who God tends to lift up for leadership. Was Saint Paul worthy of the trust of the early church? Hardly. He was their chief persecutor! Our leaders are rarely, if ever, of perfect character. They, like us, are imperfect people in search of a perfect wonder.

151

You see, stepping into the waters of trust and openness does not in any way ensure that we will be unmolested in this life. It is a lot like faith. In fact, it involves faith. Our belief in God and our trust in God's word through Jesus Christ doesn't constitute an insurance policy against the vagaries of this life. I believe in God. I love the teachings of Jesus. When my mother was diagnosed with leukemia, my faith did not halt her illness, but my faith *did* help me move through her illness, as her faith helped her.

Life without faith, life without trust, life without risking what it takes to have faith and trust, is a barren and painful thing indeed. I would suggest that each of us could use a little more trust and faith in the context of our lives. Whether it is participating in our own democratic process or stepping up to the plate as a volunteer in our community, we need to do more. Whether it is trusting a church leader or a community leader, we need to risk it so that we might all move forward.

Does this mean we are to be naive? Well, yes, a little. But the naiveté that we seek is not a purposeless and mindless wandering. It is an intentional deliberate choice to be naive. We must, as Jesus says, have the trust and openness of a child (Matthew 19:14) if we wish to participate in God's reality. Mind you, we are called to be childlike, not childish. We are called to be open and ready to trust. We are called to shed the scales of our cynicism and step forward in joyful abandon. In short, we need to be able to read this story from Exodus with the deep awareness that in this instance, God's people are not offering behavior we need to imitate.

In this Lenten time, as we journey in a wilderness of our own making, maybe we could try to trust a little more? Perhaps we could risk a little more? Maybe we could transform this wilderness of cynicism and doubt into a garden of faith and joy. Amen.

Are All Your Sons Here?

I remember sixth grade as though it were yesterday. Those shy, awkward times when we were all sliding down the slippery slope of adolescence. The young people I was growing up with, including myself, were walking this line between childhood and adulthood. One day we would step on one side of the line, and on the next day we would fall down on the other. There was no plan or intention about any of it. We were, of course, new at this stuff. Our bodies were changing; expectations of the world around us were growing. It's a bittersweet memory.

Perhaps, most clear in my mind, was the day they took us to the gym for square dancing. The teacher hauled out an old phonograph player and placed a scratched and warped square dance record on the turntable. He then lined the girls up on one side of the gym, and the boys on the other. The girls were then allowed to select their dance partner for the upcoming square dance. It was unbearable. These strange creatures began cautiously walking across the shiny wooden floor, eyeing their potential victims. Each young boy was trying to look at the floor while seeing if any of the young ladies might actually come in their direction. The horror of the scene was underscored by the lose/lose nature of it all. We were all young enough to admit — at least to ourselves — that we'd rather be just about anyplace else. We really didn't want to dance with the girls. But the truth was that the only thing worse than dancing with them was the prospect that no one would pick you!

The lucky one, we thought, was the guy who had been sent to the office earlier for passing notes in class. He, at least, was missing this slow, drawn-out torture. But even his luck failed him. One of the girls stopped, and looked around. She then padded in her sock feet over to the gym teacher and said, "Not all the boys are here." The teacher's knitted eyebrows surveyed the scene. He then nodded and sent one of the kids down to get Scottie, who had thought he was safe in the office. Upon his return, of course, the sock-footed girl snagged him as her dance partner. Who knew what she saw in him? He was, like the rest of us, pimple-faced and clumsy, but she saw something no one else saw.

Adolescent memories aside, there's something to be said for lining those boys up, I suppose. After all, if the boys had been allowed to pick, nothing would ever have happened. As it was, we each ended up with a partner, but the sock-footed girl noticed that her guy wasn't in the lineup.

There are lots of ways that we get lined up in this life, aren't there? We begin, not just with a sixth-grade gym class, but with the lineup of Jesse's sons to see which one might be favored for leadership. One after another, the sons are examined and dismissed until the question comes. "Are all your sons here?" Just as the sock-footed girl noted, it was clear that not everyone was in the room. David, of course, had not been sent to the office. But the truth is, it really didn't occur to anyone that he would be under consideration. Who would pick David? He was, after all, the youngest. We left him watching the sheep.

So David was sent for, and the rest, as they say, is history.

There's an old story about Martin Luther King Jr., and I am not sure if it's accurate or not. The story goes that he missed a meeting one day, and it was at that meeting that they put him in charge of the Montgomery bus boycott. Once again, the rest is history.

I wonder, in all the lineups we have to endure in our lives, how many folks are missing from the room? I think about when we lined up to go to college. It was actually the application process where we sent applications to our first choice, second choice, and then our "safety" school where we hoped our chances at acceptance were better than good. It was many years later that I discovered some kids in our school didn't apply because their families couldn't afford even the application fees, let alone tuition. Were there young people "not in the room" because of economics or family circumstances? You bet. Were there young people not in the application pool because of race or ethnicity? Probably so, but I never noticed.

When I lined up for my first real job, it didn't occur to me to be thinking about the Scotties or the Davids who might be under the radar for a whole host of reasons. I just wanted a job. I was thinking about me. Let the other guys take care of themselves, right? I filled out the application, showed up, and when they actually hired me, all I thought about was making sure they didn't have a reason to fire me. It never dawned on me that there might be some people who were either down in the office, or off in the field tending sheep.

So much of our lives is about this lining up to be chosen, isn't it? From those halting, uncertain days of young adulthood into our years of work and family raising, it happens over and over again. From meeting partners and spouses, to building careers, to becoming involved in church and community life, it seems that we spend a lot of time in line with someone checking us out to see if we fit the bill for this or that. With so many people in line, who ever really stops to think about who is *not* in the line up?

It seems to me that, in this life journey, we need the sock-footed girl and Samuel. We need the ones who will notice that someone is missing.

It's a question that we need to ask across the arc of our lives, isn't it? In our life as a church, "Are all our sons and daughters here?" Who is it that we have left out in the pasture, who just might end up being the best leader we can imagine? Who is it that's not at the table because it simply doesn't occur to us to invite them? Moreover, who is not with us because we have not made it comfortable for them to be present?

Are all our sons and daughters here? Sadly, we have to say, "No." Too many of our sons and daughters are not with us in the church today. Some of them are missing because we haven't counted them as important enough to involve. These are the young folk, without whom there is no church. Are we bringing them in from the pasture and including them in the lineup? Are we building ministry and mission for them? Are we providing care and comfort, education and vision? If the answer to these questions is "No," then we can rest assured that these young ones will find other things to do.

In an evermore diverse world, let us look around to see who is missing. Do we allow our own secular, cultural roots to define the community of faith? If that's so, let us hear the words of the apostle Paul telling us, "There is no longer Jew or Greek, there is no longer slave or free, there is no longer male and female; for all of you are one in Christ Jesus" (Galatians 3:28).

Are all our sons and daughters here? Look at the neighborhood in which our church is located. Are these people participating in the life of faith? Are these people included in our invitation to discipleship? Are these people being served by our ministries?

Dear friends, in Christian community, we do not have the luxury of simply lining up and not noticing. In Christian community we need to lift up the example of Margaret. That was the name, by the way, of the sock-footed girl who noticed that Scottie was missing. We need to lift up the example of Samuel, who asked the question, "Are all your sons here?"

If, as we all know down deep, all of our sons and daughters are not present, then we have to conclude something else. We are not whole.

When I sit down to dinner with my family and my son happens to be playing at his friend's house, it feels like we are not whole. His smile, sense of humor, and his particular individual take on the world are missing at our family table, and we feel it. The same is true for us as Christian community. If all our sons and daughters are not present, then we are not whole.

The evangelistic effort, you see, is a two-way street. Of course, we wish to share God's saving word in Christ. Who doesn't? But that's only half the story. Because the whole truth is that we need the participation of everyone in the community of faith. The whole truth is that we ourselves are incomplete when all our sons and daughters are not with us. Whether it is the literal sons and daughters who fall away from church because of our inattention and lack of focus, or whether it's the sons and daughters in our wider community who are not even on our radar, their absence touches us. We are less without them.

Are all our sons and daughters here? Let the invitation go forth that everyone who is a son or a daughter is welcome in our church. Let the doors fling open and let our eyes scan the horizon. Let the people of God grow in wholeness and welcome as we reach out in love and hope to places and people we may never have thought of before.

And in all of it, sisters and brothers, may we each try to be a little more like Samuel, or Margaret, as we strive to notice who is not at the table of fellowship with us. Amen.

Can These Bones Live?

I remember, not too long ago, I was reading some history about our nation and its westward expansion. This particular book had to do with the disappearance of the buffalo on the plains. Before white settlers happened upon the scene, buffalo were so numerous that vast herds stretched literally as far as the eye could see. There were millions of buffalo. So great were there numbers that it didn't really occur to people that they could ever vanish. Well, we all know how this story went. In an astonishingly short period of time, the buffalo, for all intents and purpose, were gone. Due to a frenzied and short-sighted wholesale slaughter, the likes of which fails the imagination, these millions became but a memory. Today, small herds exist here and there, but there will never again be the huge and wondrous herds that once roamed the plains.

All the while I was reading this, I kept trying to imagine the scene. But it wasn't until I came across an ancient, grainy black and white photo that it struck me. It was a picture of countless piles of bleached bones laying out on some unnamed piece of prairie land. Where once the eye was strained by living herds, here the eye was shocked by a vista of death. Everywhere there were bones. Everywhere.

As we read Ezekiel, this type of photo comes to mind. It's one thing to witness piles of bones everywhere. It's quite another to call to mind the life that those bones once supported. In our biblical passage today, the Lord brings Ezekiel out to view the wasteland. And it is not some distant glance, but an intimate tour of the valley. "He led me all around them; there were very many lying in the valley; and they were very dry." It is as though the Lord needed Ezekiel to see, not just the bones, but to sense the life that was once present.

It seems to me that most everyone sitting here today can conjure up a place in their lives that feels like that valley of bones. Most of us don't need to look too far to find the wasteland in our lives, where the bones lay in piles all around, and they are very dry indeed.

Is there a friendship or intimate relationship that has been harshly ended? Does memory find a quarrel unresolved? Do the bones of a once-tender love lay bleaching in the sun? Is there a failure that restlessly sits in the memory? A failure of integrity? A lapse of judgment? A reckless indiscretion? A stupid mistake? What must the piles of bones look like in the wastelands of our lives? Each of us knows. Each of us can feel the brittle dryness that comes when life departs; when spirit withers and blows away. It is vast. It is painful and it feels overwhelming.

I mention these closely held and personal wastelands because I believe we must be in touch with these things before we move on to the big picture. I think that too often we stuff it all down and hope that life will skip on to the next chapter as we learn how to walk around our piles of bones. But no matter how we try to move on, no matter what kind of denial we try to practice, the wasteland stays with us, and with Ezekiel we are called to take an unscheduled tour.

Take a moment now — a silent second or two — to comprehend that place that William Butler Yeats referred to in the "Circus Animals Desertion," as the "foul rag and bone shop of the heart."

As we take stock of these spaces in our life, we need to remember that Ezekiel did not take the tour of the valley alone. We need to recall that whatever devastation has befallen us in our lives, God does not call us to awareness by ourselves. No. God walks among the piles of bones with us, and the questions came to Ezekiel and they come to us, as well.

"Can these bones live?" Can life come again into the dark and brittle places within our hearts and our lives? The answer comes

160

back in the affirmative. Yes! These bones can live again. The skeletal remains can find life on one condition.

The condition is that we are to "prophesy." The Lord says,

> *Prophesy to these bones, and say to them: O dry bones, hear the word of the Lord. Thus says the Lord God to these bones: I will cause breath to enter you, and you shall live. I will lay sinews on you, and will cause flesh to come upon you, and cover you with skin, and put breath in you, and you shall live; and you shall know that I am the Lord.* — Ezekiel 37:4-6

It seems easy enough. How does the old song go? "Now hear the word of the Lord!" The trick, though, is in the prophesying. Old Testament prophecy is not prophecy the way most of us consider it these days. Ask most of your contemporaries and you will find they think of prophecy as a prediction of the future. That's not really a piece of what we are dealing with here.

A fundamental element in prophesying has to do with truth telling. This is why so many prophets got in trouble with the king. Kings, like so many of us today, didn't want truth, they wanted their own perspectives confirmed. But truth is what is called for here. In other words, the Lord calls us to say truth to the death and hurt in our lives. We are called to survey the wastelands we have within us and without, and to address them with God's word of life. The bones *can* live. God *can* place sinew and muscle back together and call life to come forth.

But we must prophesy to the bones.

Hear the word of the Lord! Where our hearts have been brittle and dry as bones, God's Spirit can move and bring new life! Where joy has been drained away, and replaced with hardened hearts, God can cause new hope to spring forth. Where we see nothing but old bones and painful endings, God envisions a riotous explosion of life.

Sisters and brothers, this is no preacher's bromide or worn-out axiom. This is biblical truth. As we prepare together to march with Jesus into the city on Palm Sunday, we know that God's word brings life! As we leave this Lenten journey, we do not depart from a valley of bones and brittle endings, but instead we leave behind a legacy of new life in God's abundant spirit.

Prophesy to the bones!

Speak truth to the pain and emptiness. Call out in the power of God's Spirit, and watch while life knits together the brittle, broken bones of your past. Do you feel sometimes that this life is like a graveyard? Do you ever feel that hope is just a word for empty wishing? Do you ever let out that heart-wrenching sigh of soul weariness and wonder where the next step will lead?

Hear the word of the Lord!

God says I am going to open up your graves and bring you forth. Even now, we can dare to hope again. Even now, we can crack open those deep and hidden places so that vision and passion can flow again. Even now, God promises new life. Look. The bones have come together and a multitude stands before us!

We can let go of tattered, old, boneyard photos. We can release the litanies of hurt and pain. We can give over to God those ancient wounded places, and we can walk once more in the land of the living. We can lift up our eyes and open up our hearts because God has breathed the Spirit upon us. God has called us out of the desert. The voice of the holy has brought us out and promises to accompany us on the journey.

Can we be too bold? Can we shout too loud? Can we miss the blooming of new possibilities as God breathes upon us? No, we cannot.

Sisters and brothers, this is not the end of the Lenten season. It is the day we have walked together out of the valley of the bones. This is not just a break in the church calendar while we decorate for Palm Sunday. We have journeyed together in a wilderness of our own making, only to stumble upon the beauty of God's life-giving Spirit. There is literally nothing that cannot be touched by it.

So hear the word of the Lord, the word of life, the word of hope, the word of new beginnings. A prelude, if you will, for what is to come.

In Jesus' name. Amen.

I Love A Parade

I love Palm Sunday. It's that wonderful day when we march boldly into town waving our palm branches and loving the parade. Yes, yes, I admit. It's probably the parade I like as much as what we're shouting about as the donkey saunters by. But I do. I love Palm Sunday. And did I say, I love parades, too?

I remember as a kid going with my mom every year to the Memorial Day parade in the small upstate New York town where we lived. It was exactly what you might imagine it to be. The high school band marched proudly, along with the veterans and the fire trucks and the mayor riding in a convertible he borrowed from the local dealership. The Girl Scouts, Boy Scouts, 4-H, and on it went. The fife and drum corps and the local National Guard unit was also present, usually with some impressive military hardware to display. Every year we sat at the curb, waving, yelling, drinking grape soda, and getting sick on cotton candy.

It wasn't until years later that I learned about the subtext of the parade. It wasn't until I was well into young adulthood that I learned in any serious way that this parade was about all the people who had died in our nation's never-ending litany of wars. My mind goes back to the gaggle of veterans who usually marched as best they could behind the National Guard unit. I never imagined or even dreamed of what horrors they might have seen. Later, after the parade, when everyone went to lay wreaths at the cemetery, my youthful mind simply didn't grasp the sense of loss that undergirded this annual celebration.

Later on, I learned that much of life operates with a subtext, or a story running just beneath the surface of what seems to be going on. I think Palm Sunday is like that. Yes, we have the parade. We have the palm branches and the coats paving the roadway. We have the people shouting loud "Hosannas," and in its own way, it is not unlike those parades I witnessed as a child.

The subtext, or underlying story, of Palm Sunday is not the past, but the near future. Everyone was shouting and cheering, but one wonders what was going through the mind of Jesus. He knew what was coming. It couldn't have been much of a celebration for him, could it?

When I read this passage from Isaiah, I read it like it's the subtext for the Palm Sunday parade. "The Lord God has given me the tongue of a teacher that I might know how to sustain the weary with a word...." I think of Jesus' ministry and how these words describe so much of his teaching. Yet, here he is on the back of a donkey. Not much more teaching left. Instead, God is the teacher, opening Jesus' ear to the realities that sit just a few days away.

Through the din of the crowd's shifting allegiances, Isaiah gives depth to Jesus' ride into Jerusalem. No rebellion or argument will be offered. There will be no resistance to the blows that are to come. The jaw is set; the direction clear. Salvation is and will always be with God and God alone. Even in humiliation and degradation, God is the vindicator. "I will not be put to shame."

It is a good thing to read this passage side-by-side with the Palm Sunday passage in John 12. Indeed, it's a good thing to try to discern the stories beneath the stories and to hold these two passages in tension. It's also a good thing for us to try to go deeper as we pass out the palm fronds and celebrate today. This is why as we ponder the heart of Jesus on the road into Jerusalem, I am moved to wonder about the story beneath the story for us as a people.

We are eager enough today to be those Palm Sunday people, aren't we? As I say, I love a parade. We spend hours decorating the sanctuary and preparing the music, just for this moment, right? Some of us, though, and I include myself here, don't really want to go beyond this joyful moment. We like it just like it is. What will come, will come soon enough, won't it? Why languish in Isaiah's dogged focus on obedience?

Could it be because, in the end, this is all about obedience? Sure, it's about Jesus who in his humanness had to have some second thought, but in the end gave it all up for us. And in turn, the obedience is offered to us, not as a collar for a puppet God to bring us to heel, but as a gift that will lead to our own salvation. In a world like the one in which we live, the idea of obedience is a hard one to absorb. We bristle at the thought. We rebel. Most of us don't like the idea of anyone being "the boss of us." We'd rather go our own way and make our own decisions. In fact, our nation is the product of a rebellion, and we hold dear the notion that we are free to pursue our own happiness pretty much anyway we want. Yet that freedom, for we who claim Christ, is tempered by the radical obedience that leads this parade into Jerusalem and to the cross.

The truth is that this freedom to do whatever we wish is really a kind of slavery. Paul writes, "For you were called to freedom, brothers and sisters; only do not use your freedom as an opportunity for self-indulgence, but through love become slaves to one another" (Galatians 5:13). Without Isaiah's subtext to ground us, it's hard to keep the obedience of Jesus before us. Without the obedience of Jesus, even to the point of death on the cross, what have we to claim except the so-called freedom of self-indulgence?

On Palm Sunday, sisters and brothers, what we begin to unwrap is the most powerful reality of our faith. That is, that self-giving love is redemptive. We see this in God's gift to us in Jesus' sacrifice on the cross. In his self-giving love, we are redeemed. All of our brokenness is lifted from us. All of it. But it doesn't stop there, because we are called to take up the wonder of self-giving love and to practice it in our lives as individuals and as church.

Jesus lays it out for us with stunning clarity. "Very truly I tell you, the one who believes in me will also do the works that I do and in fact, will do greater works than these ..." (John 14:12).

We do not have the excuse of putting Jesus on a pedestal and backing off in disingenuous awe. We have the challenge, the call to obedience, to give ourselves in love to others. In this salvation story, we have much joy to claim, but it is the deep and abiding joy that comes in willing obedience to God's call to us in Christ Jesus to take the cross and follow him (Mark 8:34).

So, as I said, I love a parade. I love parties, too. Let's celebrate this triumphal entry into Jerusalem together, today, but let's be mindful of the story beneath; the story of life-giving radical obedience to God. Amen.

To Be Passed Over

This ancient story comes down the centuries to us with power. The instructions are clear; the process plain. God is preparing to "pass through" the land of Egypt and this is one time when we would prefer that God pass us by altogether. The blood of the lamb is smeared on the doorpost so that God will know which ones are Egyptians and which ones are not.

I was reading this passage to the children and one of them raised a sheepish hand and asked these questions: "If God is God and knows everything, wouldn't God also know which houses were which? Why would God need the blood of the lamb?" The best questions always come out of the mouths of innocents.

Indeed. Why does God require the blood of the lamb? It is a multilayered and deep question. The more we think about it, the more dense it becomes. Why would God require this blood sacrifice as (he) prepares to liberate the people of Israel? And, as we look to this night as a people rooted in Jesus Christ, we are led to ask again, "Why does God require sacrifice? Why the blood of this lamb? This Jesus?"

How are we to gauge this God? How are we to understand this holy presence that requires sacrifice? It seems to make no sense.

For twenty-first-century North Americans, sacrifice is an unfamiliar thing. Few people living in the United States today have been asked to sacrifice much of anything. We tend to view it as something unpleasant and to be avoided. But it is a concept that we ought to rediscover.

To sacrifice is to give up something of importance to someone (or something) that is greater than you. A parent who forgoes a job promotion in order to keep children in the good school they are attending makes a sacrifice. A spouse or partner who scrimps and saves so that the other can attend school makes a sacrifice. We also understand this in times of war when a soldier gives up his or her life to save comrades. This is a sacrifice.

This much we understand. But when it comes to God, things get a little trickier, because for us, sacrifice and worship are very closely connected. In our earliest Hebrew traditions, sacrifice was at the core of worship. The people prostrated themselves before Yahweh and offered sacrificial offerings of food and livestock. For these people, this wasn't a check made out for an amount of money that would not be missed. It was an offering of something important to them. Food!

As Christians standing in this long line of tradition, history, and faith, we claim this God of Israel as our God, our Maker, our Redeemer. This is God. This is the one who comes to us in Christ Jesus and sits this night at table preparing to sacrifice (him)self for us! If we truly believe this, how can we do anything but fall on our knees and offer up, not just a snack, but our whole lives?

You see, it turns out that it's not so much about God demanding a sacrifice as it is that sacrifice is part and parcel of what it means to love. Sacrifice is integral to what it means to worship. Sacrifice is woven into the fabric of how we understand God.

Throughout biblical literature, of course, we see a maturing sense of this understanding. From the blood sacrifices of old to the "living sacrifice" that Paul calls the church to become (Romans 12:1), we travel an arc of revelation and learning. But the point and the concept remain clear. We give sacrificially of ourselves to that which we honor, that which we perceive to be greater than ourselves.

On this night of nights, this celebration of being passed over by God, let us reach for a new and deeper understanding of sacrifice. As God prepares in Christ Jesus to give himself up for us, let us prepare to give ourselves to God. As we come to table ourselves this night, let us stand in awe before the love of God and renew our promise to love one another.

And as we rise to leave this place, let us contemplate, let us pray, let us consider what it might mean to truly become a "living sacrifice," giving — not just a few hours or a few dollars — but our lives to God. Amen.

Where The Rubber Meets The Road

I don't need to tell you that we belong to a portion of the Christian family called the "Protestant Church." I also don't need to tell you that there's a whole lot of history behind all this, and frankly, I am going to choose to share that on another day. One part of our Protestant identity is something that we see every time we come into our church. It's something we look at every day, and don't think about too much. Take a look up on our altar. What do you see? That's right. It's the cross.

On our altar is a representation of the instrument of execution that was used by the Romans to kill Jesus. We've lost much of the power of this symbol over time. There are a lot of reasons for this, not the least of which is the fact that we no longer execute people on crosses these days. A more contemporary expression of the cross might be an electric chair or a syringe. That way people would have a clearer grip on what it is that we are focusing on tonight.

As it is, we have our cross, and I offer no complaints or radical calls to change our symbol. What I am really seeking to point out is the fact that if we went into a Roman Catholic church tonight or any time, the cross would look different. Can anyone say why? Of course you can. A Roman Catholic cross is different because it displays the figure of the crucified Jesus hanging right there in front of you. Little imagination is required there. The message is clear. The Son of God was hung on a cross for you and for me. It's called a crucifix.

In our Protestant process we did away with the body on the cross because, I was told, we focus on the *risen* Christ, which I was also told, is really the point anyway.

So there you have it. Body or no body, it's still the cross, and now that I've brought all this up, I want to say that I'm going to choose to avoid this discussion in any meaningful way except to say that tonight, it's important that we think together about that body hanging from the cross. Tonight, the image of our Lord having made that sacrifice is something we really need to consider in prayer and in worship.

Tonight, let us imagine the sacrifice that was made for you and for me.

In our life of faith, we do not have what the scholars would call "a theology of the cross." That is, we don't spend a whole lot of time dwelling on the sacrifice that atoned for our sins and brought us the chance to participate in the new life we have in Christ. But, tonight is a good time to go there. Tonight, let us walk to the foot of the cross.

This graphic reading from the prophet Isaiah that we shared this evening is the template for what we call "atonement theology." It is at the core of how we understand that on this night, Jesus died for our sins. In this much, I concur with my Roman Catholic sisters and brothers in their placement of Jesus' body on the cross. We Protestants may wish to focus on the *empty* cross and the *risen* Christ, but without the crucifixion, none of this would be possible. Indeed, some of my Jesuit friends have accused us of skipping over the tough spot and heading right for the dessert bar.

The theology of atonement puts it pretty simply. God, in Christ Jesus, went to the cross to take on the sins of the world so that we might find salvation. We can see this thinking in Isaiah as he writes, "and the Lord has laid on him the iniquity of all" (Isaiah 53:6). For most people this is a tough one to grasp, so let me put it another way.

Have you ever had someone take the fall for you? Maybe it was in school and you broke the window, but your friend accepted the blame rather than see you get in trouble. Or possibly it was someone who stood up for you and took punishment that would have come on you had this person not intervened. There are count-less stories of self-sacrifice in time of tumult and war. I am re-minded of the story of the father who stepped in front of his son so that he would go to the Nazi gas chambers in his son's place.

All of these stories reveal to some extent, what we claim in the crucifixion of Jesus Christ. What we accept, indeed, what we af-firm with power tonight is the notion that it wasn't just one thing or one error or a couple of bad things, but the sins and brokenness of the whole world that Jesus took on himself. Think for a minute of the worst thing you've done. Multiply that times humanity and then you begin to get it.

Yes, I know, atonement is not popular in some circles these days. As a culture we don't much like the idea of sacrifice in any form, let alone a blood sacrifice. Moreover, we don't much like the idea of the idea that we are broken and sinful. In an "I'm okay you're okay" kind of world, any idea that challenges this is sus-pect. The undeniable truth, though, is that we're not okay. We some-how, as Paul writes so cogently, cannot manage to do the things we know are good and right, but instead we do the things that we know are wrong.

> *I do not understand my own actions. For I do not do what I want, but I do the very thing I hate. Now if I do what I do not want, I agree that the law is good. But in fact it is no longer I that do it, but sin that dwells within me. For I know that nothing good dwells within me, that is, in my flesh. I can will what is right, but I cannot do it. For I do not do the good I want, but the evil I do not want is what I do. Now if I do what I do not want, it is no longer I that do it, but sin that dwells within me.*
> — Romans 7:15-20

Paul's insight here is startling in its honesty and openness. How often do we do things that we know are wrong, but for all manner of justifiable reasons, we do them. Likewise, how often do we shy away from doing the right thing when it's staring us right in the face? I would say, for most of us, the answer is, daily, if not hourly.

It is into this stew of human brokenness that the Son of God came to extricate us from our plight. Tonight we both grieve the loss and honor the gift. Tonight we stand in muted awe trying to find words that are adequate, only to fail and slip into a prayerful and awe-filled silence. Tonight is the night we notice that there *is* a body on the cross, that someone has stepped in and paid the price so that you and I can begin again. Tonight we confess that this sacrifice made for us is at the core of who we are as a people.

For Christianity, this is where the rubber hits the road. It is at the apex of who we are and it grounds us in every thought, prayer, and action we take. The fundamental notion that our sins are forgiven and that we ourselves are called in turn to be forgiving is really the core value of our faith. Once again, Paul gets clear with us.

> *In him we have redemption through his blood, the forgiveness of our trespasses, according to the riches of his grace that he lavished on us.* — Ephesians 1:7-8

And being forgiven, we are called ourselves to forgiveness.

> *For if you forgive others their trespasses, your heavenly Father will also forgive you; but if you do not forgive others, neither will your Father forgive your trespasses.* — Matthew 6:14-15

On this "Good Friday," let us join our hearts in a prayer of muted and awe-filled thanksgiving at the sacrifice made in our behalf. Let us, in our prayers and our lives, become the people who are worthy of such a sacrifice. Amen.

Preaching *Peace*
By Jesus Christ ...

May the peace of Jesus Christ be with you!
May the peace of Jesus Christ be with you!
Yes, yes, I know. It's Easter Sunday, and I should be greeting you with the words, "Christ is risen!" And then you all respond with the ancient response, which is, "He is risen, indeed!" This is, after all, the focus of the agenda today, isn't it? Christ is indeed risen from the tomb, and we come — Easter bunnies, colored eggs, and commercialism notwithstanding — to take note of the fact that death has been conclusively and decisively defeated. Rather than passing greetings of peace, shouldn't we be shouting out "O death, where is thy sting?" (1 Corinthians 15:55). Wouldn't it be more appropriate if we stood up and declared the power of the empty tomb and be done with it? After all, my Easter ham is waiting back home!

But no, today the Easter greeting is "May the peace of Jesus Christ be with you!"

You're probably asking yourself whatever could possess the pastor to make a shift like this when the story that needs to be told is obvious. Why would a pastor want to talk about the peace of Christ on Easter Sunday?

Well, let's look at this scripture from our lectionary. It isn't any of the traditional Easter narratives. It is a passage from Acts, where Peter is trying to make the case for Jesus. He starts out with a curious greeting. Basically, he says, "I understand that God accepts anyone who holds God in awe and does the right thing." Peter's not saying, "Come with Jesus or go to hell," is he? He's not holding a threat of damnation or judgment. Instead, he says, "I get it." God accepts everyone who stands in awe of him and who does the right things.

Wow. That alone had to catch some attention. Then, as now, there aren't a lot of people who can hold an expansive view of things in their hearts as they try to share their experiences of the holy. Most folks, regardless of their tradition, have a need to get everyone to see it their way.

Peter withholds the shaking of the finger and the scowling, scolding demeanor. Instead, he says, "You all know the story, don't you? The one that came to the people of Israel, preaching peace by Jesus Christ...."

Now, in this day of permanent warfare, when we are warned of enemies under every rock, and where those who question are lumped in with the so-called enemies; in this day, when we hear about peace, our hungry and war-scarred spirits go to the logical location. "Preaching peace by Jesus Christ," pulls us inexorably toward visions of a world where the guns are silent, and where no more children are blown to bits by landmines. Who among us does not desire such a world?

In truth, this isn't the "peace" that the writer of Acts is describing. The "peace" described here has been translated from the Greek word, *eirene*, which really means "unity." In other words, what the writer of Acts is calling for is the unity of the people of Israel in Jesus Christ. We could, of course, go deeper into the fractionalized reality of the Jewish world of the day, which was real for these people, but the point of unity applies to more than just a historical *sitz im leben* of our text. It speaks to us.

To be completely honest, I would rather deal with the other meaning of "peace." I would rather preach a rousing sermon on how on Easter Sunday, our risen Savior calls us to work for peace in the world; how our faith calls us to lay down our arms and to walk in the ways of peace. Indeed, I do believe this is all true, but fidelity to the text calls us to discuss what it means to be *unified* in Christ.

176

As we sit today claiming the reality of Christ's rising, how do we speak to *eirene*, or unity in Christ Jesus? What does unity mean to us as a church sitting here today? How, in the resurrection story that we celebrate today, do we find unity? What does unity mean to us as a broader Christian community? And more complex is the question concerning unity with those outside our faith community, outside our culture, and our experience? What does unity mean in these circumstances?

Does unity mean that we all agree on the same thing? Think about that one moment. It's a tough question, and the answer has to be both "Yes," and "No." It must be "Yes," in that fundamental agreement on basic ideas is at the root of any association we make in our lives. I volunteer for the fire department because I believe that what these people do is essentially good. I give my time and energy to the PTA at my children's school because I agree with the stated goals of the organization. Each one of us, I'm sure, could make a long list of the things we participate in because we are in agreement with their agenda or basic principles. The church is no different. Most of us are in church because we are in agreement with the basics about Christian faith. Otherwise, why would we be involved? Indeed, it's not going too far to say that without fundamental consensus on basic principles, no organization can survive for very long.

But the answer to the foregoing question must also be "No," because for us, unity is not necessarily derived from a lock-step agreement with everything that the church says or does. In fact, it strikes me that — though my experience tells me we have no reason to fear this — a community in complete agreement on all things might be just a little boring. Indeed, one might argue that respectful and loving diversity of opinion, perspective, and experience are more conducive to unity than is complete agreement.

The question, however, remains. When scripture speaks of preaching the "peace" or unity of Christ, what gives? Perhaps the best answer, in the final analysis, is balance. Perhaps, on this Easter Sunday when we look into the new possibilities brought with Jesus out of the tomb, we can look to a new kind of unity that is forged, not in blind agreement, nor in an anarchy of relativism, but

177

instead, in the gentle life-giving, grace-filled ebb and flow of God's love.

I learned the quote as one offered by John Wesley, but have found through study, that its essence came from Saint Augustine, and it goes like this:

> In necessariis unitas,
> *In essentials unity,*
> In dubiis libertas,
> *In doubtful things liberty,*
> In omnibus autem caritas,
> *But in all things love.*

Truly, is this not the essence of new life in the risen Christ? Unity in the essential embrace of new life in Christ — freedom in those things that do not hinder new life, and in whatever we undertake, to do so in love?

On this day of new life, I have to say that I stand with Augustine. And, I would call us to stand with him as we move to the graceful and flexible rhythms of the resurrection life in Christ Jesus our Lord! Let our peace, our *eirene*, our unity be in that self same love that has gone — and continues to go the distance for us. Amen.

Being A Witness

The other day I was driving along when all of a sudden, out of the blue, this car went whizzing by me on the right. The car was going about 65 miles per hour in a 25 mph zone. Just as he whipped by me, another car pulled out on my right just ahead of me. You guessed it. Wham! I was fortunate to be able to steer away from the mess and not get cracked up myself. As soon as I stopped, though, I jumped out of my car and went to check on the two drivers to be sure that everyone was unhurt. By God's grace, no major injuries! The cars, however, were another matter. Honestly, as long as everyone was okay, I didn't much care about the cars. I had a meeting to get to on the other side of town.

Just as I was leaving, though, the police arrived. One officer asked if anyone had "witnessed" the accident. Several people standing there turned and pointed to me. I smiled, turned to leave, and the police officer said, "Could you please stay a moment? We need to hear from you as a witness." So much for my meeting.

This experience, though, gave me pause as I was pouring over this scripture in preparation for today's sermon. My word was important, but not because I was a pastor. They didn't even know my profession. My point of view wasn't sought after because I was eloquent. They sure didn't want my two cents' worth because I was some sort of collision expert. No, they wanted me to share with them because I was there. I was, in the words of the police officer, a "witness."

Isn't it funny? We tend to trust the word of those who were present on the scene. Whether it's an accident, an encounter with a

179

celebrity, or just someone who attended that church council gathering that you missed last week, we believe the one who was there. Even our legal system gives high credence to an "eyewitness." I suppose it makes sense, but it is kind of strange in a way.

I remember meeting someone who actually knew one of the Beatles back in the late 1960s. Now, being a big fan, I've read lots of books about the Beatles. I've watched all the documentaries and television interviews. I own all their recordings, and I can play many of their songs on my guitar. Frankly, I know quite a lot about the Beatles, but meeting this guy who actually knew John Lennon back in London in the late 1960s? I sat mesmerized, listening to this fellow's stories for hours. Why? He was there. He was a witness. It was a step closer to the real thing. A witness brings authenticity and passion; a witness brings us closer and allows us access to what really happened.

This text from the book of Acts give us this same sense of witness. It is the testimony, if you will, of one who was there. These are not ephemeral descriptions, or vague mis-remembered sharings. These are the sharp, poignant memories of someone who was present on the scene: a witness.

But there is more to this than the witness of Peter. Peter makes it clear that he is not the only one. He says, "This Jesus, God raised up, and of that, all of us are witnesses!" What does he mean here? Was everyone in his hearing on the Pentecost day a witness to the resurrection? Not likely. And it's not likely that this was his reference point. Our time could be used to sort out the historical context of Peter's remark here. References to the wider Jewish community would have to be explored, as well as notions of the early church community that was being addressed in this writing.

Whichever way the scholarship goes, it's clear that the writer here means to expand the concept of witness beyond its normative definition. Certainly, not everyone in Peter's hearing was an actual witness. This much we know and must try to absorb. We can be witnesses to new life in Christ Jesus without having been there when he sat upon that marble slab. The witness here isn't like one who was present at the scene of an accident or a crime. It isn't like one who was present in the life moments of a great personage. We can all be — if we choose — witnesses to the resurrection of Jesus Christ. We can experience firsthand what it means to receive the newness of life that comes as we embrace the reality of the resurrection.

Then, sisters and brothers, we won't be droning on about doctrine or history. We won't get caught up in our committees or our own ego investment in church program and structure. We will no longer feel the need to be in charge of a diminishing legacy. We will possess the passion, the immediacy and the power of true witnesses. People will stop and pay attention. They'll sit and want to hear more. Ears will open, hearts will soften, and God's love will flow out because we have had the firsthand experience of new life in Christ Jesus.

Think for a moment. Where in your day-to-day living has new life taken root? Where have you found healing? How have new beginnings come upon you? Are these not the resurrection? Have you experienced forgiveness? Have you tasted the joy of grace in a relationship? All of this is of God. All of it echoes the beauty of that empty tomb, and if we can embrace it, we are witnesses to it all.

You see, cementing the resurrection of Jesus Christ into a one-time historical event robs it of its power. We get caught and mired too often in discussions and debates about the historical veracity of our biblical texts. Did this really happen? Did that happen for sure? Did Jesus really say this or that? What a waste of time! It's absurd. We treat the Bible like it's a trial record and we are going over it to find evidence ... of what? Our Holy Word is not a history book. It is the story of who we are as a people, and as such it contains sacred truth. To grind one's teeth in silly debates is to miss the whole beauty of scripture.

While debates rage and discussions put generations of students to sleep, we know that we have access to something much broader and more powerful than mere physical evidence. We have access to a firsthand encounter with the resurrection life in Jesus Christ. Hear what I just said — I called it the "resurrection life." Resurrection isn't an event. It's a way of life. We cannot, indeed we dare not, try to pinpoint the hour and day that the body awoke and sat up and wandered out of the tomb. We couldn't prove it one way or the other if we wanted to! And friends, it's not the point.

We simply need to embrace the story. It is its own truth. And when we embrace the story, we begin to get the glimmer of the way of living that turns death to life, that lifts up the downtrodden, that literally brings the spirit of life into corners where death has long held sway.

There's no denying it. We are, as Peter submits, "all witnesses." Imagine a whole church full of Christians with the enthusiasm and vigor of people who have been there, people who have seen the reality and power of the resurrection. Let us embrace Christ's rising and let us breathe in the passion and power of the new life that has been offered us. Let us step up to the plate as witnesses who can testify to the power and wonder; the reality of new life in Christ Jesus. Amen.

Converting To Christianity

"Repent and be baptized every one of you in the name of Jesus Christ so that your sins may be forgiven."

I can't speak for any of you, but I can tell you that in my twenty-plus years of ministry, I have seldom heard a preacher or a layperson stand up and call the people to repentance and baptism in the name of Jesus Christ. Oh, yes, I have heard it at a few tent meetings over the years, but in the mainline church where I have lived my life I don't think I have ever heard a pastor call upon his or her people to repent and be baptized so that they can receive the forgiveness of God. As I stand before you this morning I want to tell you that I've come to the conclusion that this is not a good thing.

My memory is dim, but it seems to me that we — in my white liberal church background — gave up such things as repentance because we felt it was too judgmental. Who among us, after all, has a monopoly on goodness? Who are we to point a finger? We have pretty much abandoned the idea that we are all sinful as well, and in its place we tried to plant the pop-psychological notion that we're all in good shape. No judgment, no real boundaries, and finally, no real clarity about belief. When conservative folk in the church charge liberals with shallow theology, friends, they have a point.

Now, before the mob attacks, let me say that there is good reason to withhold judgment concerning others. I think it was Jesus who told us to take the log out of our own eye before we remove the speck from our neighbor's eye (Matthew 7:3). Didn't he also address the idea of judgment directly when he said, "Do not judge, and you will not be judged; do not condemn, and you will not be condemned" (Luke 6:37)? Moreover, Jesus kind of took the idea of sin itself and turned it on its head, didn't he? In fact, there are innumerable times in the gospels when Jesus says that his very purpose in coming among us was to forgive sins. Who are we to point them out in others or keep track of them in some record book? Isn't it our job, with Jesus, to forgive?

Ah. The age-old conflict between the so-called liberals and the so-called conservatives. It rages on even as I write this piece. For my own part, I reject the labels of liberal and conservative. It seems to me that these polarizing tags are the work of a demonic culture that has stuck them on us in order to divide and disempower the church. It has worked so well that we even have a hard time talking about one of the most basic elements of our faith: Making disciples for Jesus Christ (Matthew 28:19).

But this scripture rests before us today and, liberal or conservative, left or right, up or down, it begs our authentic engagement.

The call to repentance is broad and deep in our tradition. We envision scenes of John the Baptist shouting to the people to repent, and we hear the words of Jesus calling the people to repentance as well, but what does that mean? Repent? For most of us, the meaning goes something like this. "I'm doing something bad. Maybe even I myself am bad and I need to stop doing what I'm doing and admit that I'm terrible ... or at least admit that what I've been doing is pretty bad...." Does that ring true for you? To repent is to admit you've messed up and messed up royally, and that it's time to come clean and admit it. Right?

Wrong.

The word here in the book of Acts has little to do with guilt, confession, and shame. It is a very different concept than this. The Greek word that has been translated as "repent" in this instance is *metaneo*, which means "to have another mind." This is a view, not of shame, guilt, and confession, but rather the utterance of a call to transformation. It is the same call that is echoed by the apostle Paul when he writes, "Do not be conformed to this world, but be transformed by the renewing of your minds, so that you may discern what is the will of God — what is good and acceptable and perfect" (Romans 12:2).

The call to conversion that we hear in this passage from Acts is not about confessing how messed up we are and then moving to the next new religion thing. It's about "having a new mind," or "transforming our minds" so that we see things in a totally new and different light. It's not changing our opinions or adopting a new ideology. It's not about moving left or moving right. The call to conversion that comes to us in this incredible passage has to do with having *a new mind*. It has to do with *transforming* our minds out of the modes of culture and ego. We become, in this process, something completely new, almost as if we were re-created. At least, this is Paul's take on the subject. "So if anyone is in Christ, there is a new creation: everything old has passed away; see, everything has become new!" (2 Corinthians 5:17).

It's not about judgment, it's about change. It's not about pointing a finger or trying to get someone to adopt my point of view of things, it's about inviting people into a transformation so complete that they will feel as though they are "born from above" (John 3:3). I have to be honest here — this feels more scary to me than the idea of pointing a finger at someone and telling them they need to "repent," in the sense that they're all messed up. How do you invite people to change from the "inside out"? (Mark 1:8, The Message).

Probably the best way to invite someone to such a life transformation is to demonstrate that change in your own life. A drunk, though perhaps a good object lesson, is not really capable of extolling the virtues of sobriety. A boxer is not likely to be a convincing proponent of nonviolence. Neither can a nontransformed Christian invite others into lives of thorough change.

Indeed, could Peter have issued the call so powerfully if he himself were unchanged? Could Paul, after pursuing the new church to persecute it, have become the apostle without having a new mind? If we hope to bring others to Christ, it must be through our own authentic faith journey of repentance and conversion. It's really that simple — not easy, it's true, but it is simple.

Can we step into this kind of repentance together? This move toward transformation and change? Can we envision what our lives would be like if we laid everything down and allowed Christ to come inside and change us? What a call! What a challenge! It moves us beyond our petty drive to convince others that we have the best religion. It shoves us outside the habitual box of judgment and condemnation, and it calls us today, this moment, to radically surrender all that we are to God's love in Jesus Christ so that we might be reconciled, transformed, and born from above.

Come, let us pray together that we might step onto this path of repentance and conversion in the name of Jesus Christ. Amen.

This Is In The Bible?

My mother saved everything from my childhood — little clay sculptures I made in church school, drawings, odd pieces of clothing, and of course, report cards. I have report cards going from high school all the way back to elementary school days. They make interesting reading, actually. And at times they are even a bit comical. One teacher noted wryly that as I got older I *might* settle down a bit. Another teacher praised my good spirit but chided my talking and passing notes in class. Then there was one that got my attention. I don't think I had ever noticed it before. Certainly, my mom never mentioned it. She probably didn't think it worth noting. But there, in red ink at the bottom of the card, my third grade teacher had scrawled, "Shares well with others...."

"Shares well with others." Sharing is an interesting thing for us to be teaching our children, isn't it? Really, it's a good thing. On the play yard or in the sandbox we want them to learn how to share toys and building blocks. We hope they will learn how to take turns on the swing sets and seesaws, and we hope, as we raise our families, that they will learn to share of themselves.

"Shares well with others." We work hard to teach this maxim, don't we? We guide the play time, share the lessons, and help our children learn that sharing is an essential component to getting along in this world. Wouldn't we like to be able to say that of our children?

But the truth of the matter is that after all that teaching, all that cajoling and guiding, we send these children who have learned how to share out into a world that does not — in fact — share well with others. The child who has learned how to share at home or in church is often the object of bullies and thieves. The child who has learned gentleness and openness at home hits the schoolyard to find suddenly that the world isn't the way Dad and Mom said it was. Ouch, ouch, and ouch again.

This is the feeling I get when I read this passage from Acts. My initial response to it is, "Is this really in the Bible? Do you know what will happen if we try this in the real world? They can't mean ... well ... that's ridiculous. It's naive! It sounds like communism!" In any discussion I've ever undertaken regarding this scripture, folks get defensive, angry, and dismissive. I am told that such things wouldn't work in "today's world," and that there's nothing wrong with making a "profit."

It's hard to confront the truth that scripture, it seems, wants us to share so well with others that we divest ourselves of the notion of private property altogether. The idea is that in Christian community the welfare of the individual is found in the welfare of the community. Thus, everyone gives everything they have to the community to be distributed according to need.

Wait. What's that? According to ... need? What if I work harder? Don't I deserve more? What if that person is lazy? They don't mean this literally ... do they? How did that get in the Bible, anyway?

Oh, yes, this is one of those "difficult sayings" that are difficult, not so much because they are problematic, in any theological or doctrinal sense, but because of the socio-political location of the people reading the text. In the United States, we consume an absurdly huge proportion of the world's resources. We are wealthy beyond imagination, while the majority of the world's population lives on less than a dollar a day. We suffer the health effects of obesity while much of the world suffers from malnutrition. Our nation is responsible for the vast majority of greenhouse gases that are accelerating global warming, and our corporations chase endlessly around the globe looking for the next nation that will let its workers be paid pennies an hour to make our shirts, sneakers, jeans, radios, and computers.

The hard truth, friends, is that the economy of the early church is hard for us because we have so much. Within that reality is the other hard truth — we don't share well with others.

Hear me on this, sisters and brothers. I live in the same world as the rest of you, and though I think sharing is great, I work hard, saving for *my* retirement. I struggle to put money aside to pay for *my* children's college. I take *my* paycheck home each week to pay for food for *my* family and to buy clothing, school supplies, and whatnot for *me and mine.* And I'll be honest, it would not be easy for me to be the first in line to give everything I own over to our church to be distributed out to all the members based on need. As I say these words, I need to confess this. I will not give it over because I do not trust. I do not — God help me — trust you. If I give everything — *everything* — over to the church, do I trust you to take care of me? My wife? My children? Do I trust the community to care for us all? Sadly, no. But it's worse than that. The real deal is that my trust in God is being put to the test. It is all, really and finally, about trust. Do I trust you? Do I trust God? Am I willing to live my life according to that trust? I feel shame as the "No" forms on my lips.

But, no matter how I might feel about it, I have to deal with the fact that this call to "share well with others" is not only here in scripture before us, it also seems pretty clear that the early church did indeed try to live this way. In fact, there are still Christian communities across the globe striving to reach for this ideal. And it's not just me. We, as a community committed to authenticity, really must confront the depth of this passage and all that supports it as we seek to be faithful.

Do we trust one another? Do we trust God?

Forgive me, but I assume that no one sitting here today is about to turn everything they own over to the church. Is that right? That being the case, I think it would behoove us to consider how we might at least make a beginning. In a Christian community where the average member gives only about 2% of their income to the church, how might we proceed? In a community where more than 20% of our neighbors have no health insurance, what can we do?

Let me make these suggestions. First, let each member of this church tithe. That's right. Let us make a solemn covenant today to give 10% of our earnings to the church. And let us do this as an indication of our trust in one another and in God. Let each person

— today — fill out a new pledge card and make sure that it's made out for 10%.

Second, let's get together and share with one another. Let's learn about the needs and the wants in our community, and let's set about devising a strategy to meet them. Do members of our community need health care? Jobs? Do the children need help in school? Let us learn about the needs and make a commitment to meet those needs. Let us make certain that those in our community who have needs are cared for by their sisters and brothers.

Finally, let's be clear that these steps are but a beginning. If we tithe this year, can we do better next year? Can we develop a fund to pay for health insurance for anyone in our church who needs it? What else can we do? What more can we give? How much more deeply might we learn to trust one another ... and God?

I put it to you as challenge and prayer. I offer it to you as grist for the mill, fuel for the fire. Let us challenge our own situation, our own circumstances, let us confront our lack of trust, and let us take the next joyful step down the road toward faithfulness to God in Christ Jesus! Amen.

Martyrdom Chic

This story about Stephen is a hard one to preach about these days. Lately, the idea of martyrdom has fallen under a bit of a cloud, don't you think? What do you think of when you hear about martyrs? In my experience, a martyr is either reduced to a psychological complex foisted off on someone who does too much for others, or it's a poor child with a dynamite vest ready to doom himself or herself and plenty of others for the sake of the cause, and the cash benefits paid to the family, after the fact. There's no question about it. The stock on martyrdom is way, way down these days.

What do you think about it? Would you be willing to become a martyr for the cause of Jesus Christ? Of course, if we are true to our faith, we would *not* be willing — or able — to take folks with us when we made the sacrifice. Just us, just us for the cause. Just us for the witness to the faith. Would you be willing?

This is a fascinating and difficult question. Today, with our young people flung out around the globe in the name of a war on terror, we know that at least some people are willing to give and to take life for a cause. This has been true since the beginning of human history. No judgment implied here, but this isn't the same as being a martyr.

In fact, I would say that the prospect of martyrdom is not illuminated by a question that asks if you'd be willing to die for the cause. My own viewpoint is that the question should be, "Are you willing to live your beliefs without compromise no matter what the cost?" Now there's a question worth considering.

How deeply are we committed to our Christian faith? How far are we willing to go, not in risking our lives — though that may be the outcome — but rather in living the life of faith fully and completely? This kind of commitment is not the path of zealotry. Zealots have a single, laser focus and seldom know much about listening, learning, or growing. Their minds are made up, their paths are set, and the goal is unshakable.

While we might say some of these things about committed faith in Christ, it is perhaps wise to look beyond the perils of zealotry and into the folds of a life lived well and fully in Christ Jesus. Again the question comes. What would such a life look like? Where would such a life begin and end?

It would seem that a committed Christian life begins and ends with the one unshakable truth of our faith, and that is "self-giving love is redemptive." Let me say that again. The core of our faith, the rock upon which our lives are built in Christ, is the sacred truth "self-giving love is redemptive." This truth bursts into our consciousness as Christians when we see the self-giving act of God in Christ for us on the cross. We see it, too, in the teachings and stories of Jesus in scripture. We also witness it in the lives of the saints down the centuries.

From Saint Francis to Dorothy Day to Martin Luther King Jr. and beyond, we see that the ultimate love we give is the gift of love that is imbued with the self. When someone loves from the inside out, with their souls, that love has impact. When we give of ourselves in love, that act has transformative power. Whether, like Mother Teresa, it is a life given in service to the poor, or someone like you or me who strives to live a life that is oriented toward self-giving, the impact of such love changes people. It has, as I said, redemptive power.

Now, as we wax eloquent about living, rather than dying, for our faith, let us be clear. Full and faithful living may well lead us to the cross. Faithfulness in life often does have a price. Whether it's honesty at the job that may cost us, clarity in caring for marginalized people, or standing in faith for unpopular causes, our living for God can lead us with Jesus to Calvary. The point, again, is the living. As Martin Luther King Jr. said on the night before his murder, "Like anybody, I would like to live a long life. Longevity has its place. But I'm not concerned about that now. I just want to do God's will, and he's allowed me to go up to the mountain. And I've looked over and I've seen the promised land. I may not get there with you, but I want you to know tonight, that we as a people will get to the promised land. And I'm happy tonight; I'm not worried about anything. I'm not fearing any man. Mine eyes have seen the glory of the coming of the Lord."

Only hours after sharing these words, Reverend King was murdered on the balcony outside his hotel room. You see, Reverend King loved life. He didn't want to die. But doing God's will and living the example of self-giving love was what was important to him, even more important than "longevity."

In this age of pop psychology and out-of-control world affairs, we must construct a new vision of what it means to go all the way for our faith. In a time where the concept of self-giving love is viewed as unhealthy by the therapeutic community, we step with clarity into lives of self-giving love. In a day when the notion of martyrdom snaps our attention to the evening news to see the shattered lives of a sacrifice that can only bring only more death, we must build a living consensus that speaks to the power of a living faith.

Together, in Christian community, we are called to go deeper in commitment and to dedicate our lives anew — not to merely die for the cause, but to live for it. We are called into transformational living that offers the gift of love and healing to anyone we encounter, no matter who they are or where they come from.

As our world spins seemingly out of control, we have answers that emerge from lives rooted in the self-giving love of Jesus. As social fabric frays and extremism rears its contorted countenance, we have the clarity and beauty of what it means to live a life of balance and wonder in the folds of God's unfailing grace.

And yes, it does begin and end with love. Then, knowing of the resurrection, we claim that it begins once again! Born in a barn, raised on the road, executed like a common criminal, and back again on the third day! It all moves around the unmovable axis of God's unfailing love for us and for the world he created.

So where do we begin?

How might each one of us step more fully and abundantly into a life dedicated to self-giving love? What healing might we offer? What hope might we engender? What new life might we participate in bringing forth? Think about our relationships. Our families, friends, coworkers, and acquaintances; where among this collection of people might we offer God's incredible self-giving love?

Think for a moment about our church community. Are there ways that we, as Christian community, might live more fully into the abundance of God's love? Are there ways we could quit worrying and — as Martin Luther King Jr. put it, "just do God's will"? What would our church community look like if we pooled all our efforts into being a community that focused all our energies on living for our faith?

In raising up this possibility, in lifting up this hope, let us make the confession together that we are and have been little more than part-time Christians. Let us lay out the truth that too often our faith ranks about as high in our lives as our commitment to the children's soccer games or our involvement in other social endeavors. Let's just lay down the masks and disguises and be real with one another about taking this faith life and living it fully.

My own suspicion is that this is what got Stephen into trouble. Sure, he was a bit of a loud mouth. It's likely that they couldn't get him to keep quiet about this Jesus thing he had found. My guess is he was a bit "over the top" at times, but my own sense of things tells me that for him, his faith was utterly central to his life.

This, sisters and brothers, is what it all comes down to in the end. Whether we are Stephen in scripture or just a regular garden-variety Christian trying to get it right, the ultimate and real call to us is to invest our lives fully and completely in the unshakable core belief that self-giving love has redemptive value. Moreover, we make this move, this investment if you will, as recipients of that love in Jesus Christ. We rise together to offer that same love to the world in beauty, wonder, and hope. Amen.

To An Unknown God

Are you one of those people who always has a backup plan? Do you make your commitments and focus your energies on one thing, but have an alternative in mind just in case things don't work out with the first one? You might call it "Plan B" or something else, but basically you're hedging your bets and covering yourself in case the situation goes south.

It's not really a bad idea. Certainly this is done in military circles, in the business community, and even in planning for church ministry and programs. Young folk applying to colleges do this as they apply for their first choice schools and then have a list of "safety schools," or backup possibilities. It is, most people would assert, simply a wise course of action.

I've heard of people doing it in their personal lives, as well. When I was much younger I remember hearing about young women who had "backup plans" or dates for the prom. If the boy of their dreams didn't ask them to the dance, then they would move on to "Plan B" just to make sure they didn't miss the dance.

As we approach this passage of scripture today, we are confronted with a similar situation. Paul stands and notes to the folks that he saw an altar to an "unknown god." This would be a relatively easy thing to ignore. After all, in a polytheistic culture such as Rome's there were many gods, some of whom might be a bit obscure, even unknown, as Paul suggests. But this unknown god was a real specific thing in Roman religious circles. It was a well-known altar and encountered frequently. It wasn't so much for a god who was not known as it was an altar to a god who might be around but people may not be aware of yet. It was a placeholder, if you will, for a god who may yet show up on the scene. Sort of a backup plan in case the gods we're working with right now don't work out as well as we had hoped.

The Romans, being not only polytheistic, but practical as well, came up with an empty seat sort of option. This way, any gods who might be wandering about wouldn't take offense at not having an altar, and the Romans wouldn't miss out on a potential deity that might be of help at some point down the road for them. Such is the focus of the "unknown god" that Paul describes in this passage from Acts.

All this is, of course, well and good for your average Roman. Good, that is, until Paul comes on the scene with these wild stories about Jesus. Paul invokes the "unknown god" in order to say that in Jesus Christ, God has become known, and the option of laying out a place setting for a God who may come along has been removed. In other words, no more "Plan B." No more backup plans or alternative strategies. For Paul, and I think ultimately for us, all the eggs go in the Jesus basket. No more hedging of our bets, no more "safety" options. This God wants it all.

This, of course, is an easy thing for a preacher to seize upon. The jump onto the rhetorical slide is easy. Down we go as we lift up the one true answer in Jesus Christ. We pick up momentum as we challenge people to throw out their carefully laid plans, rational options, and safety nets, and urge them to grab instead onto the one sure thing. Now we're really flying as we, with Paul, throw all caution to the wind and call all of you to follow a God who "does not live in shrines made by human hands."

Yes, it's a preacher's fantasy. Yet, when one stops to consider this whole Christian enterprise, the things seem almost foolhardy. Maybe the Romans had a point. Why not place our spiritual cards on a table where we can bet on any number of deities, even ones who haven't shown up yet? Doesn't it make sense to cover all the bases? Isn't it just practical in a spiritual sort of way? It reminds me of a fellow I once knew who took it upon himself to convince me that the church should be an interfaith center where all spiritual

196

options would be open to the folks who came in the door. He was well-meaning, I think, if a bit confused. I remember a conversation standing by the altar in our sanctuary one afternoon. This person looked at me intensely as we gazed at the cross on the altar, and he said, "I'll be happy when we can put a statue of the Buddha right next to the cross." The temptation of some would be to discredit this person for his lack of clarity and focus in faith. But in truth, is he any different from the Romans who Paul was addressing? Is he really any different than any of us?

Think about it. Are we able to jettison all the things that we use as backup plans in our lives in favor of our faith in God through Jesus Christ? Okay, so maybe we don't build an altar to an unknown God. But could it be that we do hedge our bets a bit when it comes to totally trusting in God? How does that old World War I song go? "Praise the Lord and Pass the Ammunition?" Maybe we aren't polytheistic like the Romans ... or are we?

Do we have a multiplicity of gods who get our allegiance and our trust, along with the God of Israel? Maybe instead of the twelve gods of the Romans, we have other gods like money. Or possibly we worship the God of national interest or patriotism? Or could it be that we bow down at the altar of social station or influence?

You see, I think we're not so different from my friend who wants the Buddha next to the cross. I think we have more in common with the Romans of Paul's day than we might imagine. I think that we, like many people, hedge our bets when it comes to our faith.

And so, easy or not, I jump onto the preacher's side and stand today with Paul.

I do think that we are called to choose.

In a world that yaks, pleads, and begs for our attention and our loyalty, the voice of Jesus bids us pick him. In a time when uncertainty clouds our judgment and we scatter like sheep without a shepherd, the good shepherd, Jesus, calls us by name. In a culture where countless gods of material wealth, power, and influence reach out in seductive song to us, the God of love stands on the solid ground of hope and new beginning and bids us sing "his" song.

Yes. There are many gods out there, both known and unknown, but we who gather here today, come to sit at the feet of the Creator of heaven and earth who has come to us in Jesus Christ. We *have* chosen. We have taken all our eggs and put them in the Jesus basket.

We do so, finally, because we trust in the message we have heard from Jesus as he stood up in the temple that day and read from the Isaiah scroll:

> *The Spirit of the Lord is upon me, because he has anointed me to bring good news to the poor. He has sent me to proclaim release to the captives and recovery of sight to the blind, to let the oppressed go free, to proclaim the year of the Lord's favor.*
>
> — Luke 4:18-19

We trust, and we believe that this anointed one who has been sent is our Savior and our Redeemer, and it is him and no other whom we follow. Yes, indeed. We have put all our eggs in the Jesus basket! Thanks be to God! Amen.

The Ascension Of Our Lord
Acts 1:1-11

Receiving The Power
Of The Holy Spirit

I love this story. It doesn't matter how many times I hear it, or how it's told, it never fails to grab me in a new and different way. It's really an incredible tale. And by incredible I mean just that. Without credibility! Who could actually buy a story like this? The disciples, cowardly and virtually faithless, abandoned the Master and scattered in the chaos of his arrest and execution. In the days that followed, as whispered rumor and innuendo turned into actual visitations by Jesus himself, the incredulous bunch slowly got it together — at least enough to meet with him this one last time. But even then they still were clueless. They figured that this must be it. Now was the time when he would act decisively, so they asked him, "Lord, is this the time when you will restore the kingdom to Israel?"

Scripture, of course, doesn't record this, but in my mind, Jesus issues a wan smile, shakes his head, and rolls his eyes slightly. Water is wet. Sky is blue. Rocks are hard. The disciples are clueless. It's just one of those things, I guess. So Jesus gently lets them know that they don't get to know the date or the time.

Instead he tells them that they will receive power. Ahhhh — power — isn't that what it's been about all along? Finally the Romans will be chased out and a new Jewish king will take over and everything will get better. The outs will be in, as they say, and the ins will be out.

But this is not the kind of power that Jesus is talking about, is it? Jesus isn't offering the power of politics or armies. He's not gifting the disciples with the power of wealth or influence. No, he is saying that when the Holy Spirit comes they will receive an entirely new thing. The Greek word is *dunamis*. The English-Greek Bible dictionary that I use for free online lists it like below.

1. strength, power, ability
   a. inherent power, power residing in a thing by virtue of its nature, or which a person or thing exerts and puts forth
   b. power for performing miracles
   c. moral power and excellence of soul
   d. the power and influence which belong to riches and wealth
   e. power and resources arising from numbers
   f. power consisting in or resting upon armies, forces, hosts

Interestingly enough, nothing here actually gets to the depth of what Jesus is trying to tell the disciples. This isn't a power like anything ever witnessed before, so language then, as now, is really inadequate to the task of describing it.

The power, however, which comes upon the disciples — and not coincidentally — upon us — is not really the power that is described by this word *dunamis*. The power that Jesus offers in the Holy Spirit is really a kind of un-power. It is the antithesis of power as we know it. It is not power shifted and given over to others. It is, quite simply, power redefined.

In Jesus Christ, power is no longer about control. It is no longer about the ability to make things happen or to exert influence. This new un-power is, in fact, so different that it is actually the literal opposite of power as we know and understand it in our culture and our world.

Paul writes best about it in 1 Corinthians:

> *For the message about the cross is foolishness to those who are perishing, but to us who are being saved it is the power of God. For it is written, "I will destroy the*

wisdom of the wise, and the discernment of the discerning I will thwart." Where is the one who is wise? Where is the scribe? Where is the debater of this age? Has not God made foolish the wisdom of the world? For since, in the wisdom of God, the world did not know God through wisdom, God decided, through the foolishness of our proclamation, to save those who believe. For Jews demand signs and Greeks desire wisdom, but we proclaim Christ crucified, a stumbling block to Jews and foolishness to Gentiles, but to those who are the called, both Jews and Greeks, Christ the power of God and the wisdom of God. For God's foolishness is wiser than human wisdom, and God's weakness is stronger than human strength.

Consider your own call, brothers and sisters: not many of you were wise by human standards, not many were powerful, not many were of noble birth. But God chose what is foolish in the world to shame the wise; God chose what is weak in the world to shame the strong; God chose what is low and despised in the world, things that are not, to reduce to nothing things that are, so that no one might boast in the presence of God. He is the source of your life in Christ Jesus, who became for us wisdom from God, and righteousness and sanctification and redemption, in order that, as it is written, "Let the one who boasts, boast in the Lord."

— 1 Corinthians 1:18-31

You see, the power of the Holy Spirit that comes upon the disciples reflects a complete reversal of the world as we know it. That which we once understood to be strong, we now know to be weak. Everything is turned upside down! In Christ Jesus, God didn't just put someone new in charge, he changed the whole power arrangement!

It's like going to the camera store and developing a roll of film. Have you ever done that? You hold up the photograph and then hold up a negative. Everything is opposite. That's the kind of power that God sends us in the Holy Spirit, the kind of power that Jesus promised his disciples and promises us, too!

201

I remember once having the high privilege of being with an extraordinary young man as he was in his last hours of life. He was dying of a brain tumor, and we had a precious few moments together that I will always remember and treasure. As he lay there we talked of silly things, and then we prayed and talked about what was coming. I will never forget him looking up at me and whispering these words. "In my weakness is my strength...."

Indeed, this young man was strong.

Friends, we stand today with the disciples of old, awaiting the mighty gift of God's power. But let us not stand there and ask when the kingdom will be restored. Let us not look simply for there to be someone else sitting at the head of the table. Instead, let us embrace the saving truth that in Jesus Christ the table is flipped upside down and the chairs and plates and silverware are strewn everywhere around the room!

In Christ Jesus, power as we know it is not just given to another, it is in itself transformed. The strength of this world is shown to be the venal weakness that it is. The wisdom of all the scholars is shown to be the pile of hooey that we always knew it was. It is this power, forged in weakness and lived out in servanthood, that God in Christ calls us to receive today.

So let's drop our quest for worldly power. Let's abandon our drive for riches. Let's leave the religious stuff behind and receive the *dunamis* of God! Let us step forward in foolishness. Let us leap ahead in weakness, and let us go together dancing and singing as we claim a newly defined and wonderful sense of power given us by our own Savior who even now disappears out of sight on a cloud.

Yes. It's a great story and, incredible or not, it's our story and we're sticking to it! This power of new life, love, hope, and wonder is ours in God's precious Spirit. Believe it or not, we are called to live into this power, to share it, and to use it to foster new life and new beginnings wherever we go in the name of our Lord Jesus Christ! Amen.

Easter 7
Acts 1:6-14

Are We There Yet?

On long family car trips, one of the favorite questions asked by children from the backseat is, "Are we there yet?" It is a question that drives certain parents to distraction, and one that kids love to ask. Even though the family has only been in the car fifteen minutes, the question comes. Even though the car is hurling down the freeway with no indication of slowing down, the question comes. And even though the kids are assured over and over again that they need to relax because it's going to be a long journey, the question comes. "Are we there yet?" They get obsessed with the destination, and miss the incredible scenery passing by the window. They focus on that point when the car will pull into Grandpa's driveway and they can spill out of the car for hugs and hoorays as vacation begins. In fact, they focus on this so much that they lose out on the opportunity to sing songs, play games, and engage in storytelling with the rest of the family as the journey continues.

The disciples, of course, are not much better than this brood of kids crowded into the backseat of the family sedan on the way to Grandpa's house. They ask pretty much the same question. "Are we there yet?" "Is this the time you're going to restore the kingdom?" Is it now? Is it now? One can almost conjure up the image of overeager ten-year-olds bouncing up and down as they fire off the question. In his answer, Jesus was preparing his followers for a long journey. "It is not for you to know the time," says Jesus. "You just need to get busy and be my witnesses."

The "time" that the disciples were referring to had to do with their expectation that Jesus would kick the Romans out and hand

Israel back to its rightful rulers. For many in the early church, as well as in today's church, "the time" referred to the return of Christ and the ushering in of a new age. It is hard for contemporary Christians to grasp the enormity of the idea of the second coming in the early church. The idea of Christ's return, the belief in Jesus' imminent return, was total. The idea that everything would soon be over and a new age begun tainted everything.

Jesus wasn't just coming someday. He was going to walk in the door any second. The return of Jesus was not something about which theologians argued or about which contemporary authors conjured up fictional stories. The return of Jesus, for these folks, was now. The power of this immediacy drove the early Christian community in its witness, in its discipleship, and in its faithfulness. Any second now, Jesus would return, so time was precious, opportunities for faithfulness were few. For these people, the voices from the backseat would not have sounded irritating or trite. "Are we there yet?" was a valid query.

Today, more than two millennia down the road, few people ask any more about the destination. Few people can conjure up a sense of immediacy after more than 2,000 years. Even those who find the second coming as a deep piece of their faith have to contend with the fact "any day now," has stretched into something over 730,000 days. Yes, of course, it is not ours to know the time. And yes, we hear the voices saying that he will return the way he came, but candidly, it's been a long time now, hasn't it?

I may be going out on a limb here, but I want to make a suggestion. Could it be that 2,000 years down the road, it might be appropriate to revisit the notion of Jesus' return? While I embrace the idea of the return of Jesus as an article of my faith, I have been moved to explore the possibility that we might have misunderstood the concept. It's certainly worth exploring, don't you think?

Think with me now. What is one of the key biblical phrases we use to refer to the church? It comes from Saint Paul, and the phrase is "body of Christ." We often refer to ourselves as the body of Christ. From our liturgy of holy communion to our church, references to the body of Christ abound. A recent search on an internet search engine produced nearly five million references to the body of Christ!

204

Paul writes in Romans:

> *For by the grace given to me I say to everyone among you not to think of yourself more highly than you ought to think, but to think with sober judgment, each according to the measure of faith that God has assigned. For as in one body we have many members, and not all the members have the same function, so we, who are many, are one body in Christ, and individually we are members one of another. We have gifts that differ according to the grace given to us: prophecy, in proportion to faith; ministry, in ministering; the teacher, in teaching; the exhorter, in exhortation; the giver, in generosity; the leader, in diligence; the compassionate, in cheerfulness.*
> — Romans 12:3-8

Consider the power of this text. "We who are many, are one body in Christ." Each of us, with our different gifts, skills, and talents, are part of the body of Christ. As members of this body, we need to ask ourselves how well we are performing our various functions. Are those who have the gift of prophecy actually prophesying? Looking around, I would have to say that there is a shortage of good prophets, good truth-tellers today. The gift of ministry? Whether it is lay ministry or ordained, we do not suffer from a surplus of gifted ministries. Teachers? Preachers? Donors? Leaders?

We can, I think, look to Paul's writings and make some sense of things.

Could it be, when we, who are Christ's body, come together in unity, faithfulness, and fullness, that this is when Christ returns? Could it be that the time that we do not know is that moment of our own collective faithfulness in Jesus Christ? Could it be, sisters and brothers, that the return of Jesus and the inauguration of the kingdom of God is bound up in us becoming the incarnate Word of God here in this time and place?

It is certainly something worth considering, don't you think? When we stop arguing about silly doctrinal concerns and come together in faith to do God's work, Jesus lives! When we stop treating the church like a club where we get to set the agenda and give

205

our hearts and our lives to the ministry of hope and love, Jesus lives!

Once again, we go to the beginning of Jesus' ministry. Once again, we go with him to the scroll of Isaiah. And once again we stand next to Jesus in the temple (Luke 4:16f) and announce with him that now is the time! This is the year of God's favor! This is the moment when we receive the power of God because "The Spirit of the Lord is upon *us*! God has anointed us to bring good news to the poor! God has sent *us* to proclaim release to the captives and recovery of sight to the blind, to let the oppressed go free, proclaim the year of the Lord's favor" (paraphrase of Luke 4:18-19).

Christ returns, my friends, when we become the incarnation of his love! Christ lives among us when we dare to place our whole lives in service, witness, and fellowship according to his teachings.

And hear me now!

When we are able to become this body together — when we are willing to hear one another, to love one another, to risk and sacrifice for one another — a new age will indeed dawn upon this earth. There will be a time when the lame will walk and the blind will see, because we have cared enough to offer them health care. There will be a time when prisoners will go free, because we chose to spend more money on schools and employment than on jails and prisons! There will be a time when the oppressed will indeed be liberated, because nations will care more about the quality of life for human beings than about the profits of a global economy!

Jesus says we do not know the time.

I want to suggest that we do not know the time because the time was, is, and always will be now!

Now is the time of our faithfulness! Now is the time of our hope! Now is the time for the body of Christ to live free and full! Now is the year — the day — the moment of God's favor. Now is the time of Christ's return. Amen.

Sermons On The First Readings

For Sundays
After Pentecost
(First Third)

Breakdowns
And Breakthroughs

Stan Purdum

The Day Of Pentecost
Acts 2:1-21

Whosoever Will

Pentecost is considered the birth date of the church universal. There was also planted that day, in the preaching of the apostle Peter, an important seed — the fruit of which was almost lost at one point in the church's history. That seed was in this statement by Peter: "Then everyone who calls on the name of the Lord shall be saved" (Acts 2:21).

Actually, Peter wasn't being original with that statement. He was quoting Joel 2:32, but that ancient prophet was talking about the salvation of the people of Israel on the great day of the Lord, whereas Peter was applying the text to the current circumstances of his audience. He was talking about their immediate salvation through their acceptance of Jesus Christ.

That was, and is, part of the good news of Christianity, but in the medieval church, that message became obscured. Its revival was part of the great Protestant Reformation of the sixteenth and seventeenth centuries.

As you probably recall, that reformation began in 1517, with work of a monk named Martin Luther, and his views unleashed a wave of change across the church. As earthshaking as Luther's reformation turned out to be, however, it was still fairly conservative compared to some of what came afterward. So for a few moments, I want to take you through a little history, but there is a point to it.

Luther's protest came to be called Lutheran Protestantism, and it was centered in Germany. Shortly thereafter a new, more radical protest arose, dubbed "Reformed" Protestantism, which grew up in Switzerland, France, the Netherlands, and Scotland. Two men

209

who were prominent leaders of that division were Huldreich Zwingli and John Calvin. They were contemporaries of Luther, but whereas Luther and his followers rejected only those aspects of the Catholic church they felt contradicted the Bible, the Reformed protestors retained from the Catholic church only what they believed was expressly allowed in scripture.

One of the doctrines formulated by these Reformed protestors, and especially by Calvin, was the emphasis on the sovereignty of God. Simply put, this means that no one controls God in any way; he is completely independent of what he has created. The problem was, however, that when that doctrine was pushed far enough, logic suggested that since God had all the control, human beings therefore had none, not even over their own destinies. In other words, God makes all the decisions about our fate.

Since some people are saved and heaven bound and others are not, said Calvin, God therefore must want it that way. God must have chosen or "elected" some people to be saved and others not to be. This idea was called "predestination," but it was not a totally new idea. Saint Augustine spoke of it as early as the fourth century, and there are a few verses in the New Testament that seem to support the idea. But it waited for John Calvin to develop it fully. Here's how Calvin actually stated predestination:

> That, God, by an absolute decree, hath selected to salvation a very little number of men without regard to their faith or obedience whatsoever; and hath secluded from saving grace all the rest of mankind, and appointed them by the same decree, to eternal damnation without any regard to infidelity.[1]

You can imagine that a lot of religious believers found that statement pretty chilling. It literally says that without regard to our own faith and practice, God chooses a few of us for heaven but most of us for hell, and that nothing we can do will make the slightest difference. As it happens, however, even the churches that have descended from the Reformed movement — including the Presbyterians and Congregationalists — don't preach that today.

210

Back to our brief history lesson: The man who challenged this idea was named James Arminius. Among the things we know about him are that he was born in Oudewater, Holland, on October 10, 1560, just four years before Calvin's death. Arminius became a theologian and minister in the Dutch Reformed church, being ordained in 1588. He pastored a church in Amsterdam for fifteen years, where he was known as a kind and devoted pastor, especially noted for ministering to his people during the devastating plague of 1602. A year later, he became a professor of theology at the University of Leiden, where he remained until his death. He was married and had nine children.

Arminius was not the first to disagree with Calvin. Others who disagreed were called "Remonstrants," and, in fact, Arminius set out to refute the Remonstrants, but ended up being convinced by them and becoming their best spokesman. So well did he defend their position that it soon became known as "Arminianism."

In contrast to Calvin, the Arminians believed that Christ died for all people, not just for the so-called elect. They said that salvation comes by faith alone, that those who believe are saved, and that only those who reject God's grace are lost.

When you think about it, that's what Peter said at Pentecost. And it sounds a lot more like the theology you and I have grown up with. Yet, back then, Arminius and his fellow Remonstrants did not win the day. Arminius himself died in 1609. Ten years later, a church synod was held in the city of Dort in the Netherlands that was widely representative of the Reformed churches. This synod formally rejected Arminianism, and a few days later, one of the leading Remonstrants was beheaded. (It was dangerous in those days to disagree!) Nonetheless, Arminianism was by no means crushed.

If we jump ahead another century, we find a man who was thoroughly convinced by James Arminius' position. He was John Wesley, who is the founding father of Methodism. In 1739, Wesley preached a sermon titled "On Free Grace" that set forth the Arminian position so clearly that at least one of his later biographers said that with it, Wesley declared war on the doctrine of predestination.[2] At the time, not all Methodists agreed with Wesley, and for a while, there existed an opposing group called Calvinistic Method-ists. But through Wesley and others of his persuasion, the doctrine, then known as Arminianism and today known simply as free will, became one of the most established of Protestant beliefs.

Okay, so much for the history lecture, but what's the impor-tance of all this today?

① For one thing, it means that God really wants *everybody* to be saved. You see, despite this long battle, free will was not a new idea dreamed up by the reformers; actually, it was a reaffirmation of what was already in the Bible, uttered by the Old Testament prophet Joel and reapplied by Peter at Pentecost. Paul repeated the idea, if not the exact words, when writing to the Romans: "... if you confess with your lips that Jesus is Lord and believe in your heart that God raised him from the dead, you will be saved" (Romans 10:9). Those are not isolated statements. Jesus himself spoke about this, saying, "... anyone who comes to me I will never drive away" (John 6:37). And, of course, there is that most well-known of Bible verses, John 3:16, "For God so loved the world that he gave his only Son, so that everyone who believes in him may not perish but may have eternal life." In other words, God excludes no one from his invitation to come to him. Some may exclude themselves, but God does not do that.

John 3:16, by the way, inspired a hymn, one that I remember from my childhood, called "Whosoever Will." The whole hymn was based on this one theme, that God is for everybody. Each verse and the chorus end with the line, "Whosoever will, may come."

② Another thing that this matter of free will means today is that it is not up to us to decide who is — and who is not — worthy of God's grace, for it is freely offered to all. This matter was really put to the test in the Church of Scotland a few years ago when a man named James Nelson applied for admission into the ministry of that denomination. Nelson had completed seminary all right and had fulfilled all of the normal prerequisites, but there was one problem: He had murdered his mother.

Fifteen years earlier, in a fit of anger over a disagreement with his mother, Nelson had beaten her to death. He was subsequently convicted and sent to prison. In prison, he heard a sermon by a chaplain that started him rethinking his life. He eventually accepted Christ, and later, after being paroled, he began studying for the ministry.

As you can imagine, not everyone in the church was in favor of admitting him into the clergy ranks, but Nelson appealed to the church's belief in salvation for all who turn to God. In the end, he was admitted by a special vote of the church's general assembly.[3]

When we are affirming the doctrine of free will, we are acknowledging that regardless of what we have done wrong, the only way we can cut ourselves off from God's invitation is to not respond to it.

Yet one more thing this doctrine means is that since we have a real choice in the matter of our destiny, not to choose is to choose. This is a fact we would probably eliminate from our religion if we could. We don't like being pushed into a corner where we have to say, "Yes" or "No." Faith would be so much easier if it just spoke words of comfort or encouragement. Instead, it confronts us with having to choose — either to accept Christ or not.

You see, because the gospel has to do with real life, it asks us to eventually commit ourselves. God simply will not be satisfied with less. There is no middle ground; so the choice is ours.

If there is anyone living today who symbolizes this matter of choosing Christ, it is Billy Graham. Here's something that Graham's son, Franklin, said:

> *Some people believe [I] ... was born a Christian. I was not born a Christian. I was born into a Christian home, I have Christian parents who set a Christian example, but I was not born a Christian. For a while I thought I was, but as I got older, I realized that I had to choose ... Jesus Christ for myself and that no one could do it for me.*[4]

Billy Graham was the subject of a CBS television feature some years ago. The program's producers had followed Graham through several of his crusades, and one of the things they noticed and pointed out in the program was how time and again, Graham used this same sentence: "I'm going to ask you to get up out of your seats ..." In other words, Graham preached for a decision. He wanted people not to leave with just some new ideas or merely having had an interesting evening. He wanted them to "get up out of their seats" and make a decision.

Of course, not every decision for Christ is made in a moment or on an impulse. Some occur slowly over time without a conscious milestone that is equivalent to getting out of one's seat. Nonetheless, there needs to be a time when we look at where we are standing and say, I am going to stand with Christ Jesus.

Many of you have made that decision. Christ invites us all, and it is critically important that we choose. Amen.

1. "Doctrinal Differences Defined at Synod of Dort 1619," Quoted by Milton S. Agnew in his supplement sheet to *The Security of the Believer* (Chicago: The Salvation Army, nd).

2. Maximim Piette, *John Wesley in the Evolution of Protestantism* (New York, 1938), p. 362, cited by Robert E. Cushman in *Methodism*, William K. Anderson, ed. (The Methodist Publishing House, 1947), p. 103.

3. *Time* magazine, August 6, 1984, p. 59.

4. *Decision* magazine, September 1985, p. 14.

To Say *Elohim*

Since we are gathered here in a church, I suspect that there are not many of you present who do not believe in God, at least to some degree. In fact, some of you may not be able to recall a time at all when you didn't believe in God. Others may remember a time — or perhaps several different times — when you questioned or even outright doubted the reality of this whole idea of God (and I'd have to put myself in that group).

But now, here we are, gathered in church for another service of worship. That may or may not signify that you have settled the matter of belief in God, but it probably indicates that you are at least open to thinking about it.

Would it surprise you if I said that as your pastor, I'm not terribly concerned about whether or not you have resolved your questions about the existence of God?

But there *are* two conclusions about God that do concern me. The first is if you say, "I've got God figured out. I know what God wants; I understand him. God is thus and so, and that settles it." I hope you see the problem with that position. If we have God all defined, if he is capable of being grasped in his entirety in the human mind, then he is less than the human mind and cannot be much of a god. That god is too small.

The other conclusion that concerns me is the one that says, "We cannot know *anything* about God" and therefore we shouldn't spend any time thinking about him. That god is meaningless.

215

It's this second position that I want to address today, and I want to do that by directing you to the very first verse in the Bible: "In the beginning, God created the heavens and the earth."

I would suggest to you that there is more than enough faith expressed in that single verse to set you on the road to finding the meaning of your life.

But let me back up a bit. We don't have the advantage of being able to read this verse in its original language — Hebrew — but if we did, we'd discover that the word translated "God" in this verse is *Elohim.* That word appears over 2,550 times in the Old Testament, and the English translations of the Bible invariably render it simply as "God." (There are many other names for God in the Bible as well. No single name can contain all that God is.)

I call your attention to the word because it helps us to understand what the author of Genesis was saying. *Elohim* is not a personal name. In fact, it is a fairly impersonal description. If we were looking for an English equivalent other than "God," we would probably have to settle for a descriptive phrase, something like, "the Supreme Being to whom all power belongs."

Now in its own time, this verse was quite remarkable. Remember that was written in a time in history when almost nobody doubted that there were powers greater than themselves. In fact, most people believed in multiple gods: gods of the weather and gods of agriculture, gods of childbearing and gods of fire, gods of health and gods of love, and so on. In the midst of all that, without so much as a sidelong glance at the multiple gods, the author of Genesis, declared that THE Supreme Being (singular!) created the heavens and the earth.

As the curtain opened on the creation of the world there was only one Actor on stage: *Elohim.* He was center stage then and he is yet today, though in our view of things, we sometimes imagine him as backstage or in the wings or not there at all.

But to make the declaration that God was not only there when the curtain went up but actually is the whole show is a starting point of faith. To say, *"Elohim* created" sets you apart at once from those who say the world is simply the result of accident or coincident. To say *Elohim* is not to say anything very personal about

216

God, but it is to say the *foundational thing* about the meaning of this life we share. This world exists — and our lives in — because God wants it to.

To say *Elohim* is to affirm that God is an objective reality apart from our ideas of God. We live in a society where we have been taught to put great stock in our own opinions — too much so, perhaps. Take the case some years back in Massachusetts of the British au pair who was accused of killing the baby in her care. Radio and television talk shows had a field day with that case. Caller after caller phoned in to state his or her opinion about whether or not the young woman actually killed the child. And some of those callers were very adamant, very certain of their opinion. By the same token, both the prosecution and the defense put forth opinions of the event as well.

Regardless of any of these opinions, there is only one truth about the death of that child, and that is whatever actually happened. In other words, there is the reality of how the child died, and any opinion of the death that doesn't match that reality is wrong, regardless of how strongly held the opinion is or of how much circumstantial evidence there is to support it.

By the same logic, regardless of our personal opinions about what God is, to say *Elohim* reminds us that there is an objective reality of what God actually is.

But there is more: If you can say *Elohim* it doesn't matter much how you interpret the rest of the verses in the creation story we read. If you take it to mean that *Elohim* created the world in six actual days, fine. If you take the day reference to mean eons of time, fine. If you take this to be a faith-story, something like a parable, that wasn't intended to teach science at all, but to teach theology, that too is fine. For in each case, we are agreeing on *the* important point: "In the beginning, *Elohim* created the heavens and the earth."

Notice two things about God from the creation story: First, this God speaks the world into existence, and second, he calls it good.

The first point: He speaks the world into existence. "And *Elohim* said, 'Let there be light'; and there was light." And so it continues

217

through each day of creation. God says, "Let there be ..." right up to the sixth day, when God speaks human beings into existence.

This story must have been a revolutionary concept to those who first heard it. Those who believed in other gods had creation stories, too, but in theirs, the world only came into being after a huge struggle on the part of the gods involved. Marduk, the god of Babylon, for example, only succeeded in bringing the world into being after a mighty battle with the goddess, Tiamat, the primal sea. After Marduk finally defeated her, he split her carcass in two to form the earth and sky out of her body. These other gods, you see, didn't really control the environment, but had to labor against it.

Against that kind of an idea, the author of Genesis 1 points out that *Elohim* spoke and the elements immediately obeyed. In this account, instead of having to do battle with sea monsters, the creatures of the sea are simply God's creation. *Elohim* gives them life and blesses them. That's a God with true godly power.

And the second point: *Elohim* declared his creation good. Again and again throughout the story, God looks at what he has created to that point and says it is good. After the creative work is done, he declares the whole matter "Very good."

That's an affirmation we sometimes forget. When we get mired down in daily problems, it is easy to forget that the world God placed us in is not a sinister place in itself. The creation, *Elohim*'s world, is good, and that is a reflection of *Elohim*'s character, goodness.

John Greenleaf Whittier stated it this way:

> *Yet in the maddening maze of things,*
> *And tossed by storm and flood,*
> *To one fixed trust my spirit clings;*
> *I know that God is good!*

Elohim is a God of true godly goodness.

It may have struck you by now that this is a somewhat odd sermon for Trinity, because the whole emphasis of this day is one — the triune nature of the one God. But think about where people

218

were in their understanding of God throughout the Old Testament and during the centuries before Jesus came, and before he spoke of the Holy Spirit. They were operating under the image of God as presented by the old stories like this one from Genesis and by God as explained by the prophets. They did not have the New Testament picture of God that Jesus later gave.

We, too, may be at this pre-Christ juncture in our personal lives. Perhaps you've never really embraced the way of Christ for your own. But if you have been able to say, "In the beginning, God created ..." you are at least where many of the Old Testament people were. There is more understanding to come, and perhaps this is the year that you will open your heart to Christ.

This is also an odd time of year to quote a Christmas carol, but I'd like to do so anyway:

> *Angels from the realms of glory*
> *wing your flight o'er all the earth;*
> *ye who sang creation's story*
> *now proclaim Messiah's birth.*

Did you catch the journey these angels made? They were present at the beginning to sing the creation story — the handiwork of *Elohim*. And then they are present to rejoice at Jesus' birth.

That's the same journey today's text from the creation story invites us to make. We are invited to move from that basic faith-starting point — that God created our world — to the faith-redeeming point — an embracing of the way of Jesus Christ and an acceptance of empowerment by God's Holy Spirit.

The recognition that we live and move and have our being at the pleasure of *Elohim* gives us a foundation for life.

The acceptance of the way of Christ gives meaning to our lives and provides a way to live in joyous appreciation and service to *Elohim* who made us. Amen.

219

The Three Dimensions Of Life

Today's reading starts in the ancient world before the great flood. It was an era when, according to the Bible, many people lived really long lives.

Take Methuselah for example. Genesis 5:27 tells us that he lived to be 969 years old. As far as we know, he lived longer than anyone else anywhere. Yet for all his years, we know remarkably little about him. We know that his father's name was Enoch and that he had some brothers and sisters. Methuselah had a son named Lamech and had some other sons and daughters. And that's about it. The most notable fact about him seems to be the number of years he lived.

I guess longevity is an achievement of sorts, provided, of course, he was a good man. But suppose he was a scoundrel. Suppose he beat his wife (or, in his case, probably a whole succession of wives) and abused his children. Suppose he was the ancient world's equivalent of a Mafia "Godfather." In those circumstances, we'd probably not consider his long life to be a good thing.

In fact, we may even guess that Methuselah was not a righteous man, for his death year appears to coincide with the year of the great flood from which his grandson, Noah, was saved by building an ark. Our scripture reading told us that story. Was Methuselah one of the great sinners who died in the flood? We just don't have enough information about him to draw any firm conclusions about his character.

221

We can say with certainty, however, that just because he lived longer than anybody else is no guarantee that he was especially good or especially wise, though he may have been.

Yet we do value longevity. I was on an airplane a few years ago, sitting in an aisle seat. I happened to glance up as an elderly man walked down the aisle. He was of no particular interest to me, but he must have noticed my glance, for he said in a loud voice, "Can't a man be 92 years old without everybody staring at him?"

I chuckled to myself for it was obvious that the old man was proud of how long he had lived and would use any excuse to announce his achievement. My second thought was, how sad. Is the length of his life all this old guy has to be proud of? True, length is one of the dimensions of human existence, but it is not, I suspect, the most important one.

In fact, it's not a factor over which we have much control. Sure, we can avoid fatty foods and tobacco and get plenty of exercise, and probably add a few years to our lives, but there are no guarantees.

In my last church, I had the privilege of preaching the funerals of two of the congregation's oldest members. Both were women well up in their nineties. I use the word "privilege" intentionally because I knew from my previous conversations with these fine women that neither considered her impending death a tragedy. Both were women of faith and both had a sense that their mission here was done, and both looked upon death as the next natural step in their journeys.

I also knew that neither one was all that impressed with longevity. They had outlived their friends, their physical strength was very diminished, and they were tired out. What, they might have asked us, is so hot about just living long? And I doubt either of them would have said that simply surviving into their nineties was in itself a fulfillment of the promise of their lives.

2. Yes, length is but one dimension of life, but breadth is another. We have only to go to the public library or the internet to get some feel for the number of areas of possible interest in this life. There are books and websites on every conceivable subject, and a person with an "inquiring mind" will find more subjects in those

222

places than can be dealt with in a lifetime, even one as long as Methuselah's. But having interests in a number of things does bring a broadness to one's life.

I had a history professor when I was in college who also wrote and published poetry. He once commented that many people were surprised when they heard his poetry and said things like, "But you teach history, don't you?" as though it were surprising for a person to have interests in more than one field.

I have to say I find it important to have some breadth in my life. In fact, one reason that I like my part-time arrangement as a pastor is because having another job as well allows me to be part of more than one creative stream. The experiences in each freshen me for the other. My own impression is that a narrowly lived life isn't much fun.

One of the observations I've made as a pastor counseling people is that one reason some people don't handle problems as well as others is because they have defined their lives too narrowly. The woman whose husband has walked out and who says, "I don't know how I can go on living; he was my whole world," has probably defined her life too narrowly. So, too, has the man who can't think of anything to do once he's retired.

③ But having said all of that, I don't think breadth is the most important dimension of life either. No, I think it is height. For it is height that determines that character of the other two dimensions, and it is height that helps us fulfill the promise of our lives.

By height, of course, I mean the relationship we have built with that which is higher than ourselves, our Creator and Lord. The fact is, this is the only dimension of the three over which we have a good measure of control. You see, almost all of us has some sense of a larger entity in life, something beyond and above ourselves that is the source of meaning. But many people choose not to cultivate this vertical relationship.

Have you known anyone who is an alcoholic but is in recovery thanks to Alcoholics Anonymous? AA has a 12-step program where the very first step is that the participants have to acknowledge that they are powerless to control the drink themselves. The second step is to turn control of their lives over to a higher power. The AA program includes a recognition that people have gotten the dimensions of their lives out of balance and have neglected the higher connection.

One of the fascinating (but by no means the only) theories about why people abuse drugs and alcohol is that on some level, people become aware of an emptiness inside themselves and the substance abuse is a way of trying to fill that which can only be filled by God. Centuries ago, Saint Augustine put it, "Thou hast made us for thyself alone, O God, and our hearts are restless until they find their rest in thee."

Of course, since I am talking to you who are here in worship, it might seem like I'm trying to convince those who are already convinced. But I've sat out there in the pews, and I know it's possible to be here and enjoy the culture and fellowship of the church without developing that higher connection to the God of the church and of the universe.

The author of the Psalm 61, feeling lost and alone, prayed:

> Hear my cry, O God; listen to my prayer.
> From the end of the earth I call to you, when my heart
>   is faint.
> Lead me to the rock that is higher than I;
> for you are my refuge, a strong tower against the enemy.
> — Psalm 61:1-3

The "rock that is higher than I" is a metaphor for God. This psalmist knew where his help and the meaning for his life lay. Only by climbing that rock, only by developing the height dimension of his life, could he find that which brought him security and peace and could the promise of his life blossom.

We cannot build that relationship by nurturing only the length and breadth dimensions of life, even if that is what our culture most encourages.

Height is the factor that determines whether, when we finally come to our grave, people will say, "Thank God he's gone," or " To have known him was a blessing."

Height is the factor that determines whether the broader interests of our life enrich us or lead us into trouble.

You see, life can be great without length — many people we remember as giants on the earth didn't live all that long. Jesus lived only 33 years.

Life may still be significant without breadth. Some single-minded people have made great contributions to society. Consider Mother Teresa. Basically, she was only focused on the sick and those who suffered.

But without height, there is always something missing.

The dimension of height means that we live our lives conscious that we are not the end in ourselves — that our values are connected to something outside ourselves. We are conscious that we have the need to worship something beyond ourselves, and that when we go seeking that something, we find it is God.

Nikos Kazantkakis, author of *The Last Temptation of Christ*, tells of visiting a saintly monk on a secluded island. He asked the monk, "Father Makarios, do you still wrestle with the devil?"

"Not any longer. I have grown old and [the devil] has grown old with me. He does not have the strength. Now I wrestle with God."

"With God? And do you hope to win?"

"No. I hope to lose."

Is that not what it means to develop the height dimension of life? To surrender to God and let him direct us.

Methuselah lived 969 years. Did he fulfill the promise of his life? We have no way of knowing. But we know what *we* need to do to fulfill the promise of our own life. And God invites us to do just that by reaching for him.

The height dimension of our lives is something that no flood can wash away. Amen.

God, What Are You Up To?

One of the better programs on television from 2003 to 2005 was a series on CBS called *Joan of Arcadia*. Like many thoughtful shows, this one did not score high enough to stay on the air for long, but it did last two seasons.

The title alludes to Joan of Arc, the fifteenth-century teenager who believed she heard the voice of God urging her to save France from England during the Hundred Years War. That Joan led an army into battle, successfully forcing the British to retreat from Orleans. Later, captured by the British, she was tried for heresy and burned at the stake.

The Joan of the television show is a modern girl, struggling not only with the usual issues of being a teenager, but also with the problems of being new in town and having a brother who recently became a paraplegic as the result of an auto accident. Then her life is suddenly further complicated when God starts speaking to her. God comes to her not as an inner voice, but disguised as other people and showing up in the midst of Joan's day. One time, God comes to her as a cute boy on the bus. Another time, it's as a woman with attitude working in the cafeteria of Joan's school. Other times, it's as a maintenance worker, a little girl, a fellow student, a lecturer at her school, a liquor-store clerk, and so on. Joan never knows when someone she encounters will turn out to be God, for he appears as individuals of various races, ages, and of either gender.

Initially Joan questions her sanity, but she eventually follows God's instructions, although they make no sense to her. Each time she does, however, something further down the line works out for

227

the good, demonstrating the truth of the old adage that God works in mysterious ways. Still, Joan remains enough of a skeptic to not share this new relationship with anyone else. Joan feels that her family is already dealing with a lot of heavy stuff, including serious pressures with her father's job as a police chief and the complexities brought on by her brother's injuries. She realizes that she can't suddenly reveal that she's literally running into God and having conversations with him. Her family already has enough issues to deal with.

It was a pretty well written show, and one that didn't leave you wishing you hadn't watched it, but what I found most interesting about the series was the role God played. His instructions to Joan were almost always confusing and counterintuitive. Joan often questioned them, and over the course of several shows, she eventually asked the questions most of us wish God would resolve. But God is not in the business of providing answers, not about his instructions or about himself or about his methods. The show's executive producer, Barbara Hall, said, "[In] trying to write God, I obviously don't know what he's thinking. On the show, God says he won't answer any direct questions because he chooses not to explain what is going on — because he's a mystery. The show is really a lot about posing theological and philosophical questions and not about answering them."[1]

Well, isn't that about how it usually is when we try to reconcile the complexities of our lives with the ways of God? Don't we usually find ourselves with more questions than answers? Isn't it true that when we get to places where there are no solutions forthcoming, we have to proceed on one of only two conclusions? Either 1) there are no answers and life actually has no meaning or 2) someone higher than us knows the answers and we can operate on the basis of faith in that someone.

The Old Testament reading this morning is a case in point. It concerns Abram, later to be known as Abraham. Without warning, Abram hears from God that he — Abram — will father a great nation. God tells Abram that through him, all the families of earth will be blessed. What's more, says God, Abram is to take his wife, servants, and herdsmen, and migrate to Canaan.

228

Abram obeys, but the whole circumstance must have struck him as strange. Nothing in his life had prepared him to receive direct instructions from God. We know from reading on in Genesis that as the years roll by, Abram puzzled over how God's promise would be fulfilled. Sarai, his wife, would become an old woman, and they had no offspring. Abram asks God how a new nation could arise by direct descent from the two of *them*. But God repeats the promise, and Abram trusts God.

Actually, the encounters between God and Joan on the television show almost seem modeled on this old story from Genesis. There are the elements of the scripture account that also occur in Joan's meetings with God: First God shows up unexpectedly with surprising news or instructions. Second, God's instructions puzzle and even trouble the person receiving them, leading the person to question God. Third, God doesn't seem to mind the questions, but refuses to answer them. Fourth, the person decides to obey, and that satisfies God.

There is one more point of congruence, but we have to go beyond this particular passage of scripture to see it, and that is when the results of what God instructed eventually become clear. In the Bible, even after his later visit from God, Abram still has to wait several more years before his son Isaac is born, and even then Abram is only seeing the beginning of the fulfillment of God's promise. In *Joan of Arcadia*, however, we see how God's instruction works out for the good by the end of each episode. In one episode, for example, God told Joan to go get a job, even though it made no sense with her schedule and responsibilities. When she finally did what God asked and took a job, her wheelchair-bound brother was inspired by her example to break out of his depression and anger and get a job himself, his first step back into resuming his life. As a viewer, I concluded each episode with a sense of "Oh, now I see why God wanted Joan to do that."

It is in this final point that the television show is probably the furthest from the actual experience of most of us who try to obey God. Generally, God's purposes do not become clear for a long time, and sometimes not in this lifetime. In that regard, the Genesis story is a more realistic model than the television show. In fact, it's not difficult to understand why, as the series developed, Joan came to obey God somewhat more readily; it's because she saw how his previous instructions worked out.

In our lives, God's purposes often remain a mystery. During the opening credits for *Joan of Arcadia* each week, we heard the song "What If God Was One of Us?" being sung by another Joan — Joan Osborne. Actually that song was written back in 1996, and was a hit for Osborne then. Although the credits sequence didn't give time for us to hear the entire song, another part of the full lyrics asked a question similar to this: "If you were facing God, and all his glory, what one question would you want to ask?" Well, the question we might pose is the one that I've used to title this sermon today: *God, what are you up to?*

While often we cannot answer that, the New Testament gives us an important affirmation about God's purposes. Writing to the Roman Christians, the apostle Paul said, "We know that all things work together for good for those who love God, who are called according to his purpose" (Romans 8:28). We need to look at that verse carefully, for it is often misunderstood. It is *not* saying that everything works out for the best no matter what. In fact, the verse is not about *our* circumstances; it is about *God's* sovereignty, his total independence of humankind. His purposes, the verse says, will be accomplished through any means God chooses.

Let me give you an example: the old hymn, "God Moves In A Mysterious Way." The words to that hymn were written in 1774 by the poet, William Cowper, who — though a sincere Christian — suffered periods of depression and on more than one occasion attempted to end his life. Now there is a story behind the writing of the hymn that's been told many times.

One evening, an impenetrable fog had settled over the city of London. In a dismal flat in the heart of the crowded East End, William Cowper stood gazing into the fireplace. Then suddenly, overcome by emotions of discouragement, gripped by fears that he could not name, he threw on his cloak and walked out into the night.

In the dense fog, Cowper groped his way across the pavement, guiding himself by the curbstone until he reached the corner where he knew a horse and cab always waited. He opened its door and ordered the driver to take him to the Thames River, for in his deep depression, he had decided to jump from the bridge and end it all.

The trip should have taken fifteen minutes, but after an hour and a half of negotiating the dark and foggy streets, Cowper realized they were hopelessly lost. In frustration, Cowper got out, paid the driver and started out on foot. Almost at once, however, his arm struck a familiar object. It was the iron horse's head of the hitching post in front of his own home. After an hour and a half of wandering around, he had ended up right back where he had started.

As the story goes, Cowper was so impressed by this turn of events that he climbed the stairs to his flat, lit the lamp, and knelt to ask God to forgive him for what he had planned to do. Then he wrote the words to the hymn, which begins, "God moves in a mysterious way his wonders to perform."

It is possible that the story is true as told, but it's equally possible, as one of Cowper's biographers has suggested,[2] that the cab driver was not lost at all and that he had purposely driven Cowper all over the city, pretending not to be able to find his way so as to charge a bigger fare (as some cabbies today have been known to do). Then, after an hour and a half, he deposited Cowper back at his front door.

Although Cowper apparently thought arriving back at home was an act of God's providence and wrote this great hymn to express that, we could just as easily conclude that the hymn came about because of the deceitfulness and greed of a London cab driver. But even if that's the case, it changes nothing about the testimony of the hymn, for whatever the cause of the event, God enabled Cowper to see some meaning in it that helped him face life again.

You see, God's purposes cannot be overridden by anything we can do. That's what the verse really means: "We know that all things work together for good for those who love God, who are called *according to his purpose.*" God's intentions will be fulfilled, regardless of actions or inactions on our part, because God is in ultimate control.

In the second verse of Cowper's hymn he says:

Deep in unfathomable mines
Of never-failing skill
[God] treasures up his bright designs,
And works his sovereign will.

In the television show, God chooses to use actions in Joan's life to accomplish his purposes, but only if she is willing to trust him enough to cooperate. In the Genesis story, God chooses to use Abram's descendants, but only if Abram is willing to trust him enough to hang in there. But here's the point: Even if Joan or Abram had refused, God would have worked his purpose out some other way. He is not stymied by our unwillingness to trust him.

We, however, can miss great riches and blessing by refusing to cooperate with his purposes. Cowper puts this positively:

Ye fearful saints, fresh courage take;
The clouds you so much dread
Are big with mercy, and shall break
With blessings on your head.

We may have questions for God, but he has one for us, too. It is "Will you trust me?"

As we've said, we don't always know what God's purposes are, but we have a clear enough view from the Bible and the teachings of Jesus to understand some of them. Aligning ourselves with those things about him that we do understand and trusting him for the ones we don't is a big part of what the Christian life is all about. Amen.

---

1. www.joanofarcadia.com/theshow.

2. Albert Edward Bailey, *The Gospel in Hymns* (New York: Charles Schribner's Sons, 1952), pp. 133-134.

God's Laughter

Okay, who knows how Joan of Arc died? Right. She was burned at the stake. Keep that in mind; it will come up again in a few minutes.

Today's text is about Sarah laughing, and it strikes me that it would be better if the lectionary had scheduled this reading for sometime in April instead of during the summer. That's because April is National Humor Month. This observance was started in 1976 by humorist Larry Wilde, author of 53 books on the subject of humor, and director of The Carmel Institute of Humor, whatever that is. According to Mr. Wilde's website, National Humor Month "is designed to heighten public awareness on how the joy and thera- peutic value of laughter can improve health, boost morale, increase communication skills and enrich the quality of one's life."

Wilde says, "Since April is often bleak and grim and taxes are due on the fifteenth, it can be one of the most stressful times of the year. Besides it's the only month that begins with All Fool's Day — a day which has sanctioned frivolity and pranks ever since the 1500s."[1]

Another good date for this text would be the Sunday after Eas- ter. There is an old tradition in the church to call that Sunday "Bright Sunday" and to observe it as a day of joy and laughter, with parties and picnics to celebrate Jesus' resurrection. Sometimes parishio- ners and pastors even played practical jokes on each other. People told jokes and had fun.

The custom of Bright Sunday got its start in the writings of early church theologians like Augustine, Gregory of Nyssa, and

John Chrysostom. They noted that on Easter, God played a practical joke on the devil by raising Jesus from the dead. Easter was "God's supreme joke played on death." *Risus paschalis* — "the Easter laugh," is what the early theologians called it.[2]

My standup routine this morning is not aimed at launching a new career as a comic, but I am a carrier of the joyous good news that Christ defeated death, and I suspect that God continues to have a good laugh about it. (The writer of Psalm 2, by the way, observed, "He who sits in the heavens laughs ..." [Psalm 2:4].)

But we have this text now, and it invites us to think about God's laughter. The incident in our reading today began when Abraham noticed three men standing near his tent. Following the hospitable customs of the day, he invited them into his compound to rest and eat. Abraham didn't know it at the time, but it turned out that these three were God himself and two angels, making this one of the strangest stories from those early times.

In any case, after the three had eaten, they inquired where Abraham's wife, Sarah, was. The fact that they knew her name gives away that they are more than three ordinary men. Sarah had not been seen to this point because again, following the customs of the times, she remained out of sight while her husband carried out the hospitality duties. She is not out of earshot, however, and has been inside the tent listening to the conversation between Abraham and the three visitors.

It is important to know before going further that at this time, Abraham was 100 years old and Sarah was ninety. She had never had any children, which was the great disappointment of her life.

Then God says to Abraham, "I will surely return to you in due season, and your wife Sarah shall have a son."

Well, at her advanced age, this announcement struck Sarah's funny bone, and, the Bible tells us, she "laughed to herself." It was either a laugh of skepticism or a laugh at the incongruity of the idea, but it was a laugh. And though it was not out loud, God heard it, and said to Abraham, "Why did Sarah laugh, and say, 'Shall I indeed bear a child, now that I am old?' Is anything too wonderful for the Lord?" That is posed as a rhetorical question, but the intention is to elicit the internal reply of "No, nothing is impossible for God."

234

At that point, Sarah somehow joins the conversation, and probably out of embarrassment at being perceived as rude, she denies that she laughed. But God says, "Oh yes, you did laugh."

That's the end of the conversation, but if we jump forward a few months — nine months, to be exact — Sarah has a baby boy whom Abraham named Isaac, which means "to laugh." Sarah saw that name as quite appropriate, for she said, "God has brought laughter for me; everyone who hears will laugh with me."

Now there is no denying that religion is a serious matter and that what you believe makes a significant difference in how you live your life. But following Jesus is not only about carrying a cross; it is also about sharing in God's belly laugh at death.

We are not accustomed to thinking of going to church for a good laugh, but to miss the merriment of the gospel is to miss out on the lift it gives us in this life, long before we see the grave. The late author, E. B. White, who wrote the well-know children's book, *Charlotte's Web*, discussed this matter of humor in one of his essays. He noted, "... the infinitely fascinating question, which nobody has managed to answer, of why Americans believe that if a thing is funny it can be presumed to be something less than great, because if it were truly great it would be wholly serious!"

White maintained that a humorous response to life can be just as serious as a humorless one:

> *How it has come about that a nation which produces humor in such abundance, and lives by it to such an extent that it would be unrecognizable without it, has concluded that humor is inferior nonetheless both in form and depth — this is either a most bewildering paradox or can be explained simply by itself: that of which there is no end, and which comes so easily to so many, cannot matter as much as a gravity which lies outside the reach of the vulgar....*[3]

My intention is hardly to tell you to take laughter seriously — that's an oxymoron if there ever was one — and the Bible itself reminds us that there is, in addition to a time to laugh, also a time to weep (Ecclesiastes 3:4). What's more, some types of laughter are quite ungodly, including that laughter that is mocking or ridiculing, or the kind that finds glee in the pain or troubles of others, or the kind that tries to excuse wrongdoing by dismissing it as "just having fun."

Nonetheless, I want to remind you that the gospel is at root *good* news and that Christianity is a faith that proceeded into the world carried on the joy of the first disciples.

Here's something else. Good humor and faith are connected. Reinhold Niebuhr, one of the great theologians of the twentieth century, explained it like this:

> *Humor is concerned with the immediate incongruities of life, and faith with the ultimate ones.... Laughter is our reaction to immediate incongruities and those which do not affect us essentially. Faith is the only possible response to the ultimate incongruities of existence which threaten the very meaning of life.... Humor is, in fact, a prelude to faith; and laughter is the beginning of prayer. In the holy of holies, laughter is swallowed up in prayer and humor is fulfilled by faith.*[4]

In other words, clear joy, the wholesome spirit of gladness, is the sign of God with us. Or as Martin Luther put it, "We are sad by nature, and Satan is the spirit of sadness. But God is the spirit of gladness and preserves us."[5]

God is the spirit of gladness, and he preserves us. That's my point today, but I want to conclude with a few stories:

The missionary and author, E. Stanley Jones, tells about a missionary in China who was to be beheaded during one of the waves of persecution of Christians in that country. As she was being walked up a hill to her place of execution, she got to thinking about how funny it would be to look back and see her head rolling down the hill as her spirit was going off to heaven, and she laughed out loud. Her captors wanted to know what she was laughing about, and so she told them. So they said to her, "Well, if it is going to make you so happy, then we aren't going to do it." So she laughed her way out of her execution![6] She could testify, I suspect, with Sarah that "God has brought laughter for me."

236

One Sunday, a mother woke up not feeling well, so she was not able to accompany her family to church. After they returned home, the mother asked her young daughter what the sermon had been about. The girl responded, "It was 'Laugh. You'll get your quilt.' " The mother was puzzled by that, so she later asked her husband what the pastor's sermon title was. He answered, "Be joyful; your Comforter is coming."

Dr. Samuel Upham was a professor of theology at Drew University years ago. He died in 1904 at the age of seventy. In his last hours, he was lying on his bed, surrounded by friends. At one point, it seemed that he had died, but one woman touched his feet and said, "No, he's not dead. Feel his feet. They're warm. No one ever died with warm feet." At that, Dr. Upham opened his eyes and said, "Joan of Arc did!"

Those were his very last words — and evidence that even in his final moments, he was preserved by God's spirit of gladness.[7]

And so are all of us who follow Jesus. Amen.

---

1. http://www.larrywilde.com/month.htm.

2. This information from the website of the Fellowship of Merry Christians, www.joyfulnoiseletter.com/hhsunday.asp.

3. From *Essays of E. B. White*.

4. Cited in *Context*, April 15, 1992, p. 5.

5. *Ibid.*

6. E. Stanley Jones, *The Divine Yes*.

7. Thanks to Duane E. Snyder, "The Smiling Master," August 24, 1980.

A Way Of Seeing

Remember your childhood suspicion that both your mother and your teacher had eyes in the back of their heads? As you got older, you realized it wasn't literally true, but it was a way of describing their awareness of what you were doing. Well now, we are coming to a place where it could be a much more literal statement. In fact, they could even have eyes in the back of their *mouths*.

There have been some interesting developments in the field of perception, spurred in part by research to help the blind, but also by a need to help people who have so much to see that their eyes cannot take it all in — aircraft pilots, for example. As aviation technology has evolved, cockpits have filled up with many new instruments, to the point that in some flight applications, pilots have so much to keep track of that they are visually overwhelmed. The visual workload has gotten so high that there has been an increase in the number of human factor-related mishaps.

One way to solve that, however, is to feed some of that information to the brain through paths other than the eyes. As far as anatomy is concerned, the eyes are merely input devices that feed data to the brain, but there are other ways that the brain perceives information, as well. You know that cookie you ate the other day tasted good not because your eyes passed that news along, but because your tongue did. In the words of Paul Bach-y-Rita, professor of rehabilitation medicine and biomedical engineering at the University of Wisconsin, "A nerve spike is a nerve spike. The brain doesn't give a d___ where the information is coming from."

The latest technology Bach-y-Rita has been working on sends information besides the usual taste and texture stuff through the tongue to the brain. The device consists of a video camera worn on a strap on the forehead. That camera converts images to pixels and sends them to a small box called a "Tactile Display Unit," which also is attached to the forehead strap. That unit converts the pixels to electrical impulses that flow down a wire inserted into the mouth, and tingle the tongue. From there, the tongue's natural sensors carry the image to the brain. This device is still in a primitive stage, but in lab tests, blind people using it have been able to "recognize letters, catch rolling balls, and watch candles flicker for the first time."[1]

And you see, it doesn't matter where that video camera is placed. You could wear it backward and have eyes in the back of your head, or you could place in on the tail of an aircraft and "see" other planes approaching from behind.

What I want to talk about is a different way of seeing. In some sense, that has been a major theme behind all my sermons. I've no doubt even stated it directly in a sermon or two, but going on the assumption that a crucial point bears repeating, I want to say it again, and illustrate it with some examples.

Now to say that I can even sum up several years of sermons in one makes me sound a lot more organized than I am. I did not arrive here with a 3 x 5 card in my pocket with that theme written on it. I had no notebook or computer flow chart with a plan worked out for how to present it. Nothing nearly that planned took place. But as I look back over some of the things that have reoccurred in my sermons, I see that I have promoted one major theme as a foundation for the other things I've said.

That overall theme is that religious faith is a different but valid way of seeing the world and life. For example, I have preached previously from Hebrews 11. That is a passage commonly referred to as the "faith chapter," but as I read it, it often strikes me that it is really about "seeing" something that not everyone sees. In the first verse of Hebrews 11, the author says, "Now faith is the assurance of things hoped for, the conviction of *things not seen*." He then points out Abel, Enoch, Noah, Abraham, Sarah, and others as examples of people of faith. Of them, the Hebrews writer says, "All of these died in faith without having received the promises, but from a distance they *saw* and greeted them" (Hebrews 11:13).

In faith, we, too, believe that God is real even though we cannot see him. We believe that God "rewards those who seek him" (Hebrews 11:6) even when that reward is not apparent at present. In other words, faith is not some mustered up belief or desperately held position. It is a way of seeing. When we apply the Christian faith to the world we live in, we could say that *faith does not change the facts about the world, but it does change the conclusions we draw about those facts.*

For example, two people can look at the same facts and arrive at opposite conclusions. If two people visit a hospital that treats those with serious crippling injuries, they will both see patients with missing limbs, patients in great pain, and patients suffering other ways. One might look at all of this and conclude that the world is a mess and life is a nasty joke. He might even decide not to allow himself to care too much for anyone because of the possibility of pain when a loved one suffers.

The other person might see in all of this the incredible courage and resilience of the sufferers and decide that the illnesses are an outrage precisely because God's gift of life is so good.

From another church I served, I took a work team to the mountains of eastern Kentucky to help build homes for low-income families. Back in one of the "hollars," I met a woman named Edna. She was a poorly educated backwoods woman who had been impoverished all her life. But she was rich in faith. She told me about another woman, a friend of hers, who recently separated from an abusive husband. The woman was angry and bitter at God. Then Edna told me that she'd had a similarly unhappy marriage and had left her husband. But the effect of that for her was different than from her friend. "It drives me to hold on tighter to God," she said. "I need it to help me get through this."

In our reading from Genesis, Hagar is the wronged woman. She had borne Abraham a son. Hagar was the maid of Sarah, Abraham's wife, but because Sarah was childless, she had encouraged Abraham to produce an heir with Hagar. Yet, once her own son was born, Sarah became jealous of Hagar and demanded that her husband send Hagar and her son, Ishmael, away. Abraham does this, and Hagar and Ishmael were banished into the desert, where, they were soon lost and out of water. Eventually, Ishmael was at the point of dying of thirst. Hagar put him down under a bush, turned away, and began to weep. God heard her, and, "God opened her eyes and she saw a well of water, and she went and filled her bottle, and gave the boy to drink."

God did not perform a miracle for Hagar in the usual sense of the word. He did not create new resources that were not already there on the scene. Rather, he *opened her eyes* so that she saw the well that she had not seen before. When that happened, the same environment that had looked so hopeless and barren to her was now seen as a life-sustaining place. The well had been there all along, and the place had never been as "godforsaken" as she had thought. But until God opened her eyes, Hagar missed all of that.

The last church I served included some farmers in the congregation. In 1988, that part of Ohio suffered a drought, and those farmers watched their fields dry up and their crops die. That was their livelihood, of course, but I was impressed that they did not stop attending church and they continued to put money in the offering plate. A cynic might look at that fact and say, "Well, the farmers don't want to offend God and cause him to withhold more rain." But I looked at the same facts and concluded, "Look at their remarkable faith. They know that whether it rains or not, God is with them."

I was able to say that because faith shapes how I see the world. During that 1988 drought, I preached a sermon where I stated plainly how I see things. The sermon was based on a drought story from the Old Testament, where Elijah the prophet challenged the prophets of the false god Baal to bring rain, something they were unable to do. Then Elijah prayed, and the rains came (1 Kings 18). Here is something from that sermon:

> But like Elijah we need to hold on to our belief in God's goodness. God will again send the rain on our land. We will continue to pray for it. Perhaps it is already too late for this year's crop, and we need to be ready to

care for the farmers and others who will be most directly hurt by this dry summer. We need to find ways to do that even while we maintain our faith in the goodness and providential care of God.

To repeat, religious faith is a way of seeing the world and life. That above all, is why I remain a Christian, for Christianity helps me to interpret life with a sense that it is good and that despite the pain and hurt of our world, it will come out right in the end.

In his classic book, *The Varieties of Religious Experience*, William James, writes of "once-born" and "twice-born" people. This is not the same as what we mean when we say "born again." The once-born people are those who move through live without ever experiencing anything that seriously challenges their faith, nothing that causes them to say, "What I was taught was true about my religion is a lie." They may have some problems, but nothing that causes them to essentially think of God differently from when they were children.

Twice-born people, on the other hand, are those who have experienced some faith-shattering event or challenge, and have lost their faith. Then, they have eventually found their way to a more mature, tried-by-fire faith. It is a less simplistic God they now envision, but one who helps them through the storms of life. They have, in short, learned to see the world differently.

To the eyes of such faith, another reality can be perceived behind the pain and trouble of the present time. We can see God at work and his grace in effect.

Christian faith is a way of seeing the world through more than just our eyes. Or to say it differently, it is having eyes in the back of our mind, in the front of our heart, in the depths of our spirits, in the palms of our hands, and in the soles of our feet. It is a way of seeing God in the world. Like the grandfather who took his grandson fishing, and while they were sitting together on the bank, the boy asked, "Grandpa, can anyone see God?" The old man answered, "Sometimes I think I never see anything else." Or, in the words of the priest in the novel, *The Diary of a Country Priest*,[2] "Grace is everywhere."

As the author of Hebrews says, "By faith we understand that the worlds were prepared by the word of God, so that what is seen was made from things that are not visible." That's clear statement about faith-seeing from someone with twice-born faith. Amen.

---

1. Michael Abrams, "Eyes in the Back of Your Mouth," *Wired*, December 2002, p. 46.

2. By George Bernanos, 1937.

Breakdowns And Breakthroughs

There are some recent studies on racism that offer important information about our thinking processes for all of us no matter to what race we belong. These studies challenge the older idea that racial prejudice is something we are born with — something inherent in our makeup. They show that even when we have a negative gut reaction to someone based on race, we can override that reaction with our rational thought processes.[1]

Racism is not my subject this morning, but I mention these studies about racism to highlight its important conclusion about our ability to modify our emotional responses by how we think. That also means that in other areas of life, our minds can take us beyond gut reactions and beyond passionately held conclusions.

Chances are I am not telling you anything you don't already believe. But here's where we may be breaking some fresh ground: *This same principle of our thought processes carrying us forward in terms of how we live together as a society needs to apply in our understandings of religious faith as well.* I say that because when it comes to Christianity, some people view the Bible, which was completed about 1,900 years ago, as God's final word on all subjects. As though it timelessly answers all questions of concern to us mortals without the need for any further input from God — and that no matter what new information or experiences we encounter as a human community, it is already addressed in some way in the scriptures.

That is simply not the case. The Bible is invaluable and our best resource for learning about God. To us who seek to follow Jesus, the Bible is irreplaceable and even precious. It is God's word — but not God's *final* word.

It is important to acknowledge that because as we go through life we encounter new situations and gain new information. Thus it is important that we process these things in ways that are faithful to our Christian commitments without acting as though God has nothing further to say to us.

The ability of the rational part of our minds to move us along, then, becomes a tool of our religious and spiritual growth.

In that regard, the scriptures themselves give us two excellent examples.

The first is this strange story from Genesis about God telling Abraham to slay his son Isaac and offer him as a sacrifice, a story in which there are, admittedly, several things that are difficult for modern people.

For one thing, the story tells of the voice of God and later the voice of an angel coming to Abraham *from outside himself*. Actually, the idea to offer his son could be from Abraham's own imagination. Today the same events might be told in terms of inner conflicts, convictions, and insights, for this is a way God communicates with us today. Still, we get the point that Abraham believed that God wanted him to offer his son, Isaac, as a sacrifice.

For another thing, the whole idea of God requiring a human sacrifice is totally foreign to our understanding of God. But we must remember that Abraham lived in Canaan about 4,000 years ago, in a time and place where the sacrifice of children was practiced by many of the other peoples around him. They did so in hopes of appeasing gods they thought of as angry or unpredictable. Also, Abraham did not have benefit of much previous knowledge of God. He did not have the Old Testament. He did not have the Mosaic laws, including the Ten Commandments, which weren't given until some 650 year later. He lived in a culture that believed in many gods, and so he was just learning what the Lord God, whom the Bible calls *Yahweh* (among other names), was like.

Therefore, this idea to offer his son did not astonish Abraham. He probably believed that God had as much right to ask for Abraham's son as his neighbors' gods did of theirs.

So Abraham prepared to obey, but then, at the last minute, God stopped him from killing his son and directed him to instead sacrifice a ram caught in a thicket nearby.

What is of interest for us this morning is what happened to Abraham's understanding of God. When the angel stopped him from slaying his son, the angel said, "Do not lay your hand on the boy or do anything to him; for now I know that you fear God, since you have not withheld your son, your only son, from me."

At that moment, Abraham understood that the whole incident was a test of faith, and he realized that it was not God's will that he should offer his child as a sacrifice. He learned that what God wanted instead was trust and obedience. This new awareness was an important point in not only Abraham's personal development but also in the entire Judeo-Christian history ever thereafter. The Old Testament Israelites repudiated the whole practice of human sacrifice, and Christians today believe that every human being is valuable in God's sight.

But to return to Abraham: What happened to him in that incident was breakdown of an old idea about God — that he was as bloodthirsty as the gods of Abraham's neighbors — and the breakthrough of a new understanding of God that placed Yahweh above other gods.

Abraham was presented with new information. To deal with it, he had to let his thinking processes override his old ideas and perceptions. The old ideas broke down because they were found to be inconsistent with new information. That was a spiritual giant step forward for Abraham.

The other example is from Acts 15, but to get the point, we need a bit of background first: Jesus was Jewish and almost his entire ministry was among Jewish people. Thus, after the resurrection, when Christianity started to spread, it was among Jewish people. The 3,000 converts on the Day of Pentecost were virtually all Jewish. In essence, the earliest Christians saw their faith as a further development of Judaism. And later, when Paul and Barnabas went on the road as Christian missionaries, they started their ministry in each town by preaching in the synagogues, the Jewish houses of worship. They soon discovered that a lot of non-Jews — Gentiles — were listening to the Christian message, too, and many were responding in faith and becoming followers of Jesus.

This was a new development and created a situation in the church. Nobody wanted to prevent the Gentiles from following Jesus, but since the first Christians' own experience of Christ was in the context of Judaism, some of them believed that Christianity could not exist outside of Judaism. So what these Christians said was that yes, the Gentiles were welcome but they first had to convert to Judaism.

But people like Paul and Barnabas, who had witnessed the sincere conversions to Christ of many Gentiles, had come to the conclusion that requiring a move into Judaism as well was an unnecessary obstacle on the road to Christ.

What we read in Acts 15 is part of the debate over this matter that took place in the mother church in Jerusalem, where not only Paul and Barnabas, but also the apostle Peter, all spoke in favor of welcoming Gentiles into Christianity without requiring conversion to Judaism. Acts 15 also includes the ruling of this church council, issued by the church elder, James, who decided the question in favor of freely welcoming the Gentiles.

This is another example of an established idea breaking down because of new experience and of a new understanding breaking through. Now that Gentiles were clamoring to join the church, Christians had to consider what was happening. They concluded that God was in this situation and some new direction was essential.

That same principle of old ideas breaking down and new ones breaking through is still a major way in which we grow spiritually as individuals and in which the church grows in its understanding of what it means to be the body of Christ in the world.

It is not that we usually go looking for some new concept. Instead, we actually hold tightly onto the ones we are already comfortable with until we reach some point where they become untenable, inconsistent, or unworkable — or until some new light is shed on the subject.

For example, in our individual lives, God as we envision him now, should be different from how we envisioned God when we were children. We adults cannot easily worship the concept of God that exists in the mind of a child unless we are prepared to deny our own experience of life.

Think of the image of an insect in the larva stage. It has a shell, but as it grows, the shell becomes too tight. Eventually the shell cracks and the insect sheds it and grows a larger shell. Many of our ideas of God and our understandings of what it means to live a Christian life are like that shell. They suit us for a while, but eventually, if we are to mature, our ideas must allow for some expansion.

The church's experience in the last couple of centuries is instructive. There was a time when many in the church thought that races could not worship together. We have, thankfully, rethought that idea.

There was a time when a majority of people honestly believed that women were unfit for many jobs traditionally held by men, including church leadership positions, until some women came along and did those jobs well. Then the old concept did not fit the new information. So the old concept broke down and the new concept broke through.

In both of those cases, it was not simply a matter of saying the church needed to be more inclusive. It took new information, arguments from experience, and some brave persons pioneering a new way that helped us as a church to see that certain old ideas were no longer helpful. Eventually, former understandings broke down and new ones broke through.

The church is going through a similar experience today as homosexual people are asking to be fully integrated into the life of the church, and the church is struggling with that issue. While we cannot predict where it will all come out, we can recognize that we have a lot of new information that we need to process while we listen for God's word today.

It's not a matter that at one point we are not Christians and after rethinking a position we suddenly are. Rather it is that a growth process is taking place. Abraham was being faithful to God both *before* and *after* he realized that God did not want human sacrifices. The Jewish Christians in the first-century Jerusalem church were being faithful to God both before and after their decision to open the church to Gentiles. Most of the people in earlier generations who denied women leadership roles in the church did so from quite sincerely held commitments to Christ. They were attempting to be faithful to the light as they saw it at that point. When they finally dealt with new information, some were able to revise their position.

It is of interest to me that Methodism's founder, John Wesley, had changing views about his own Christianity. His journals have been preserved, and in them he occasionally expresses a view of his own growth and development that he himself later challenges. One of Wesley's biographers, Richard Heitzenrater, writes:

> *We must assume that what [Wesley] believed about himself at any given time is true for him at that time. Later reflections upon his earlier conditions must be accepted for what they are, an indication of his self awareness at that later time ... Thus in 1725, he thought he was a Christian, for a while after 1738, he thought he had not truly been a Christian in 1725; by the 1770s, he was willing to admit that perhaps his middle views were wrong, and that he could understand himself as having been in some real sense a Christian in 1725.[2]*

In truth, most of the growing in life, spiritual and otherwise, takes place by this process of old concepts breaking down and new ones breaking through. It is important therefore that we not be afraid of this process, but that we recognize it as natural, helpful, and necessary.

Of course, not all new ideas are better than old ones, and not every change should be made. Both of these incidents from the Bible suggest that the breakdown-breakthrough process is one way in which God speaks.

So both Genesis and Acts ask us to consider these questions: What strongly held convictions that arise from our faith are becoming too tight and beginning to break down? What gut reactions need to be overridden by our rational thought processes? Could any of that be God calling us to grow? What new understandings are trying to break through?

The answers to those things are found in prayer, in study, in experience, and in thought — all of which are tools God has given us to help us grow in faith and walk loyally in the way of Jesus. Amen.

---

1. See Sharon Begley, "Racism Studies Find Rational Part of Brain Can Override Prejudice," *The Wall Street Journal*, November 19, 2004, B1.

2. Richard P. Heitzenrater, *The Elusive Mr. Wesley*, vol. 1 (Nashville: Abingdon Press, 1984), p. 32.

Choosing To Love

The popular notion in our society is that the best way to choose a marriage partner is to wait until we "fall in love" with someone. By that, we usually mean that we wait for some kind of feeling, some emotional response to a person of the opposite sex that convinces us that we can never be truly happy again unless we can spend the future with that person. And often the feeling we experience is one of ecstatic joy and excitement.

But there are a couple of realities about falling in love that aren't quite as exciting. One is that we are just as likely to fall in love with someone with whom we are ill-matched as with someone who is a good match for us. The emotional experience we call falling in love is absolutely no guarantee that the object of our affection is in any way a good marriage choice. We are just as likely to fall in love with someone with whom we will be miserable as with whom we will be happy.

The second reality about falling in love is that sooner or later, just about everybody falls back out of love — or at least out of the state of high excitement that characterized the first blush of romance. This is because the experience of romantic love is basically an emotion, and emotions are changeable. Whether we like to admit it or not, part of falling in love is physical attraction, which by itself, is pretty shaky ground on which to build a relationship.

But even beyond that attraction, the feelings related to falling in love generally do not last. In fact, at least one author who has written on marriage describes falling in love as a kind of temporary insanity.

253

In some parts of the world, marriages are still arranged by parents, with the marriage partners themselves having little or no say in the selection of their mate.

Several years ago, I was the associate pastor at Trinity United Methodist Church in a large downtown area. That large church contained a marriage chapel built by donations from several denominations as an ecumenical chapel. One marriage I had there was for a young Muslim couple. The groom was from a country in the Middle East and had come to the States to study at a university. His bride was from the same country, but the groom had only met her a few days prior to the wedding. His parents had selected her and flown her over to America to marry their son.

I asked this young man how he felt about that, and he said he felt good about it. He said that his parents were wiser than he was and had more experience of life than he did. So, he believed, they were able to make a better choice for him than he would by himself.

Well, that kind of arrangement would not be my preference, but apparently it works. And by all evidence, the ratio of happy to unhappy marriages in cultures where arranged marriages are practiced is at least as good as in ours.

In the scripture for today, Abraham arranges a marriage for his son, Isaac, who, we note, is not consulted in the process. Abraham and his clan live in Canaan, but he does not want Isaac to marry a Canaanite woman. So he sends his servant back to Mesopotamia, where Abraham himself was born, to find a suitable bride.

When the servant arrives in Abraham's old home region, he uses a rather unique process of selection. He waits to see which maiden will draw water for him and for all his camels from the local well. The young woman who does this is Rebekah, daughter of Bethuel. The servant speaks with her family, who in turn, asks Rebekah whether she wants to go to Canaan to marry Abraham's son. She agrees, and travels to Canaan with the servant to meet her husband to be. Sort of the ultimate blind date!

When Isaac meets Rebekah, he seems quite satisfied with the selection. He proceeds to marry her, and *then*, the Bible says, he loved her.

He married her; *then* he loved her. Given the circumstances, the Bible has the order of things quite right for Isaac. For I doubt that the word "love" as used in this context referred to falling in love. No, it was something else.

Whether we have selected our mate through the falling-in-love experience or had our mate selected for us as Isaac did, what happens after that is very much the same. When the initial excitement wears off, as it almost always does, we are faced with a choice: "Will I love this person or not?"

"So [Rebekah] became his wife, and he loved her." The Bible is telling us that when it came to his marriage, Isaac acted like a grown-up! He realized that *real love is a choice*, and he chose to love this woman he had married.

So it is for us. We either choose to love or we choose not to. And that kind of decision is something quite apart from any particular emotions we may feel about our mate — which, as we all know, can come and go like the wind. Real love is a commitment of loyalty and faithfulness to another person, not rooted primarily in emotions.

One very important adult task is coming to terms with the reality that as pleasurable as it is, falling in love is a temporary thing. Falling in love gets us started in a relationship but it is seldom what sustains it. And unless we make peace with this fact, we are apt to waste a lot of time and energy trying to make our relationships conform to some preconceived notion of "the perfect romance."

Of course, there is still plenty of room for romance in our marriages, and we ought to do loving things for each other. Let us not despair because we don't always feel lovingly toward our mate. In fact, it's a revealing picture of our choice to love when we treat our mate lovingly on days when the feelings of love are not particularly strong.

What exactly do we choose when we decide to love?

For one thing, we choose a primary loyalty. The scripture, after telling us that Isaac loved Rebekah, says, "so Isaac was comforted after the death of his mother." One way to read that is that Rebekah helped to fill a void in Isaac's life left by the passing of his mother, Sarah. And there's nothing wrong with that.

2. Another view is that Isaac realized his primary loyalty on earth now was to his new family rather than his old one. "For this reason a man will leave his father and mother and be united to his wife, and they will become one flesh" (Genesis 2:24). That's how God set things up when marriage was instituted in the beginning. That's how God intends it.

How exactly that works out will vary from situation to situation, but one thing it always means is choosing our primary loyalty among all the people we love.

I know a couple whom I'll call Andy and Sharon. They experienced a lot of difficulties after they first married. They lived not far from Andy's parents. His father had a physical handicap, so when Andy had lived at home, he had learned to handle many of the handyman chores around the house that his father was unable to do.

After he got married, Andy's mother got into the habit of calling Andy at work whenever something at her house needed to be repaired. Like a dutiful son, Andy would stop at his parents' house on his way home to make the repair. Since he was already there, his mother made supper for him. Meanwhile, Sharon had supper waiting on the table at home. Sometimes Andy didn't get home until bedtime.

You can imagine the stress this pattern put on their marriage. Several evenings, Sharon had to cancel plans the couple had made together because Andy wasn't there.

Eventually it all came to a head. Andy had to make some choices. As their pastor, I was involved in helping Andy do that. Andy made the right one. When it was not feasible for him to assist his mother with a chore, he learned to tell her to call a plumber or the appropriate repairman. He's still a good son, and his marriage has improved. Andy and Sharon visit Andy's mom and dad together and there is a healthy relationship between the generations. But it is healthy because Andy chose his primary loyalty.

3. Still another choice real love requires is choosing to love the actual person we've married. Because falling in love is such a wild and crazy emotional ride, we sometimes fail to see the other person as he or she really is. In other words, we may fall in love with

a romanticized ideal image of the other person instead of the actual person. Then later, when the flames of romance have diminished somewhat, the blinders fall off and we discover that we've fallen in love with a phantom, an ideal image that doesn't exist. You discover your wife is neither a goddess nor a vixen, but a human being with both glories and faults. You discover your husband is neither a knight in shining armor nor the most sensitive guy to ever live, but a human being with both glories and faults.

That's the point at which lasting love needs to take hold. That's the point at which the scripture places Isaac. After he had married Rebekah, he loved her. That's when he decided to love not who he wanted Rebekah to be, but who she really was.

The pattern God set from the very beginning was that a man and woman should choose to love each other. So when we do so, we are following the intention of our creator.

"Isaac ... married Rebekah. So she became his wife, and he loved her." That was the decision of a grown-up. Amen.

A Man Of The Moment

Do you remember the movie 1988 movie, *Twins*? It was comedy that starred Arnold Schwarzenegger and Danny DeVito as, of all things, twin brothers. Even if you know nothing about the plot of the movie, the mental picture of those two actors standing side-by-side as twins is itself pretty funny.

The setup for the move is that the brothers are the result of an experiment to grow a perfect man, who is the Schwarzenegger character, named Julius. But in the course of manipulating his genes when he's in the prenatal stage, the scrap that is not used develops into the smaller brother, Vincent. Thus Julius is planned and grows to athletic proportions. Vincent is an accident and develops from the leftovers. While Julius is taken to a south sea island and raised by philosophers, Vincent is placed in an orphanage. Grown up, Vincent becomes a low life and is about to be killed by loan sharks when Julius discovers that he has a brother and begins looking for him. The plot takes off from there.

That movie was lighthearted and in the end, the twin brothers end up as good friends.

Take a similar scenario, where twins are born, destined not only to have unequal physical proportions, but also to have different fates, with the divine balance set against one of them. That's because of God's declaration to their mother while they are yet in her womb that the elder will serve the younger. Under those circumstances, the scenario is not funny, and the brothers go through years when there is great anger between them. Finally, they are reconciled, but it is an uneasy peace, and neither has much to do with the other. It's not a particularly happy ending.

That story is not a movie, but is the biblical account of Esau and Jacob, the twins born to Isaac and Rebekah. The part of their story we are considering today is when both brothers are still young men living in the family compound and before the great division developed between them. They are very different from each other, both physically and in personality. Esau, the twin born first, is a rugged outdoorsman and a hunter. He is his father's favorite, especially because the old man has a taste for the meat Esau brought home from his hunting forays. Jacob, however, is more of a homebody, and a quiet person more given to the pursuit of personal advancement than of wild game. Jacob is his mother's favorite.

There is also one more thing that sets them apart: the issue of primogeniture. That is the principle practiced in their society whereby the firstborn son — Esau in this case — is the one designated to take over leadership of the family clan when the father dies and also to receive a double portion of the inheritance. That is his birthright. It was a big deal in the ancient world.

Then comes the incident in today's reading. Esau has been out on a hunting trip and when he comes home, he is really hungry. In fact, he is so famished that getting some food quickly is all he has on his mind. It so happens that at that very moment Jacob is cooking up a pot of red lentil stew, so Esau asks for a plateful. Jacob is willing to give him some, but only for a price. "First sell me your birthright," he says. Esau reasons that he is better off with a full stomach and no birthright, than dead from hunger but in possession of his birthright. So without any more thought than that, he agrees.

Now this was a very shortsighted decision on Esau's part. In the first place, it was an exaggeration that he was about to die from hunger. He'd been out in the field all day and probably had not carried enough lunch with him, so that upon arrival at home, he was in one of those hungry stages where you say something like, "I'm so hungry I could eat a horse." Considering only how he felt at that moment, he agreed to exchange something of great value for bowl of red stew. It was a supreme example of short-range thinking, and even worse, it had long-range consequences; it set the stage for the later bitterness between the brothers.

One indicator that Esau was thinking only of his present moment is captured in the Hebrew language in which this story was originally written. Our NRSV translation has Esau saying to Jacob, "Let me eat some of that red stuff," but rabbi and author, Burton Visotzky, says that a better translation of what the hungry Esau said is "Gimme some of that red stuff." In fact, Rabbi Visotzky points out that the Hebrew verb he translated "gimme" is generally employed in the Bible for the act of providing fodder to animals.[1] That Esau used that word indicates that he was hardly being a connoisseur here. He just wanted something to fill his belly.

There are five more verbs that report that rest of Esau's behavior in this incident. They are *ate*, *drank*, *rose*, *departed*, and *despised*. The first four tell us that he did not savor his costly meal; he just shoveled it in and left. The last verb, "despised," is the narrator's comment on Esau's awful decision. In trading off his valuable birthright for a meal — and a pretty ordinary one at that — he, in effect, despised his birthright, treated it as though it wasn't worth much. There is a Yiddish folk expression that comes out of this biblical story. When someone is rude at the table or just "stuffs his face," it is said pejoratively that he "eats like Esau."[2]

I have called Esau a "man of the moment," and it is in that description that he is most like many of us today. It is quite natural and appropriate for little children to be focused on what excites them at that instant in time, but lots of people never seem to outgrow that. We continue to want what we want right now, even if fulfilling the momentary urge will affect our longer-term goals. We often seem to be unwilling to delay immediate pleasure even when it is in our best interests to do so.

Think of it as eating our dessert before we eat our vegetables. That's okay occasionally, but always filling up on dessert so that there is no room for vegetables is very bad for our health. Going outside to play instead of doing our homework is acceptable now and then, but make it a habit and it likely will doom you to low-paying jobs when you grow up. And the same is often true of other things that give their rewards immediately but keep us from reaching our longer-term goals later.

Psychiatrist/author, Scott Peck, points out that life presents us with a series of problems, some of which are painful to deal with. Nonetheless, to avoid a miserable existence we need to deal with them, because most of them do not go away on their own. One of the basic tools that we need to solve those problems is the willingness to delay gratification. He defines delaying gratification as "a process of scheduling the pain and pleasure of life in such a way as to enhance the pleasure by meeting and experiencing the pain first and getting it over with. It is the only decent way to live."[3] Another way to define delaying gratification is simply as "putting off pleasure until your work is finished."

In my own life, one of my personal rules is "Do the hard stuff first." I have not always lived by it, but when I have, it has made my life better and has let me encounter fewer problems.

David Laibson, a professor at Harvard University who was a researcher and collaborator on a brain study in 2004, sees the matter as a battle between emotions and reason: "Our emotional brain has a hard time imagining the future, even though our logical brain clearly sees the future consequences of our current actions. Our emotional brain wants to max out the credit card, order dessert, and smoke a cigarette. Our logical brain knows we should save for retirement, go for a jog, and quit smoking."[4]

Of course, both Dr. Peck and Professor Laibson describe this matter of delayed gratification in behavioral terms, but you didn't come here this morning to get a lesson in human behavior or psychology, so why talk about delayed gratification in church?

One reason is simply that this scripture reading itself brought the subject up. In Esau, it gives us a clear example of someone who lived so fully in the moment that he messed up his future. Another reason to think about this in church is that for spirituality and Christianity itself to have their full effect on us, we need to be able to link to the future. Christianity does have a great deal to say about how we live in the present. In fact, the Bible doesn't say very much about the future in its meaning of the time ahead on earth in a person's life. In the old King James Version of the Bible, the word "future" does not even occur. Nonetheless, underlying Christianity's focus on serving God in the present is the confidence that God's kingdom will eventually come. And living morally and spiritually today sometimes means delaying or even rejecting some pleasures in favor of receiving a heavenly reward.

We don't often talk about the Christian life that way — living God's way to inherit the kingdom of God. We'd rather talk about commitment and loving God as their own reward, but we don't all function the same way, and it is not wrong to work for a spiritual long-range goal. We are saved by God's grace, not by any good works on our part, but good works are essential to our faith. As James wrote in his biblical book: "What good is it, my brothers and sisters, if you say you have faith but do not have works?" (James 2:14). Sometimes that means doing good that is inconvenient or unpleasant in the present moment but which is in line with the promise of God's kingdom.

We've been talking about Esau as a man of the moment, but let's think for a moment about his brother. Jacob wasn't a model of righteousness either, but he clearly did have the ability to delay gratification and to work for long-term goals. If you follow Jacob's story, you'll see that he worked for seven long years to obtain the wife he wanted. After his father-in-law pulled a sneaky trick on him, he worked another seven. It could not have been easy, but he did it. Jacob was the brother through whom the people of Israel descended, and in part, he was able to fit into God's plan because he was willing to take the long view.

- It is good to remember that about Jacob when we are inclined to be impulsive with our spending or to take our present good health for granted. Recall the proverbial old person in poor health who said, "If I had known I was going to live this long, I'd have taken better care of myself."
- It's good to remember that about Jacob when there's school-work to be done at the same time there is an entertaining program on television or a new video game on hand.

- It's good to remember that about Jacob when we are tempted to take moral shortcuts or to get away with something shady "just once."
- It is good to remember that about Jacob when the choice is between doing a good deed today and putting it off to a more convenient time. That's when we need to be people of the moment in the positive sense, doing the thing that helps and heals right now rather than putting it off.

We need to practice our faith moment by moment, very much in the present, and to that end, we should not confuse delaying gratification with delaying to do what will help others or what will fix a troubling situation. But we also need to keep the long view — the kingdom view — in mind so that the ways we spend ourselves today are not just for the immediate kick, but also as an investment in God's kingdom to come. Amen.

---

1. Dr. Burton L. Visotzky, *The Genesis of Ethics* (New York: Crown Publishers, Inc., 1996), pp. 131, 138.

2. Shlomo Riskin, "Shabbat Shalom: Parshat Vayetze," November 24, 2001, www.ohrtorahstone.org.il/parsha/5762/vayetze62.htm.

3. M. Scott Peck, *The Road Less Traveled* (New York: Simon and Schuster, A Touchstone Book, 1978), pp. 15-19.

4. Steve Bradt, "Brain takes itself on over immediate vs. delayed gratification," *Harvard University Gazette*, October 21, 2004, www.news.harvard.edu/gazette/2004/10.21/07-brainbattle.html.

The Ladder From Our House

There is a wonderful story about a city mayor. It happened that during one particular year, the mayor made trips to both Washington DC and to Israel. According to the story, while in Washington, the mayor visited the president in the oval office. During the visit, the mayor noticed three telephones on the president's desk and inquired about them.

"Well," said the president, "The black one is a regular telephone, the white one is for calls within the White House and the red one is a hotline to God."

"Gee," replied the mayor, "with all the problems my town is having, I could certainly use some advice from God. Could I possibly use that hotline for a few moments?"

The president was happy to oblige and left the mayor alone in the oval office to make his call. And so the mayor talked to God.

Afterward, he asked the president how much he owed for the call. The president called the White House operator and got the time and charges. The mayor immediately paid the charges, considering it money well spent.

Later that year, while in Israel, the mayor also had an audience with Israel's prime minister. He noticed that the prime minister had three telephones in his office as well, so he asked about them.

"Well," said the prime minister, "The black one is a regular telephone, the white one is for calls between government offices and the red one is a hotline to God."

Remembering how helpful his last conversation with God had been, the mayor asked for and received permission to use the prime minister's hotline for another call to the almighty.

After completing his call, the mayor asked the prime minister how much he owed for the call. The prime minister looked a bit surprised and then said, "You don't owe anything. Over here, phoning God is a direct call."

Ah, well, we all have times when we wish we could have our direct hotline to God. In fact, in a more serious vein, aren't there times of personal crises or of momentous decision when we sincerely wish to God that he would contact us and tell us what to do? At least it would be helpful if he told us what the consequences of each of our choices would be.

Jacob, who found it expedient to leave his father's house in a hurry after having defrauded his brother Esau, stopped one night to sleep in the wilderness. In his dream that night, he saw a ladder that reached from earth to heaven. Angels were traveling up and down this ladder and God himself was standing at the top of it. God spoke to Jacob and extended to him the covenant promises that he had already made with Jacob's father Isaac and with his grandfather Abraham.

When Jacob awoke, he realized that he had had an experience that is granted to only a very few. That ladder had been his own hotline to God.

It seems remarkable to us that God would choose to extend a vision to such an unsavory character as Jacob, but the point is, the only way such direct access to God can be had is if God himself offers it. There is nothing we mortals can do to establish this link.

There are some points where we can identify with Jacob's story. In the first place, Jacob was in exile from his home. Now we may not feel too much sympathy for him since his exile was the result of his own wrongdoing. Still, some of us know what it is like to be cut off from people we love or to know that some of our actions have troubled or even ended certain relationships.

We ought to note, however, that there is nothing in Jacob's demeanor as he camps out that night to suggest that he had a guilty conscience or desired to mend his ways. He may have been apprehensive for, as far as he knew, his brother could have been pursuing him. He was probably despondent. And since he wasn't at home, there was no chance of him actually receiving the inheritance he had won by treachery. Yet, he does not appear to be sorry for what he had done.

We may be able to identify with Jacob at this point, too. Have any of us ever said, "Well, what I did may have been wrong, but I am not about to apologize"? Or, "The church would not approve of what I did but I sure taught that nasty so-and-so a lesson"?

The remarkable thing about this whole account is the fact that God comes to Jacob in this dream without first demanding any kind of contrition on Jacob's part. God does not rebuke Jacob for his sin. On the contrary, God confirms to Jacob the inheritance that he thought he had lost, assures him of divine help and promises to be with him.

Yet even after this powerful dream, Jacob shows little evidence of conversion. In fact, demonstrating what a conniving rascal he still is, he responds to the dream with the following vow:

> If *God will be with me, and will keep me in this way that I go,* and *will give me bread to eat and clothing to wear,* so that *I come again to my father's house in peace,* then *the Lord shall be my God....*
> — Genesis 28:21-22 (emphasis added)

Nothing Jacob did made him deserving of a vision of God, but he needed that vision, and God gave it to him.

But that is a point for us, too. Even if we have never done anything as dastardly as Jacob did, none of us have been deserving of the grace of God, and yet God gives it to us anyway.

In John 1:43-51, which tells of Nathanael's call to be an apostle, Jesus tells Nathanael that he knew Nathanael had been sitting under the fig tree when he first heard about Jesus. That Jesus knew this astonished Nathanael, but Jesus then startled him even more. Jesus referred to the Old Testament story of Jacob's dream and then said to Nathanael, "... You will see heaven opened, and the angels of God ascending and descending upon the Son of Man."

267

In other words, Jesus was saying, "I can do more for you than read your heart. I can be for you and all people the ladder that leads to God."[1]

Here again is the affirmation that this direct link with God occurs only as God's gift to us, for surely Jesus was sent by God to lead us to the Father. Jesus is the ladder from our house to God. Jesus said as much when he stated, "I am the way, and the truth, and the life. No one comes to the Father except through me" (John 14:6).

It is extremely hard for us to really feel the impact of those words, "I am the way." We who have been raised in the Christian faith have been taught for so long that God is accessible to us that we take it for granted.

But think for a moment what our lives would be like if we did not know the way to God. In the ages before Christ, more primitive people did not know the way to God. In Mesopotamia, those who practiced the Babylonian religion built multitiered towers for worship with ramps joining each tier. These ramps were intended by their builders to be stairs joining heaven and earth, a route by which their gods could descend to help them and receive their worship. These worshipers hoped that these ramps and structures would prove to be the way to their gods. Some of the other peoples did things like sacrifice their children in an attempt to reach their gods.

In our age, even though these old and sometimes barbaric practices have been abandoned, there are still plenty of people who don't know how to reach God. Although in one perspective, this doesn't seem to be a very religious age we live in, in another perspective it's a time when people are hungry to believe in that which is beyond themselves.

Some time ago, I attended a conference in Chicago. The speaker at one session was Lynn Garrett, the religious book editor at *Publisher's Weekly*, the "bible" of the book-publishing industry. She explained that there is an explosion of interest in religious and spiritual books, and that sales of such books are stronger currently than they have been for decades. "One Spirit," one of nine specialty clubs of the Book of the Month Club, is the fastest growing club in the company's history. And Ingram Books, the nation's largest book wholesaler, saw a nearly 250% growth in the religious book category starting in the mid-1990s.

Book sales are a sign of the religious hunger in America, but note that I said "religious and spiritual" books, not just Christian books. To be sure, sale of Christian books are on an upswing, but the "religious" books category includes New Age, Scientology, believe-in-yourself, and a host of other titles on spirituality that are far afield from Christianity. You see, many people are hungry to believe, to connect with that which is beyond themselves, *but they don't know the way.* As a result, people swallow all sorts of stuff — everything from astrology to crystals to UFOs to Elvis sightings. People want to connect with a "higher power" but have no idea of how.

Then, too, even among those of us who have some inkling that Christ is the way, some of us perhaps don't grasp what that means. We may be relying on a record of good deeds to get God's attention and thus fail to realize that God may be reached through faith in Jesus.

There may also be some of us who feel we are too sinful or have done something too terrible for God to listen to us. We may think that we can't come to God until we've "cleaned up our act." We may not understand that God calls us to come just as we are, and that Jesus is the way.

How would you feel if, in the midst of a crisis, you could think of no way to reach God? Would you not feel even more abandoned and alone? But Jesus says to us, "I am the way. I'm the ladder from your house to the Father."

Jesus as the ladder does not mean that he provides instant answers to prayer, but he provides an instant audience with whom to share our burden, and he provides instant access to God. He is the ladder by which we ascend to God and the ladder by which God's love descends to us.

Perhaps the most helpful part of Jacob's story for us is the knowledge that Jacob's sinfulness did not stop God from communicating with him.

Some time ago, I read of a minister's son, named Chris, whose mother had died when he was seven. His father eventually remarried and although Chris' stepmother was good to him, the young boy was deeply hurt by the death of his mother. He felt as if he had been deserted. As a result, this boy avoided attachments with others for fear of being hurt again. Resentment and rebellion churned in him. He became difficult to live with and hard to understand. He was so impossible to deal with that he was expelled twice from school before he was in the seventh grade. He began drinking and using drugs while still in his teens.

At 23, despite the fact that he was still a very mixed-up person, Chris got married. A child was born in the first year and somehow Chris found a job as a policeman. He found the job nerve-racking. He had to deal with people at their worst: those who were drunk and threatening, those who stole, parents who beat their children, spouses who attacked one another, kids in crime and so forth.

All of this made him even harder in his spirit. He viewed compassion and tenderness and love as signs of weakness. He became a tough, cold-hearted man.

He drank a great deal, but the alcohol did not assuage the terrible turmoil in his inner man and he contemplated suicide. He could find no ladder out of the pit of despair he lived in.

Finally, he recalled that a minister who was a friend of his father's lived in a nearby city, and Chris called for an appointment. When there, he described in detail his inner agony. When he finished, the pastor said, "Chris, the only help that can do you any good must come from Jesus Christ." The minister was telling Chris that Jesus was the way, the ladder to God.

That was precisely what Chris did not want to hear. He left in anger and disgust.

But, apparently the pastor had planted a seed. A week later, Chris came across a book titled *Authentic Christianity* and felt compelled to buy it. He soon found himself engrossed in the book, and while reading, he began to cry. He fell on his knees and asked Jesus to come into his life.[2]

That's exactly what Jesus did, and that was the beginning of Chris' journey toward inner peace.

This man found that the ladder from God had been extended down into his home all along. Christ had been there throughout all the pain. The pastor and the book simply helped Chris to see the ladder, Jesus Christ. As Chris started to climb up, he found that God was already climbing down to meet him.

And that's what God does for each of us, too. He sets the ladder named Jesus Christ down into our lives and stands near the bottom rung, ready to hear our pleas and strengthen us, and help us to climb to God.

That is one of the treasures of our faith: Jesus is the ladder to God. Amen.

---

1. William Barclay, *John*, Vol. 1, *Daily Study Bible Series*, p. 94.

2. Thanks to Dr. Charles Ferrell for this illustration.

Sermons On The First Readings

For Sundays
After Pentecost
(Middle Third)

Appointment
With Thunder

David J. Kalas

Proper 12
Pentecost 10
Ordinary Time 17
Genesis 29:15-28

A Match Made In Heaven

One of the great privileges of being a parish pastor is the opportunity to officiate at weddings. Most folks only know how beautiful a wedding is from the pews. I want to tell you, though, that a wedding is even more beautiful from the vantage point at which I get to see it. I get to stand here in the front. And from here, I get to see the faces.

I am always touched as I watch the faces of the bridesmaids and the groomsmen while their best friends — or, often, their siblings — come to this long-awaited moment. More than that, I love to watch the faces of the bride and the groom as they speak their vows — those profound promises — to one another. And, from where I stand, one of the most interesting faces that I get to see is the face of the bride's father.

In our tradition, there is that moment, just after the procession, when the father of the bride stands in the front, situated between his daughter and her husband-to-be. I am just sentimental enough that I always find that picture to be a very lovely and poignant one.

"Who gives this woman to be married to this man?"

That is the picture with which our Old Testament reading ends. Laban gave Jacob his daughter, Rachel, to be Jacob's wife.

See the three of them standing there at the wedding ceremony: Rachel, the lovely and shapely young bride. Jacob, the young man so in love. And Laban, the father of the bride, standing between the two of them.

I tell you, that scene features a match made in heaven. It is a lovely scene. Lovely, that is, unless you know the story that leads up to it.

The truth is, it's hard to find a good guy in that picture. It's hard to find someone that you like and want to root for. Jacob is reputedly a cheat (Genesis 27:36; 31:1). Laban is a master manipulator and shrewd to the point of being dishonest. And Rachel herself shows a treacherous side along the way, too (Genesis 31:32b-35).

In truth, it was Jacob's propensity for cheating that got him involved with Laban and Laban's family in the first place. Jacob was born and raised in Canaan, where he lived with his father, Isaac; his mother, Rebekah; and his twin brother, Esau.

From the very beginning, Jacob and Esau were at odds. Even while they were still in the womb, they noticeably wrestled with one another. When Esau came out first, Jacob was not far behind. Because he came out holding onto his older brother's heel, his parents named him "Jacob," which meant "heel holder" or "one who supplants." It was an unfavorable name, and Jacob lived up to it.

As the boys grew, Esau became more and more his father's favorite. Jacob, meanwhile, was mama's boy. Esau was rough and outdoorsy. Jacob was more refined, and more of a homebody.

The Bible does not chronicle their childhoods together, but it is not hard for us to imagine, is it? I imagine that, like all brothers, they scrapped with one another, wrestling that was sometimes playful, and sometimes hurtful. I imagine that, just as he did in the womb, Esau usually prevailed in those wrestling matches. He was stronger and rougher, and I expect he beat up his slightly younger brother more than a few times.

No need to feel sorry for Jacob, though. He was not so brawny as Esau, but he was far more clever. Jacob could always fool Esau: talk him into things, con him, and put him at a disadvantage. For every time that Esau hit, tripped or tackled Jacob, I imagine that Jacob tricked, swindled, or cheated Esau.

When they were boys, the hitting and the cheating were perhaps inconsequential. When they were young men, however, the stakes were considerably higher. Jacob cheated Esau out of far more substantive things. And Esau was no longer satisfied to beat up Jacob; he wanted to kill him.

So it was that Jacob had to run away from home. First, he had tricked the gullible Esau into signing over his extensive benefits as the firstborn son. Then, later, he had fraudulently taken from Esau their father's special blessing — a most valuable commodity in that time and place.

Esau resolved to kill Jacob, so Jacob was sent packing. He was directed by his parents to go to northern Mesopotamia, to live with his mother's brother, his Uncle Laban.

Do you believe in love at first sight? If you do, then you have a kindred spirit in Jacob. For from the moment Jacob saw Laban's younger daughter, Rachel, he was, shall we say, motivated by her. Jacob had his eye on Rachel from the beginning, and as soon as he saw the opportunity, he asked to marry her.

In that day, of course, such a marriage proposal was not made to the young woman, but rather to the young woman's father. He would be the one to determine his daughter's partner for life. Jacob asked Laban to give him Rachel in marriage.

The conversation, as we have it recorded for us in our scripture reading, was initiated by Laban. "Because you are my kinsman," he said to Jacob, "should you therefore serve me for nothing?"

The reader does a double take. What did I miss? It seems that Jacob — Laban's nephew and guest — has been working for his uncle, and not even working for pay. Somehow or other, out of the goodness of Jacob's heart (which seems hard to believe), or out of some clever manipulation by Laban (which is much easier to believe), Jacob has been roped into helping with the chores. After some time in that arrangement, Laban pretends to be magnanimous by offering to pay Jacob for his work.

Jacob, meanwhile, is very clear about the salary package for which he wants to negotiate. "I will serve you seven years for your younger daughter, Rachel."

The Bible reports that Jacob loved Rachel, and as the story unfolds we discover that Rachel was the one true love of Jacob's life. She was the sole object of his desire for years before they were married. Even though there was another woman, Leah, to

whom he was married for many more years, and though he produced offspring with two other women, besides, and though he
had many children and grandchildren; we see evidence, even years
after her death, that Jacob's life was still being shaped by his love
for Rachel.

Jacob loved Rachel so much that he was offering to work seven
years for her. Multiply your annual salary by seven. That's a lot of
love. But he was so taken with her that he was willing to devote
seven years of his life to laboring, knowing that all he would have
to show for it in the end was a wife. No savings. No belongings.
No flocks, no herds, no children. Not even seven years of enjoying
being married. But that's what Jacob was willing to do; he set the
terms.

Laban, with another slick imitation of generosity, replied, "It
is better that I give her to you than that I should give her to any
other man."

Always the consummate bargainer, Laban raises the specter of
another customer waiting in the wings. He uses the term "give"
rather loosely, considering the steep price he is accepting from his
nephew for his daughter.

Years before Jacob was born, we get our first glimpse of what
kind of man Laban was. A servant of Abraham arrived to propose
that Laban's sister, Rebekah, become Isaac's wife. The biblical
author introduces Laban this way: "Rebekah had a brother whose
name was Laban ... As soon as he had seen the nose-ring, and the
bracelets on his sister's arms, and when he heard the words of his
sister Rebekah, 'Thus the man spoke to me,' he went to the man"
(Genesis 24:29-30). It's easy to be suspicious of Laban when we
see how prominent the jewelry adornments were to him. Like the
cartoon character whose eyes become dollar signs, Laban seems
always to see the profitability of relationships.

Still, in spite of the cynical Laban, love prevailed. The Bible
says that Jacob's seven years of labor "seemed to him but a few
days because of the love he had for [Rachel]." In a world of arranged marriages, where woman were often treated like property,
and in a culture where polygamy was not uncommon, here is a

refreshingly romantic note. The years seemed like a few days because of Jacob's love for Rachel.

In addition to being romantic, the verse rings true for us. We know from our own experience that labor is made lighter by love. Something within us resonates with Jacob as he toils cheerfully day after day, looking forward to the day when both his love and his labor would have their reward.

When that day finally arrived, however, there was a terrible surprise. In a brash and heartless move, Laban substituted his older daughter, Leah, for his younger daughter, Rachel, on the wedding night. It was morning before Jacob realized what had happened. And Laban's response to Jacob's indignation was a bit of small-print that was never actually printed: "This is not done in our country — giving the younger before the firstborn."

In the end, Laban managed to get another seven years of labor out of Jacob for the privilege of marrying the daughter for whom he had already worked seven years in the first place.

So we return to the picture with which we began: the wedding of Jacob and Rachel, with Laban standing, symbolically, in between.

This episode from Jacob's life does not seem to be a particularly spiritual one. These verses are not the stuff of inspirational posters, and these scenes do not become pictures on the walls of our Sunday school classrooms. These are not the profound moments of encounter with God, like Bethel or Penuel. In fact, God is not mentioned at all in this story. His hand is not obvious in the events that unfold, and his influence is certainly not apparent in the behavior of these people.

This story does not seem like natural Sunday morning material.

It does, however, seem like Monday morning material — and Tuesday afternoon — and Friday night. This story is the stuff of real day-to-day life. We see here the stuff of work and wages, of love and marriage, of celebrations and conflicts. While we may not immediately recognize God's role in the story, we surely recognize everything else about the story.

That picture — Jacob and Rachel on their wedding day, with Laban standing in between — does feature a match made in heaven.

279

But it is not necessarily Jacob and Rachel. Rather, the truly providential match is the relationship between Jacob and Laban.

Jacob met his match in Laban. After the Triple-A competition of Esau through his growing-up years, now Jacob was in the big leagues. And, he was repeatedly bested by his senior con artist, Laban.

Could this have been part of the wisdom that Isaac and Rebecca saw in sending Jacob to his uncle's house — like the parents who know that the "real world" of work or military service will bring necessary virtues to their undisciplined child? Or was it entirely the hand of God that put Jacob and Laban together?

Whatever the cause, it had a good effect. When Jacob left Laban's house, after twenty years of having his own heel constantly grabbed, he did not revert to his old ways. He was honest with God about who he was (Genesis 32:27; cf Genesis 27:19-24). He was genuine and humble with Esau in their reunion (Genesis 33:1-11). And, he was properly troubled by shrewdness and duplicity in his sons (Genesis 34:1-31; 49:3-7).

We are naturally grateful to God when he gives us what we desire: our Rachel. We ought also to be grateful to God, however, when he gives us what we need: our Laban. Amen.

A Blessing In Disguise

I wonder how many of us here are named after someone.

Chances are that a good many of us carry family names. We are named for a parent, a grandparent, an uncle, or an aunt somewhere on the family tree. Others of us had parents who named us after a character in the Bible, or perhaps some other significant character from history.

All told, I expect a pretty fair number of us are named after someone else.

When Isaac and Rebecca had their twin boys, they took an unusual approach to naming their babies. They named the boys for the boys themselves. They took a look at each boy when he was born, and they gave him a name based on what they saw.

Typically, we don't get named for ourselves until much later in life, and then we call it a "nickname." There is some feature, some trait, some characteristic, some behavior that we become known for, and that results in a nickname. We are, thus, named for ourselves.

But Jacob and Esau — the two boys born to Isaac and Rebecca — were named for themselves right from the start.

Esau was born first. The Bible reports that baby Esau came out noticeably red and unusually hairy. And so they named the boy "Esau" because, in their language, that sounded like the word for "hairy." They named Esau for himself.

Then, right after Esau, came Jacob.

We have an expression when one person arrives right after or right behind another person, we say the second person is "right on his heels." Jacob arrived, literally, right on Esau's heels. That second baby boy came out holding onto the heel of his slightly older brother, and so Isaac and Rebecca named him "Jacob," meaning "heel grabber." They named him for himself.

I suppose it is hard to trace the cause-and-effect relationship between what parents perceive their child to be and what that child is. To what extent does a child earn the reputation he has within his family? And to what extent does the reputation he has with his family continue to shape and condition the child?

Isaac and Rebecca called him "Jacob," and their boy lived up to — or down to — that name, that identification. Jacob was a heel-grabber. He was forever trying to supplant or usurp, to trip up or outmaneuver, to get ahead, or to cheat someone nearby.

Jacob's name suited him well. From his birth on, he was a heel-grabber. And indeed, for his early years, it continued to be his older brother, Esau's, heel that Jacob kept grabbing.

There was an occasion when they were both young men living at home that Esau came in from the fields and found Jacob in the kitchen making some sort of stew. Esau was hungry, and so when he walked inside, smelled the aroma, and saw the food, he asked Jacob for some of it. Jacob responded by suggesting a trade: He would give Esau a bowl of the stew if Esau would give Jacob his birthright.

The birthright was the entitlement that belonged to the first-born son. It carried authority, and it carried property and financial advantages. Jacob's proposition — to trade a birthright for a bowl of stew (or a mess of pottage, in the old vernacular) — was an absurdity. To give away a significant future inheritance, as well as a position of authority, for a lunch? Only a fool would agree to such a preposterous deal.

Enter Esau.

Esau, in a response that no doubt seemed like cleverness to him, said to Jacob, "What good will my birthright do me if I die of starvation right now?" And so, the writer of Genesis ominously concludes, "Thus Esau despised his birthright" (Genesis 25:34).

Jacob tricked his stomach-driven brother out of his birthright.

282

Then, some time later, Jacob cheated him out of his blessing, too.

The blessing, incidentally, is a spiritual currency that has lost its sense of value in our culture. We don't use blessings in our day-to-day life anymore, apart from when someone sneezes, and even then, we do not much take it seriously. It is more politeness than power.

I don't think that blessings have lost their value in heaven, however. In the Old Testament, there is no question about the power and the importance of a blessing. The blessing was a serious enough business that Isaac wanted to give his to Esau. And the blessing was serious enough business that Rebecca coveted it for Jacob.

Esau, you see, was Isaac's favorite son: rugged, outdoorsy, a man's man. Jacob, however, was Rebecca's favorite: cleaner, more civilized, more brains than brawn.

When Isaac was an old man — blind, feeble, and presumably about to die — he sent for Esau to give him his blessing. But before Isaac would bless him, Isaac instructed Esau to go hunting, prepare a meal, and then bring it to his father. Then, after eating the meal, Isaac would give Esau his blessing.

Rebecca overheard the plan, and she immediately put a plan of her own into action. Eager for her preferred son to receive the coveted blessing, Rebecca arranged for Jacob to disguise himself as Esau, and then to carry in a meal she prepared for Isaac to eat. Because Isaac was old and blind, the disguise did not have to pass the sight test; only the touch and smell test.

(Rebecca found, incidentally, that she could achieve both of those results by draping Jacob's arms and neck with goat skins, which gives us a sense for what Esau must have been like.)

While Esau was still out hunting, Jacob entered their father's tent, and effectively stole his father's blessing, disguised as his hairy brother, Esau.

Now we fast-forward the story twenty years.

Jacob is a middle-aged man, married, a dozen children, and wealthy with flocks, herds, and servants. He and his household are traveling — making a major move, really — uprooting themselves from what had been their home in northern Mesopotamia, and going to create a new home for themselves in southern Canaan.

One night, Jacob is in the midst of a personal crisis, and he senses the need to go through it alone. He separates himself from the rest of his group. He sends his family, his flocks, and his servants across the River Jabbok, and then he stays behind, alone, through the night.

As it turns out, he is not alone for long. Someone — some man, some at-first unidentified personage whom we later discover is the Lord or the angel of the Lord — appears out of nowhere and wrestles with Jacob through the night.

Charles Wesley tells the story in song.

> *Come, O thou Traveler unknown,*
> *whom still I hold, but cannot see!*
> *My company before is gone,*
> *and I am left alone with thee;*
> *with thee all night I mean to stay*
> *and wrestle till the break of day.*[1]

Jacob wrestles with God. A compelling image, and very probably an experience familiar to some here.

When daylight begins to break, the mysterious visitor tries to leave, but Jacob holds on. Like the stubborn newborn holding his brother's heel, Jacob holds on.

Jacob says, "I will not let you go until you bless me."

And the Lord responds, saying, "What is your name?"

I wonder what flashback Jacob experienced in that moment. A young man, slinking into his father's tent, bringing his misleading meal, and wearing his makeshift disguise, seeking his father's blessing. His father asked him who he was, and he lied: "I am your firstborn son, Esau."

Now Jacob seeks a blessing from God himself, and now God himself asks him who he is.

Isaac had been old and blind: He didn't know who had entered the room. But God? God is not old and blind. God knew. This omniscient wrestler in dawn's light knew who Jacob was. Ah, but see the honesty — the confession, if you will — that is a prerequisite for God's blessing. *Who are you? What is your name?*

This is the same God who asked the guilty, leaf-clutching couple, *"What have you done?"* He does not ask what he needs to know. Rather, he asks what we need to answer. He asks Jacob, *"Who are you? What is your name?"*

We human beings are torn creatures, at this point, you know. We long, on the one hand, to tell who and what we really are, while at the same time we are so desperate to hide it.

The hostess works hard to clean the house for guests. She says she'd be mortified if they saw what a mess it was. But then, when they arrive and remark how lovely everything is, what does she do? She says, "Oh, you should have seen it a few hours ago" or "Just don't look in the closet where I stuck everything." She doesn't want them to see her mess, but somehow she is still eager to confess it.

A couple with trouble at home tries hard to be on their best behavior in public, not to air their dirty laundry. But then they freely make jokes in public — jokes that nibble around the edges of their painful truths.

We are a mixed bag: so eager to hide our blemishes, and yet so needing to get them out in the open. We suffer from the conflict of a fundamental fear and a fundamental longing. I fear that if so-and-so really knew me, he wouldn't like me, wouldn't accept me, wouldn't respect me, or wouldn't love me. And, at the same time, I long just to be loved and accepted for who I really am.

We wear our own facades, like Jacob in his smelly goatskins, seeking to be accepted or respected because of who people will think we are. We seek their blessings in disguise.

Then comes the time to do business with God, and he won't let us get away with it.

Before God will bless Jacob, Jacob has to tell him his name. Before God will bless Jacob, Jacob has to say — indeed, has to confess — "I am Jacob. Heel-grabber. Manipulator. Selfish. Cheat." *Then* God will bless him.

This is swimming upstream against both our instinct and our experience. Our instinct and experience in the rest of life is that we

285

fare better when we cover our blemish, when we conceal our weakness, when we hide our vices. But God will not bless us in disguise. God required Jacob to tell him his name, before God would bless him.

And *how* does God bless him? Glory be, God *changes* his name!

The Lord says, *"No longer shall you be called Jacob ... Now you will be called Israel — prince — for you have persevered with man and with God, and prevailed."*

Jacob has a new name: a name — an *identity* — born out of an encounter with God.

In the name "Israel," you see, the last syllable "el" represents one of the Hebrew words for God. "El." So, for example, "Beth-el" means "house of God." "Emmanu-el" means "God with us." "Ishma-el" means "God will hear." "Dani-el" means "God is my judge." And "Isra-el," the name that God gave to Jacob, literally means "God prevails."

So Jacob was changed from being named for himself and what he did to being named for God and what he does.

We come to do business with God this morning. We come to receive blessings from him. We find that there is no opportunity for a disguise with him. And, much to our relief, we discover that there is no *need* for a disguise with him!

We must confess our name — who we are, what we are — and we discover that, unlike the world around us, he loves us even knowing the truth about us.

Then he changes our name, our identity — from sinful to forgiven — from filthy to clean — from distant to close — from lost to found — from Jacob to Israel. Amen.

---

1. Charles Wesley, "Come, O Thou Traveler Unknown."

The Land Where
Our Fathers Had Lived

The story begins innocently enough. The writer of Genesis simply sets the stage with a reference to geography: "Jacob settled in the land where his father had lived as an alien, the land of Canaan" (37:1).

He settled in the land where his father had lived.

Jacob is the third generation of patriarchs by whom Israel's God was henceforth known. Several centuries later at the burning bush, for example, the Lord introduced himself to Moses as "the God of Abraham, the God of Isaac, and the God of Jacob" (Exodus 3:6). Jacob, his father, and his grandfather were the honored primogenitors of God's chosen people.

Abraham, you remember, was the Mespotamian man with whom God first initiated this covenant. Abraham's descendants would be God's people, and he would be their God. The covenant was not one of mutual exclusivity, however. For while God did intend to be their only God, and therefore exclusive in that sense, he did not necessarily intend to have them as an exclusive chosen people. Rather, he expressed to Abraham a more global purpose and mission: "in you all the families of the earth shall be blessed" (Genesis 12:3).

A key element of God's covenant with Abraham was the issue of land. Abraham was living in the land of Mesopotamia when God called him, but God required him to leave that land (Genesis 12:1). At several points along the way, God assured Abraham that he intended to give a different land to him and his descendants (Genesis 12:7; 13:14-17; 15:18-21; 17:8).

Abraham lived out his days as an alien there in that land of Canaan. By the time he died, the only plot of land that he could claim as his own was a field he had purchased so that he could acquire the cave within it as a burial ground for his wife, Sarah. But while only an acre or two may have been registered in his name at the county courthouse, God had promised to give his descendants possession of that whole land, as far as the eye could see.

Abraham and Sarah's son, Isaac, was the child of God's promise and the heir of God's covenant with Abraham. He, too, lived out his days as an alien, a sojourner, there in the land of Canaan.

We do not see much of Isaac in his own right. His character, it seems, is always as a supporting actor, never the star.

First, he plays the part of Abraham's son: the fulfillment of God's promise, the object of Ishmael's antagonism, and the symbol of God's great test of Abraham's faith and obedience.

Isaac's next major role is almost entirely offstage. Like those occasional television characters (Carlton, the doorman on *Rhoda*, Norm's wife on *Cheers*) who are recurring in their series and yet never actually seen, Isaac is invisible during the marvelous story of how God provided a wife for him.

And that marriage, then, leads to Isaac's third costarring role: dad.

Isaac married a woman named Rebekah, and she gave birth to twin boys. They were not identical twins, however. In truth, they could not have been much more different.

The firstborn was Esau. He came out conspicuously red and uncommonly hairy, and his appearance gave rise to his name, "Esau," which meant "hairy." At first blush, the name seems disappointing. In the preceding stories from Genesis, we have been introduced to marvelous and meaningful names. The baby Noah was named with profound expectation. Abraham's original name, Abram, was noble, and his new name from God was full of promise. Isaac's name was marked by good humor and joy. But "Esau"? How unimaginative. How ignoble.

And yet, Esau's name was a sight better than his younger brother's.

When the second child was born, in dramatic contrast to Esau, he was smooth skinned (see Genesis 27:11). And because he came out right on Esau's heels — literally — his parents named that second boy "Jacob," meaning "heel holder" or "supplanter." While Esau may have been named for a rather superficial trait, Jacob, it seems, was named for a character flaw.

As they grew up, the two young men were as different as their appearances. Esau was an outdoorsman — a hunter — a man who smelled like animals and fields. Jacob, however, was more manicured and genteel. In one episode, when Esau comes in from the fields, he finds Jacob in the kitchen. That snapshot captures each man in his own natural habitat.

With boys as different as Jacob and Esau were, it's easy to imagine that parental preferences and prejudices formed early. Unless parents are vigilant to avoid it, reputations in the home harden quickly, as each child stakes out exclusive claim to some territory. The smart one. The athletic one. The troublemaker. The clown.

Esau was out in the fields; Jacob was inside in the kitchen. Jacob was brains; Esau was brawn. And Jacob was mama's boy; while Esau, the man's man, was his father's favorite son.

What is it like for a boy to grow up knowing that his father prefers someone else? A growing boy so deeply and so naturally needs the approval and affection of his father. Young Jacob must have lived his childhood in a constant but futile effort to get the same kind of smile, the same rapport, the same approving slap on the back that Esau enjoyed from Isaac.

Finally, one day Jacob got from Isaac precisely the kind of treatment typically reserved for Esau. Indeed, Jacob quite literally took something that had been reserved for Esau: Isaac's special blessing. That moment of deception — that one final, desperate, heel-grabbing effort to come out first — was the last straw. Jacob had to run away from home, while Esau stewed, murmuring threats, and promising himself revenge.

Paternal favoritism — and being on the short end of it — was the harmful environment in which Jacob grew up. Then Jacob himself settled in that place, that pattern, where his father had lived.

We fast forward to today's Old Testament reading, and we see Jacob as a father himself. He has twelve sons and a daughter. He had lived for two decades in northern Mesopotamia with his uncle, Laban, but now he was back in the same land where his father had lived before him, living the same way.

Though Jacob himself had grown up with the pain of paternal favoritism, he still introduced that same pattern into his own home and inflicted that pain on his own children. Joseph was Jacob's favorite, and everybody knew it. And as though the disproportionate affection and approval were not apparent enough, Jacob's preferential treatment one day took on a visual aid.

Jacob gave Joseph a coat. On first hearing, that seems like a small thing, but in a day when new clothes were not so commonplace as they are today, this gift was a big deal. Furthermore, in a family of twelve sons, one suspects that hand-me-downs were the order of the day. Yet, here was an article of clothing that bypassed the older brothers and went straight to the favored Joseph. To make matters still worse, this coat was a distinctive one: colorful, distinguished, and probably expensive.

In a world of browns and grays, Joseph's colorful coat was as conspicuous as his father's preferential love. With that coat on, the other sons of Jacob literally could not look at Joseph without being reminded that he was the favored one. That fact, combined with Joseph's own precociousness, gnawed at them.

How striking is the phrase "they saw him from a distance." For the prodigal's father, that sight on the horizon set him running to embrace his beloved son (Luke 15:20). For these under-loved brothers, however, that sight was enough to prompt a murder conspiracy.

We get a measure of the brothers' animosity toward Joseph both in what they did and in what they almost did.

What they almost did was kill their brother — just as Esau had pledged to do to Jacob a generation before. What they did do — their alternative to outright fratricide — was to throw Joseph into a pit. Deep and dry, it would be a terrible and inescapable death. Reuben had a more merciful plan; but no one else, including Joseph himself, knew about it.

Perhaps the most telling image of Joseph's brothers came not in the moment when they threw him into the dreadful pit, but in what they did next. "Then they sat down to eat." It is a portrait of indifference and complacency. While their little brother cried out for mercy, they were filling their stomachs. Most of us find that our appetites are diminished by unpleasantness, tension, or strife, but not these boys. Nothing wrong with their stomachs; just something terribly wrong with their hearts.

Then, providentially, Joseph's life was spared by the arrival of a caravan. Judah reasoned with his brothers: "What profit is it if we kill our brother and conceal his blood? Come, let us sell him to the Ishmaelites, and not lay our hands on him, for he is our brother, our own flesh." Here is the motto of selfishness masquerading as ethics: What is the profit to us of this action or that? And here is the utter poverty of their consciences: that they conclude Joseph ought to be sold rather than killed since, after all, "he is our brother, our own flesh."

Long before modern social scientists began to talk about family systems and dysfunctional family patterns, God referenced the terrible phenomenon of the parents' iniquity affecting their children "to the third and the fourth generation" (Numbers 14:18). We see the tragic pattern played out here in this unredeemed display by the sons of Jacob. Isaac had played favorites among his sons, and it eventually erupted into the one brother seeking to kill the other. Then one brother had to leave home. Then that fugitive became a father, who also played favorites among his sons, where murder was also narrowly avoided.

Jacob had settled, you see, in the place and the pattern where his father had lived.

The stories about Jacob come rather early in Old Testament history. Further down the road, in the era of the divided monarchy, we find quick sketches and summaries of so many kings who ruled in Israel or Judah along the way. The biblical author employs a telling standard for offering a quick, thumbnail evaluation of those kings: The kings are compared to their fathers.

Abijam, the son of Rehoboam and great-grandson of David, is summarized thus: "He committed all the sins that his father did before him; his heart was not true to the Lord his God, like the heart of his father David" (1 Kings 15:3). Later, the Bible reports that King Asa of Judah "did what was right in the sight of the Lord, as his father David had done" (1 Kings 15:11). Meanwhile, King Ahaziah of Israel "did what was evil in the sight of the Lord, and walked in the way of his father and mother, and in the way of Jeroboam son of Nebat, who caused Israel to sin" (1 Kings 22:52).

What is the land where our fathers lived? What was the example, "the way," of our fathers and mothers?

Perhaps it was a life of faith, wisdom, and charity, and we do well to settle there, too. But perhaps it was not. Perhaps, instead, some of us are heirs to a legacy of addiction or abuse; of uneven love or misplaced priorities. Perhaps we have seen in ourselves how easy, how natural it is to settle in the same places and patterns — in the land where our fathers had lived.

Each generation must hear God's call anew. For some of us, that will mean a deliberate departure from the land — the life — where our fathers had lived; a departure to go to a new and different land that God will show us (Genesis 12:1).

Proper 15
Pentecost 13
Ordinary Time 20
Genesis 45:1-15

God's Providence:
The Long And Short Of It

We human beings are naturally fond of happy endings. We have an innate sense of the way things ought to be, and that part of us is profoundly satisfied when things turn out that way.

The episode that we read today from the story of Joseph is a classic happy ending.

It's a beautiful scene. The nearly blameless hero of the story, Joseph, has been finally rewarded for his wisdom and faithfulness, exalted to a high position of authority and prestige. After years of unjust suffering, he is comfortably situated. After almost unspeakable enmity between him and his brothers, we see this marvelous and emotional reunion. People who had been cruel are forgiven. People who had been antagonistic to one another now embrace one another. And a father whose heart had been broken by tragedy — and whose family had been broken by enmity — will see his son again and have his whole family reunited.

The events that lead up to this happy ending were entirely guided by the providence of God. Joseph is quite clear on that point. Five times in as many verses, Joseph makes explicit reference to what God has done: "God sent me before you to preserve life" (v. 5). "God sent me before you to preserve for you a remnant on earth, and to keep alive for you many survivors" (v. 7). "So it was not you who sent me here, but God" (v. 8). "(God) has made me a father to Pharaoh, and lord of all his house and ruler over all the land of Egypt" (v. 8). "God has made me lord of all Egypt" (v. 9).

But this happy ending was improbable — and the providential hand of God invisible — in the events that preceded this moment.

293

Rewind the tape just a little, and see how far removed Joseph once was from this good place and this happy ending.

Joseph grew up as the favorite son of a wealthy father. But he was not the only son of his father, and his father's favoritism worked against him in the minds and hearts of his older brothers. They resented Joseph's most-favored status. They objected to the special treatment he received, and they found intolerable the precociousness with which he spoke and conducted himself. Indeed, Joseph's brother so resented him that they sought to get rid of him. Permanently.

Their original plan was simply to murder him. It was unapologetic, unsophisticated, and cold-blooded. But after the one brother with a conscience intervened, they adopted Plan B: Throw Joseph into a pit in the middle of nowhere, where presumably he would starve to death and there would be no blood on their hands.

But then, over the horizon, along came a still-better option. A caravan appeared, and the traveling merchants provided a non-violent and happily profitable way for the sons of Jacob to rid themselves of Joseph. And so, not long afterward, Joseph was hundreds of miles from home, sold as a slave to Potiphar, an important and wealthy Egyptian.

Back home, the brothers took advantage of Joseph's distinctive coat to create an alibi. Pouring animal blood on it, they took it to their father as apparent evidence of Joseph having been attacked and devoured by some wild animal. So he was given up for dead. No one was out looking for him. There were no "Have you seen this child?" posters being distributed. No one was going to find him or rescue him. His situation was inarguably hopeless.

By any reasonable expectation, young Joseph knew that he would never go home again. He would never see his father again. And he would probably never be a free man again.

Then things got worse!

One day, while Joseph was doing his chores around his master's house, his master's wife approached him. Apparently this had happened before, on several occasions. When Potiphar was not around, his wife would flirt with Joseph and try to seduce him. And on this particular occasion, she was more insistent than usual.

The Bible recommends that we flee from temptation, and that is precisely what Joseph did. He did not hang around to indulge the flirtation, engage in witty repartee, or toy with double entendres. He did not go toe-to-toe with temptation; he ran away from it. As he sought to escape, she caught hold of his cloak and held on tight. Determined to get away, Joseph slipped out of that outer garment, leaving it behind in her hands.

Now, for the second time in his life, Joseph's outer garment was used to suggest an untruth about him. Angry and hurt, Potiphar's wife took Joseph's garment to her husband, claiming that Joseph had attempted to rape her. The article of clothing left behind was interpreted as tacit proof of her claim.

There's not much hope for justice when the master's wife brings an accusation against the foreign slave. Joseph was arrested and put in prison.

This part of the story, of course, is half of the reason why Joseph became one of the favorite characters for the children of Israel. Throughout their history, they identified with his experience of unjust suffering. They understood the righteous being wronged. When Jews through the centuries looked back and saw the honorable young man suffering, the innocent young man being punished, they nodded knowingly.

Meanwhile, the other half of the reason why the story of Joseph became a favorite for the people of God was the way that Joseph's troubles turned into Joseph's testimony. For in the end, the story of his suffering became a story of God's providence.

While Joseph sat in prison, he had occasion to meet two men who had been officials serving in the court of the king of Egypt. Joseph had a significant encounter with both of them during their briefly overlapping prison sentences, and one day, years later, one of those royal officials remembered Joseph, and brought him to the attention of the king.

By the end of Joseph's story, this foreign-born, one-time slave, one-time prisoner is the second-in-command over all of Egypt. He rides in the king's chariot, and he wears the king's ring. He is an internationally known figure, whose wisdom and leadership influences the entire region, saves countless lives, and changes the economy and shape of Egyptian life for generations to come.

That brings us to the beautiful happy-ending scene that is our Old Testament lection today. Joseph is reconciled to his brothers, who repent, and whom he forgives. He is able to invite his whole family to join him in Egypt, where they settle on the best land in the entire country. He is reunited with his father: able to live with and provide for his father during the final years of his life, able to have his father meet and bless his own children, and able to be at his father's side when he dies.

But go back and consider again Joseph sitting there in that Egyptian dungeon. Calculate how far he was from every good thing. How far was he from his home back in Canaan? He had no realistic hope of returning there ever again. How far was he from his family? His brothers hated him, and his father thought he was dead. How far was he from Potiphar's elegant home — from that pleasant environment, from that level of responsibility, from that degree of freedom, such as it was? All of that was gone for good. A foreign slave convicted of attempted rape on his master's wife: that profile isn't given a second chance.

As he sat there in that dungeon, how unimaginably far was Joseph from the king's throne and chariot? From power and importance? From the best land in all of Egypt? An impossible distance.

Here is a thing we need to understand about ourselves: Distances are very important to us. From the time we are children, we pester our parents from the back seat: How much farther? Are we there yet?

But that standard fare from children is not limited to children. When something we hope for as adults seems a long way off, we get discouraged and wonder if we'll ever get there. When we sense that it's close — that we're close, that we're almost there — then we take heart and feel encouraged.

The only reason children are always asking, "How much farther?" is because they can't calculate it for themselves. As adults, however, we are always calculating how much further something is, for distances are very important to us.

Distances are important to us, you see, because we believe that distance makes a difference. And, of course, it does make a difference to us.

But it doesn't make a difference to God. As people of faith, that is a truth that we need to embrace. In God's providence, a thing is not more likely because it is close, and it is not less likely because it is far away.

At first blush, that seems like foolishness. What manner of blind faith is required to ignore reality and to deny improbability? But this is not ignoring the earthly reality; rather, it is affirming God's reality.

In some science class along the way, we learned about the concept of significant numbers. If I am measuring the distance between my house and my children's school, a tenth of a mile is a significant number. If I am measuring the distance from the Earth to some other galaxy, however, a tenth of a mile is no longer significant.

Likewise, against the vastness of God's knowledge and God's power, the seemingly great distances in our lives are just tenths of miles. They are not significant numbers to him.

So, let me ask you: What are the impossible distances in your life today? What good thing seems so far away it is unreachable? It may be in your marriage or some friendship. It may be in your finances or your physical health. It may even be in your relationship with God.

From where you're at this morning, it may be very easy for you to imagine where Joseph was at, for you may also be at a place where you don't want to be and didn't expect to be. You may be in a place that is a long, long way from where you once were or from where you want to be.

Trust that distance to the providence of God. Then hold on for an unbelievable ride. Amen.

Proper 16
Pentecost 14
Ordinary Time 21
Exodus 1:8—2:10

Endless Line Of Blunder

Turn the page, and the story is suddenly different.

When we close the book of Genesis, the descendants of Jacob — that is, the children of Israel — are comfortably situated as honored guests in the land of Egypt. And the very best part of the land of Egypt, at that. Jacob's son, Joseph, is a local hero, having navigated the nation (and much of the region) through a devastating period of famine. The Egyptians, along with his own kin, mourn his passing.

But turn the page, and the story is suddenly different.

We open the book of Exodus, and in almost no time we see that the Israelites' circumstances have changed dramatically. The Bible reports that "a new king arose over Egypt, who did not know Joseph." Joseph was gone; the Pharaoh who knew Joseph's significance was gone. And so, under the rubric of "how soon they forget," the new administration casts a dim eye toward those relatives of Joseph who comprise a significant minority within the land of Egypt.

It seems to come naturally to human beings to be afraid of minorities within our midst. The pages of history books and newspapers reflect our uneasiness with minorities. That is true not just in the United States, but all over the world.

Almost by definition, the minority threatens the status quo. They represent something different, so their growth in number or in influence signals change. What will become of our neighborhood, our community, our country, our way of life if "they" take over?

299

That is the natural fear of the majority. And that was the fear of Egypt's pharaoh.

He observed (and probably exaggerated, as our fears and prejudices tend to do) the foreign population within his land. "Look, the Israelite people are more numerous and more powerful than we." If that had been factually correct, of course, then the Egyptians could not have so easily conscripted them into forced labor.

Then the pharaoh looked down the road and imagined the danger that those foreigners represented. "They will increase and, in the event of war, join our enemies and fight against us."

The biblical author, who, as a rule, does not airbrush the blemished people of God, gives us no indication that the pharaoh's fears were well founded. Yet, the large minority in one's midst is intimidating. What could conceivably happen morphs in our minds into what will certainly happen, and something has to be done to stop it. And so, in effect, the dog that has never bitten anyone is put down simply because he has the teeth to do it.

Is the threat to our security mere rationale for our racism, or is the racism born out of insecurity? Whatever the chicken and egg, the pharaoh devised a plan — "Come, let us deal shrewdly with them" — in order to solve the perceived problem.

Our fears, distilled, are not necessarily hateful or unreasonable. And our desire to maintain the status quo, our way of life, or our sense of security, is not innately sinister. But when our fears carelessly personify the threat that they feel, they turn into sloppy and odious prejudices. Then begins a vicious cycle: Our prejudices expand our fears, and our fears fuel our prejudices.

It serves us right then, I suppose, that our hatreds so often turn around and haunt us. The Egyptians forced their former guests into bondage, but only to find that "the more they were oppressed, the more they multiplied and spread." So what began as fear turned to prejudice; and prejudice turned to hate and cruelty; but in spite of their cruelty, the oppressors only experienced more fear: "the Egyptians came to dread the Israelites."

Pharaoh himself showed how easily haunted we are by our hatreds. When the midwives were unwilling to carry out his murderous instructions, they crafted a certain lie about the Hebrew women: namely, that they were "not like the Egyptian women; for they are vigorous and give birth before the midwife comes to them." It was not true, but it was plausible, you see, to the prejudiced. For in the fearful component of our hatreds, we are willing to believe extraordinary things about "them," whoever they may be.

We recognize that this is one of the calling cards of racist propaganda. "We" are warned about what "they" are like; what "they" can do; and what "they" could become. Their physical prowess, their financial shrewdness, their conspiratorial connectedness, their duplicitous character; even their quiet, workmanlike ambition: Whatever their broad-brush characteristics may be, we can paint it as a suspicious and treacherous trait.

So it is that this large community of dangerously prolific and mysteriously strong Israelites haunted pharaoh. So he turned to this drastic measure: "Every boy that is born to the Hebrews you shall throw into the Nile."

The scene is almost too gruesome to imagine: the helpless and innocent children, the grieving families, the carnage. We are reminded of the New Testament tyrant who also ordered the murder of baby boys (Matthew 2:16), although he failed to kill the one baby he so feared. And, likewise, this pharaoh's edict did not eliminate the baby who would become the greatest threat to Egypt's security.

Obviously, the pharaoh did not know the God with whom he was dealing. In his typically human calculations, he feared the size and strength of the Hebrew people, and so he sought to reduce their numbers. But ask Goliath how much size matters. Ask Gideon what difference numbers make. Ask the boy with the bread and fish how much the Lord can do with a small amount. The pharaoh sought to thin out the Israelite community, but one baby got through, and that one baby was enough for God to free the entire nation.

In the short-term plot of Exodus' story, this hideous decree from the throne serves as the backdrop for God's providence. The baby Moses is miraculously spared the death sentence. The very water that was death to his generation becomes his transit to the providential setting God had for him: namely, that he was discovered and adopted by the pharaoh's own daughter.

In the long-term plot of human history, however, the pharaoh's decree to kill the baby Hebrew boys plays a different role, for there is a larger pattern here. This anonymous king of Egypt is the first in a very long line of antagonists who have endeavored to snuff out God's chosen people. In every epoch, it seems, some tyrant has made this his mission. And every one of them has failed.

From Haman to Hitler, the Jews have been targeted by those who wanted to eradicate them. As with Israel, the church has always had enemies seeking its extinction.

In the Old and New Testaments alike, there is something marvelously improbable about the people of God.

In the Old Testament, God begins with an old man, who has no children and owns no land. How many millions of anonymous men have lived and died like that, and their footprints have been completely erased by the passage of time. But God chose this particular wandering Aramaen, and 4,000 years later whole nations trace their lineage back to him.

Likewise, in the New Testament, the Lord began with a handful of Galilean nobodies. By human standards, they had no power, no importance, and no influence. In short, they were, by any ordinary standard, insignificant. And yet, taken as a group, Jesus' twelve disciples are arguably the most famous group of men in history. They are portrayed in more paintings, windows, and statues than any other collection of human beings. Around the globe, hospitals, churches, cities, and countless people are named after them.

How feeble did Judah look as Assyria was bearing down on it? Jerusalem figured to be just one more notch in Sennacherib's cruel belt. Yet to this day, Jerusalem and her inhabitants still stand. For centuries, most of what we knew about the once mighty (and long gone) Assyrians was the record of them preserved in the books of those seemingly feeble people whom they sought to conquer.

How puny and vulnerable did those early disciples look when the local potentate, Herod, beheaded John the Baptist, killed James, and imprisoned Peter? Yet now, two millennia later, Herod's only real legacy is at the points where he crossed paths with these seeming nobodies within his jurisdiction.

The same leaders who had conspired to have Jesus arrested and crucified endeavored to silence his earliest followers. Then, a few years later, the Roman emperors began to set their aim against the church. Employing the considerable resources, cruelty, and coercion at its disposal, Rome sought to crush the followers of Jesus. Yet the Sanhedrin is gone; the Roman Empire is gone; and the Church of Jesus Christ lives on in every corner of the globe.

Within the relatively narrow confines of the twentieth century, the Soviet Union came and went. The God it sought to outlaw continued to be worshiped. The gospel it sought to silence continued to be shared. And the church that was there for centuries before the Soviet Union existed continues now for decades after its demise.

Turn the page, and the story is always the same. Small-minded and frightened antagonists, who endeavor to snuff out God's word and God's people. Pharaoh and Nebuchadnezzar, Sennacherib and Haman, Nero and Trajan, Hitler and Stalin, and more today, and more tomorrow — the tyrants come and go. Their plots prevail for a moment. But God's purpose endures — and therefore God's people endure. So Samuel Stone sang:

> *The Church shall never perish!*
> *Her dear Lord to defend,*
> *To guide, sustain, and cherish,*
> *Is with her to the end:*
> *Though there be those who hate her,*
> *And false sons in her pale,*
> *Against both foe or traitor*
> *She ever shall prevail.*[1]

When the Sanhedrin was weighing their options against the early followers of Christ, old Gamaliel cautioned them: "I tell you, keep away from these men and let them alone; because if this plan or this undertaking is of human origin, it will fail; but if it is of God, you will not be able to overthrow them — in that case you may even be found fighting against God!" (Acts 5:38-39).

The pharaoh did not have Gamaliel's wisdom whispered in his ear. And so, as he tried to crush the people of God who lived in his midst, he became the first in a long line of fools: tyrants in every age who have endeavored to fight against God. An endless line of blunder. Amen.

---

1. Samuel J. Stone, "The Church's One Foundation," 1866.

The Names By Which He Is Known

When I was about six years old, I made friends with a boy named Danny. At the lake community where our family spent our summer vacation, the house where Danny's family stayed was right across the street from the house where we stayed. Because we were not year-round neighbors, the families did not know each other at all, but Danny and I eventually met and began to play together.

One day, when we were playing catch together, the ball got away from us and rolled over near where my sister happened to be sitting. Not knowing my sister's name, Danny called out to her, "Hey, David's sister, could you please toss us that ball?"

My sister, who was seven years older, was amused by the appellation, and so it stuck. From that time on, among the kids in the two families, she was known as "David's sister."

And the pattern grew. Next there was "Danny's brother." Then "Danny's other brother." And then, of course, there was "Danny's mother" and "Danny's father," as well as "David's mother" and "David's father." We even had "David's sister's dog."

The pattern continued for several summers as our families vacationed across the street from each other. It was a playful way that the members of the two families referred to one another.

What we did playfully for a few years, however, is what Israel did quite seriously for centuries. Danny's brother, Jeff, was not known by his own name: He was known as Danny's brother. And, likewise, the Lord was not known by his name: He was known as Israel's God.

Our Old Testament text for today is a portion of the famous burning bush event. Moses, who was a fugitive from Egypt where he had killed a man, had settled among the Midianites. There he met and married a woman, and he lived with her family, caring for the flocks of his father-in-law, Jethro.

One day, while he was tending the flock, Moses' attention was suddenly captured by a strange sight.

The occasion reminds us, of course, of the marvelous versatility of our God. He appears to and calls Isaiah in the temple, but he is not limited to working in such a designated sacred space. He calls Gideon in his hiding place, the fishermen and the tax collector at their work, young Samuel in his bed, and Saul/Paul right on the path of his well-meaning and zealous opposition to God. So, here, Moses is walking along, literally minding his own business, when the Lord gets his attention with this strange phenomenon.

The sight that Moses turned aside to see was a bush: specifically, a bush that was on fire. Yet while it appeared to be burning, it was not burning up. Moses moved toward it to take a closer look, at which point the Lord called out to him from the bush.

The Lord began by calling Moses by name. We may take that for granted, and yet it remains an unnecessarily personal touch. Calling someone by name may be required in order to get a person's attention, the Lord already had Moses' attention there at the bush. He could have begun speaking without personally naming Moses, much as the angel over Bethlehem began speaking without calling the shepherds by name.

Interestingly, the Lord speaks Moses' name twice. Obviously, most salutations do not repeat the person's name, but it is a pattern that occurs several times in scripture. And the repetition — "Moses, Moses!" — seems to convey a certain affection and urgency: Samuel, Samuel (1 Samuel 3:4); Martha, Martha (Luke 10:41); Simon, Simon (Luke 22:31); and Saul, Saul (Acts 9:4).

Next, the Lord introduced himself to Moses. This strongly suggests that Moses had not heard the Lord speak to him prior to this occasion. Introductions are the sort of thing that only occur once between two people, unless they have forgotten each other; and that doesn't happen with God.

While the record we have of Moses' early life surely assumes God's providential hand in his life, there is no earlier indication that God had spoken to him. This appears to be the first time. And on the numerous subsequent occasions when the Lord spoke to Moses, he did not introduce himself again as he does here in this, their first meeting.

This encounter at the burning bush is especially distinctive, for in the end the Lord introduces himself twice.

At the outset, God introduces himself this way: "I am the God of your father, the God of Abraham, the God of Isaac, and the God of Jacob." Then, as the episode unfolds, God calls Moses to return to Egypt as the instrument of his deliverance, and Moses responds with resistance. He feels unqualified and ill-equipped, and so he raises a series of objections. And among them, Moses expresses this concern: "If I come to the Israelites and say to them, 'The God of your ancestors has sent me to you,' and they ask me, 'What is his name?' what shall I say to them?"

God had called Moses by name. And God had introduced himself to Moses. Still Moses did not know God's name.

This detail may elude us in our reading, for we may have lost, in our own practice and prayer, the distinction between names and titles. We use his titles freely — God, Lord, Savior, Redeemer, Father, and such — and we may use them as though they were his name. But Moses perceived the fact of the matter: He did not know God's name.

On this occasion, therefore, God disclosed his name to Moses and, by extension, to his people: "I AM WHO I AM.... Thus you shall say to the Israelites, 'I AM has sent me to you.'"

Several eventful months later, Moses was back on that same mountain to meet with God. With the Israelites camped below, God gave to Moses there on that mountain his commandments, which would form the basis of his covenant with his people. Included among those fundamental commandments was this high-ranking instruction: "You shall not make wrongful use of the name of the Lord your God, for the Lord will not acquit anyone who misuses his name" (Exodus 20:7). And, somewhat later, the penalty phase of this important command is revealed: "One who blasphemes the name of the Lord shall be put to death; the whole congregation shall stone the blasphemer. Aliens as well as citizens, when they blaspheme the Name, shall be put to death" (Leviticus 24:16).

So it is that the Old Testament people of God had a sense for the importance, the holiness, and the power of God's name. They knew it as majestic (Psalm 8:1), as their protection (Psalm 20:1), as their source of help (Psalm 124:8), as their refuge (Proverbs 18:10), as their pride (Psalm 20:7), and as worthy of praise (Psalm 113:3).

That wonderful name was revealed to Moses at the burning bush. And that episode presents us with a noteworthy sequence of events: a sequence that may be a universal pattern.

At the end of the episode, Moses knows God by name. It's personal and it's powerful. But at the beginning of the episode, that's not the case. God knows Moses by name, but Moses does not know God in that personal way. In order to introduce himself to Moses, God says, "I am the God of your father, the God of Abraham, the God of Isaac, and the God of Jacob."

In short, before Moses knows God by his name, he knows God by other names: specifically, the names of other people.

This is not a mystery; this is quite natural. We understand this sequence from our own day-to-day human interactions. For when we introduce ourselves to another person for the first time, we often do it in reference to some third-party. Since we are unknown to the individual we're meeting, we identify ourselves, if possible, with someone who is known to them.

To a friend of my daughter, I introduce myself as "Angela's dad." To a friend of my wife, I introduce myself as "Karen's husband." To the nurse outside a patient's door, I introduce myself as that patient's pastor.

If I say, "Hello, I'm David," that might mean nothing to one of my daughter's friends. When I introduce myself as Angela's father, however, then I make a connection. Such was God's approach with Moses. He did not begin by introducing himself by name;

Moses didn't know him yet. Instead, he began by introducing himself by other people's names: Abraham, Isaac, Jacob.

This is, you know, always the nature of our experience with God. You and I were not born with a knowledge of the Lord; we came to know him. And we did not come to know him in a vacuum; we were introduced to him by someone else. We were taught about him, led to him, and nurtured in our relationship with him by someone else. Indeed, probably by dozens of other people.

Before he is known by his name, he is known by someone else's name. Before he was my God, he was the God of my father. Before I know him as my God, I might know him first as "Danny's God."

See, then, how our testimony circles around to become our responsibility.

When I bear witness to God's work in my life, I discover that his work has been done through so very many people along the way. Some of them have an idea how God used them in my life. Some others have no idea. But they are the names by which he was known to me: He was their God before he was my God.

And now he is my God. He and I have been introduced. It is a personal relationship. I know him by name.

Since he is my God now, there is a good chance that he will be known by my name. There are a great many people who don't know him yet, but they know me. And for some, I may be their only association with him.

Likewise with you — for some friend or family member or neighbor or coworker — someone in your life who does not know the Lord personally only knows him right now as your Lord. You and I are among the names by which he is known. Amen.

Eat And Run

At some time or another, we've all had to hurry through a meal and hurry away from the table. And so, at some time or another, we've all found ourselves saying, "I hate to eat and run, but...."

Everybody has done it. Everybody knows what it's like.

But even though everyone says he hates to eat and run, the truth is that not everyone does hate it. Some folks rather like it.

As a little boy, I liked to eat and run in the summertime. When the weather is warm and it stays light later, dinner is just an interruption for a young boy. And so I'd be reluctant to come in from playing when my mother would call me for dinner; and as soon as I was finished, I would look for the first opportunity to be excused so that I could go back outside and play some more.

As a boy, I liked to eat and run.

Children so often do, you know. Parents are forever telling their children not to wolf it down, to chew their food properly, and not to eat so fast. I think of my three young daughters as rather civilized eaters, and yet the first one to finish dinner on a given evening is likely to call out, "I won!" Children like to eat and run.

And there are a good many of us adults who like to eat and run, too. We feel so busy, or so pressured, or so involved in our work that stopping to eat feels like an interruption. Consequently, some folks stop working just long enough to sit down and eat, and then they go right back to work. There are still others who do not even stop to eat: They eat while they work, and they work while they eat. They don't so much "eat and run" as they do "eat on the run."

Truth be told: We live in a culture that likes to eat and run. We are surrounded by fast-food restaurants, drive-thru windows, restaurants that promise speedy delivery, and microwaveable food. It's an eat-and-run culture.

I suspect that that's not best for us. I'm not an expert on either digestion or nutrition, but I do suspect that eating and running — or eating on the run — is not the healthiest way to do it. Rather, I imagine that it's healthier to take time to eat, and time to digest. And I suspect that the eat-and-run approach of our culture is partly to blame for our indigestion, our heartburn, our overeating, and our fat.

Still, for all of that, God wants his people to eat and run. Or at least he did one night some 3,000 years ago.

That night — and that meal — was the occasion we know as Passover. That was Israel's night to eat and run.

The children of Israel had been slaves in Egypt since the generation after Joseph. By this point in the story, their bondage had lasted 400 years, with no end in sight. But on this particular night, Moses gave the people specific and unusual instructions from God. There was a certain menu that they were to prepare: lamb, bread, and bitter herbs. There was a specified way of preparing it, as well: the lamb was to be roasted, and the bread unleavened. And, too, there was a certain way that they were supposed to eat this prescribed meal: "This is how you shall eat it: your loins girded, your sandals on your feet, and your staff in your hand; and you shall eat it hurriedly."

See the picture in your mind's eye of elegant dining. You arrive at a fine restaurant where you get out of your car at the front door, leaving your vehicle to be parked by the valet. Just inside the door, an attendant checks your coat. You are greeted and seated. You sit comfortably, perusing a menu of select delicacies. And, as your server graciously brings course after course, you enjoy a leisurely dining experience.

By contrast, see this Passover. No valet will park your car; instead, you'll need to keep your keys in hand as you eat so that you'll be prepared to make a hasty exit. Your coat is not checked, either. On the contrary, you'd better keep it on while you eat, for you may have to leave at any minute. It's not a broad menu to peruse: There's just one dish we're serving. There's certainly no time for enjoying a leisurely meal: shovel it in, eat it quickly, and wolf it down, for you may need to be out the door in a matter of moments.

The hurry-up feel of that evening meal was in stark contrast to all that had come before. The children of Israel had been in bondage there in Egypt for four centuries. Imagine that: the equivalent of continuous slavery from the time of Rembrandt's birth to the present! Four hundred years of the descendants of Jacob sitting down, night after night, year after year, to their meager evening meals in bondage. The pain and drudgery of living and dying in slavery; and night after night passed without relief; generation after generation passed without deliverance.

But now, suddenly, they had to hurry?

It's possible, too, that the people were feeling more despairing than hopeful that night. After all, even when it seemed that deliverance finally arrived, it became an exercise in patience and waiting.

How high were their hopes when Moses first appeared on the scene: when he went to Pharaoh on their behalf, speaking God's word and performing God's wonders? Yet, Pharaoh was unmoved, and their situation was unchanged. Except that, initially, it actually changed for the worse.

The treadmill continued, plague after plague. Egypt and her king were like a boxer who kept taking body blows but refused to go down. And while you and I know how the story turned out, for the people who were living it, the prospect of freedom must have seemed more and more remote with every setback into Pharaoh's stubbornness and hard-heartedness. So often the people had had their hopes up; and so often those hopes had been dashed, as their ball-and-chain reality persisted.

But now, after so much fruitless waiting, suddenly the Hebrews were put on high alert. After an eternity on the tarmac, now the captain wants us to fasten our seat belts and believe that we're actually going to take off?

Across their slave ghetto in Egypt that night, the Hebrews slaughtered their lambs and slathered the blood on their doors. With coats on and walking sticks in hand, they ate their meal in haste. Outside, the wails of grief could be heard from Egyptian households, and in the middle of the night, Moses was summoned to Pharaoh's presence. It was over. The king of Egypt surrendered to the singular God of Abraham, Isaac, and Jacob. The Israelites were finally free.

For us as Christians, the occasion of the Passover meal naturally reminds us of Jesus' Last Supper and, by extension, the sacrament of the Lord's Supper. Jesus and his disciples were in the midst of celebrating that commemorative holiday meal, when Jesus embarked on words and actions so familiar to us, but undoubtedly strange and troubling to the disciples.

The Jewish observance of the Passover meal had acquired layers of symbolic elements and practices, and from its inception it was clearly understood as a teaching tool — "When your children ask you, 'What do you mean by this observance?' " (Exodus 12:26). But in Jesus' association of the bread with his body and the cup with his blood, the old Jewish Passover meal took on new meaning for us as Christians. For us, it is not the symbolism of unleavened bread that is meaningful but rather the symbolism of broken bread. We do not partake of the lamb and the bitter herbs, but only the bread and the cup.

The Lord specified to Moses and the people that "this day shall be a day of remembrance for you. You shall celebrate it as a festival to the Lord; throughout your generations you shall observe it as a perpetual ordinance." And we are reminded likewise of the ordinance of Christ at the Last Supper: "Do this, as often as you drink it, in remembrance of me" (1 Corinthians 11:25).

Meanwhile, the symbolism of the original Passover event plainly reminds us of our salvation. The central role of a male lamb without blemish and the idea of being saved by "the blood of the Lamb" is part of our gospel vocabulary as Christians. Even in New Testament times, the earliest Christians had already begun to identify Jesus as "our paschal lamb" (1 Corinthians 5:7).

While the occasion of the Passover meal reminds us of Jesus' Last Supper, and the symbolism of the Passover event reminds us of our salvation, the style of the Passover meal should prompt us to think of something else. Something future, not past.

You and I do not await our deliverance from slavery in Egypt. Neither do we need to wait for the salvation that is offered in Christ. Yet we do wait. Night after night, generation after generation, century after century, we wait.

One day, Jesus told his disciples what would happen to him in Jerusalem, and within a few months it had occurred. Jesus told them that he would rise again, and within three days of his death he had. Jesus told the disciples to tarry in Jerusalem until they were clothed with power from on high, and within two months came the Day of Pentecost.

Jesus also told his followers that he would return.

It did not happen as quickly as they expected.

Soon the apostles needed to begin answering the churches' questions about the believers who had died, about Christ's delay, and about life in the meantime.

After so long a wait, it would be an easy thing — natural, really — for us to live with diminished expectations. To let one day flow mindlessly into the next, with no real hope that today might be the day.

Jesus anticipated that possibility, that risk. He noted that the servant might observe, "My master is delayed in coming" (Luke 12:45), and consequently neglect his duties. But scripture warns us again and again that his coming will be sudden and unexpected (see Matthew 24:44; Mark 13:36; 1 Thessalonians 5:2). And so we are exhorted to "be ready" (Luke 12:40), "keep awake" (Matthew 25:13), and "be alert" (Luke 21:36).

The ancient Israelites were told, on the night of Passover, to eat the bread of haste, to dine with coat on and staff in hand, and to eat quickly, for they needed to be ready to leave. You and I, today, are not told to eat like that; we are instructed to live like that. To live each day with a posture of readiness, "because your redemption is drawing near" (Luke 21:28). Amen.

315

Proper 19
Pentecost 17
Ordinary Time 24
Exodus 14:19-31

Do You See What I See?

In 1956, director/producer Cecil B. DeMille tried to do in motion pictures what artists had attempted to do for centuries on canvas: capture this moment.

It is the ancient writer of the book of Exodus who reports and describes the moment for us. And the children of Israel, in prayers and songs for centuries afterward, remembered the moment, and the God who brought it all to pass.

The Hebrew people, newly freed from their slavery in Egypt, had just begun their journey toward the promised land. They would go by way of Mount Sinai, where they would receive God's law.

If the people had charted their own course, their logical choice would have been to travel the shortest distance between the two points of their origin and their destination. Leaving Egypt in the west, they would have traveled due east across the northern edge of the Sinai Peninsula, and straight into the land of Canaan, which God had promised to their ancestors, Abraham, Isaac, and Jacob.

But the people were not charting their own course. Instead, God led them on this journey, guiding them daily with a massive pillar. In the daytime, that pillar was a cloud that they could see and follow. In the nighttime, the pillar was made of fire, enabling them to travel even in the dark.

It must have been a great comfort to Moses and the people: this visible phenomenon that accompanied and led them all along the way. Perhaps there are times in our lives when we wish God's guidance were not so obvious. But for his people in the wilderness, that daily pillar must have been greatly reassuring.

While their destination was to the northeast, God began by leading them south and southeast. He had made an appointment to meet with them at Mount Sinai, which was in the southern part of the Sinai Peninsula. And, too, he knew that the more direct route would also mean more battles for the people (Exodus 13:17-18). And so, in order to keep them from becoming discouraged, the Lord detoured his people around those conflicts.

The decision to head south, however, soon appeared to be a strategic mistake. At least to human eyes. The Egyptian pharaoh, for whom surrender was the momentary exception rather than the rule, had reconsidered his decision to let the slaves go. And so, with an army of chariots in his wake, the pharaoh set off in hot pursuit of the Hebrews. When he caught up with them, he found them camped by the shores of the Red Sea.

The Israelites seemed trapped. On the one side was the dominating military force mustered by the king of Egypt. On the other side was the substantial body of water. And caught in the middle were the children of Israel, whose recent feeling of deliverance and victory turned suddenly into despair.

If God had led them by the more direct route, they would not have encountered the Red Sea, and they would not be trapped. In DeMille's movie, *The Ten Commandments*, the pharaoh sees the situation and observes, "The God of Moses is a poor general to leave him no retreat."

Retreat, however, is a relative thing. What looked like no escape to the pharaoh — and to the panicking Hebrews, for that matter — was no problem for God. For the Lord did not intend for his people to retreat, but to move forward. That massive pillar, which had been exclusively in front of the Israelites up until that moment, moved around behind them, protecting their flank. It separated the Hebrews from their pursuers all night long. Meanwhile, back at the beach, the Lord sent a strong east wind to blow across the waters of the Red Sea. All night long, the wind blew. And it blew with such force and effect that it created a path of dry ground, in the midst of what had been the sea, on which the people could walk to the other side.

Every portrayal of this event is necessarily abbreviated. A portrait can only be a snapshot, and a movie scene can only be a few minutes long. But this was an event that lasted all night long, and it must have been a sight to behold.

I certainly believe that God could have provided a more instantaneous way to defeat the Egyptians or to deliver the Israelites. If by saying "Let there be," he brings whole worlds into being, then he certainly did not need an entire night to part the Red Sea. Yet rather than a miracle in a moment, he chose a process that took all night. Perhaps there was some mercy in that, for it afforded the Egyptians plenty of opportunity to recalculate and retreat. They did not. But then their king was stubborn and proud, and those two traits seldom recalculate and seldom retreat.

Skeptics have long been uneasy with this miraculous account. The parting of the Red Sea seems, on its face, so improbable to them that they search for alternate explanations.

Of course, finding an alternate explanation does not, by itself, rule out the hand of God or the purpose of God. In *The Ten Commandments*, the pharaoh tries to find alternate explanations for the plagues that had beset his land. "When the Nile ran red, I too was afraid," he admits to Moses. "Until word came of a mountain beyond the cataracts, which spewed red mud and poisoned the water.... Was it the wonder of your God that fish should die and frogs should leave the waters? Was it a miracle that flies and lice should bloat upon their carrion and spread disease in both man and beast? These things were ordered by themselves, and not by any god."

The skeptic believes that if events can be explained by nature, then they were natural; not supernatural. Meanwhile, if the events seem to contravene nature and its laws, then the report of those events must be fabricated or exaggerated.

Belief came late to the skeptical Egyptians. Too late.

After the Lord had blown a dry path for the Israelites, they began their journey to the other side. Meanwhile, after giving his own people a good head start, the Lord must have removed the barrier from in front of the Egyptians. For while they were kept away from the Israelites through the night while the wind blew, pharaoh's chariots were suddenly free to pursue the Israelites down into the dry bed of the Red Sea.

Then the Bible reports that the Lord "threw the Egyptian army into panic" and "clogged their chariot wheels so that they turned with difficulty." At that late moment, the doomed enemies of God's people finally came to a great realization: "Let us flee from the Israelites, for the Lord is fighting for them against Egypt."

Surely this is among the most slow-witted statements in all of human history.

Egypt had suffered a series of plagues that had left it decimated, and each step had been predicted by that man of God, Moses. That same God had sent darkness on the land, which distinguished between the Egyptians and the Israelites for three days. He had sent a pestilence that killed Egyptian animals but spared the animals of the Israelites. And then, in the final, lethal blow, that same God had caused the death of the firstborn in every Egyptian household, while the Hebrew homes had been passed over.

Then, some few days later, at the site of the Red Sea, that God had created a barrier to protect the children of Israel from the chasing chariots of the pharaoh. And then, in the meantime, he parted a body of water so that those people could cross to the other side on dry ground.

After all of that, when their chariot wheels are stuck in the mud and their fate is sealed, finally it dawned on the Egyptians: "The Lord is fighting for them against Egypt."

Very good. What gave you your first clue?

Jonathan Swift wrote, "There's none so blind, as they that won't see."[1] Pharaoh and his cohorts would not see. Miracle after miracle, they just would not see. Or at least they did not recognize and understand what they were seeing.

They are not alone. Some of those who witnessed the Day of Pentecost event there in Jerusalem saw the Spirit manifest and move in unprecedented ways, yet they chalked it all up to wine (Acts 2:12-13). Some who watched Christ himself going about doing good reckoned that it was the work of Beelzebul (Luke 11:15). So very often people see God at work without recognizing it; without recognizing him.

But where the magicians saw magic, where pharaoh saw nature, and where the skeptic sees exaggeration, Moses and the Israelites saw the hand of God. They all looked at the same things, but they did not see the same things.

I once created a kind of word search puzzle on a blackboard for a church youth group. I carefully designed it so that it had no English words of more than two or three letters in length. What it did have hidden within it, however, was the standard conjugation of the Latin verb "to love." Any first year Latin student would recognize the familiar forms. Anyone who didn't know Latin, however, would be stupefied.

The assembled group of teenagers sat and sat, trying to find words of significant length in the word search puzzle that I had created. Then, like a dream, one young man — the only one in the group, it turned out, who had taken Latin — walked in a few minutes late.

"Mike," I asked him, "what do you see here on the board?"

"I see the conjugation of *amo*," he replied immediately, "but I don't know what all those other letters around it mean."

He had made my point for me. You can only see what you know, but you don't always know what you see. If you know Latin, you see it in the puzzle. But if you don't know Latin, then you don't know what you're looking at. It's still there, but you don't recognize it, because you don't know it.

Likewise for us human beings: for pharaoh and Moses; for the skeptics and the believers. The man or woman of God looks at circumstances and events, and they recognize the hand of God there. The person who does not know God, however, doesn't see him, even though he is at work. Amen.

---

1. Jonathan Swift, *Swift's Polite Conversation*, with introduction, notes, and extensive commentary by Eric Partridge (London: Andre Deutch, 1963), p. 61.

Proper 20
Pentecost 18
Ordinary Time 25
Exodus 16:2-15

Sentimental Slaves

Let me ask you to do a little remembering today. I don't know specifically what it is that I'm asking you to remember: that will vary with each individual. In general, though, here is the assignment: I want you to remember "the good old days."

What comes to mind when you hear that phrase? What time? What place? What period of your life and experience first occurs to you when you hear a reference to "the good old days"?

When our oldest daughter was just five years old, she was sitting with my wife and me watching some of our home movies from the time when she was a baby and a toddler. After we had watched for a while, she sighed wistfully, and said, "I wish I could be a baby again!"

At that moment I recognized that you don't have to have lived very long — you don't have to be very old — in order to have the experience of looking back with longing, of remembering some "good old days."

I think it comes naturally to us as human beings. I don't believe that every yesterday is better than every tomorrow, but I do think that it is part of our nature to long for former times. Perhaps that was an instinct the human race acquired when our first parents were evicted from Eden. Perhaps it has been part of our emotional DNA ever since to long for better days gone by.

If you've found yourself in a group of people who share a common past, you know the group dynamics of reminiscing. The memories, the stories, and the laughter. I have watched three older couples recount, with tears in their eyes from laughing so hard, the story of

323

the three men running to catch a bus together one winter night so many years ago. It was not an extraordinary event — not a wedding or the birth of a baby — but it was a simple slice of life from a friendship of many years, and the mere recollection and retelling of it was full of fondness and joy.

Then there is, too, the inevitable bittersweet quality that comes with the remembering and reminiscing. For in our revisiting of the past, we are forced to recognize the people that are gone and the circumstances that have changed with the passage of time.

I am a terrifically sentimental guy. I have joked with friends that, perhaps by the time I'm an old man, I will have raised the bar a bit, and I will only be sentimental about things that are twenty or more years past. As it is right now, I can work up a good deal of nostalgia for something that happened just last week.

The 1973 movie, *The Way We Were*, is a marvelously sentimental tale. Near the end of the story, we see two old friends, J. J. and Hubbell, sit back in a sailboat together and reminisce about times and places gone by. They had been through college together, World War II, overlapping careers, marriages, and divorces. Now, relaxed and laughing together, they enjoy an exercise of nostalgia. "Best Saturday afternoon?" "Best month?" "Best year?"

Hubbell is able to answer the first two with confidence. When J. J. asks, "Best year?" however, he pauses. This one is not so easy to single out. Finally, tentatively, he answers, "1944." Then, quietly and without explanation, he amends his answer: "1945." His voice trails off and the scene fades away as he says, "1946," and perhaps more.

As viewers, we have seen Hubbell live some of those years. They were actually difficult years, in many respects. "It was never uncomplicated," he admits in another scene. And yet, in hindsight, the years melt together into a single, beautiful memory, and he is unable to distinguish the "best year" from among them.

This is the nature of memory, of course. Sentiment and nostalgia soften, or completely excerpt, the difficulties of a time and place in the past, highlighting only what was beautiful and precious then and there.

You and I are accustomed to the juxtaposition of "before" and "after" pictures. We've all seen photos of the same person before and after a certain diet, photos of a room before and after some redecorating project, photos of an individual before and after some radical makeover. All of those before and after photos track a certain kind of improvement.

At the other end of the spectrum, we have also seen and been moved by photos of a neighborhood before and after a tornado, or photos of an entire city before and after a hurricane. These photographs record loss and devastation.

The pictures we are not so conscious of — though we all have them — are not the "before and after" variety, but rather the "during and after" pictures. This, you see, is the stuff of memory. How does a time, a place, or an experience look to us in the present — that is, "during" our time there? And, by contrast, how does that time, place, or experience look to us sometime in the future — "after" our time there?

The years right after the war looked very good to Hubbell. Better than they actually were. I know that my sentimental reflections on earlier times in my life are equally gilded.

But let us adjust our picture of reminiscences just a bit. Imagine friends who are remembering fondly a time gone by: their version of "the good old days." They cannot say with certainty which year was best, for they were all so good. Then rewind the tape and discover the lost era for which they long.

It is not the halcyon days of high school or the vibrant years of college. It is not the simple, early days of marriage or the fun and fast years when the kids were young. No, these friends are among the children of Israel, and the place about which they are feeling nostalgic is none other than Egypt. Egypt!

Ah, the difference between the "during" and the "after" pictures.

For hundreds of years, the descendants of Jacob had been oppressed foreigners within the land of Egypt. For generations, they had called out to the Lord for deliverance. Their bondage was cruel. Their labor coerced. And they longed for God to fulfill the promise he had made to their ancestors, delivering them out of their slavery and leading them to the promised land.

While he is still in chains; while he labors in the mud; while he is being watched and whipped by some cruel taskmaster, ask the Hebrew slave where he would like to be one year hence. And he will answer, "Anywhere but here!"

Less than one year later, he and his fellow Israelites are free. They are en route from the land of their bondage to the land of God's promise. The journey, however, includes miles of wilderness, and the people are feeling the pangs of hunger. As they sit and talk together, they say, "If only we had died by the hand of the Lord in the land of Egypt, when we sat by the fleshpots and ate our fill of bread."

In the end, this episode from Israel's exodus experience becomes a story of God's abundant and miraculous provisions for his people. For their attitude, they probably deserved punishment, but God taught them a lesson in a different way: overwhelming them with his gracious supply.

For our purposes today, though, I want us to consider the trap into which God's people had fallen. "If only," they said longingly. "If only we had died by the hand of the Lord in the land of Egypt, when we sat by the fleshpots and ate our fill of bread."

What's wrong with our memories that we should long for Egypt?

To daydream, however unrealistically, about a place we have never been is somewhat excusable. To fancy that the "someday" future will be infinitely better than the present may be delusional, yet it is at least understandable. But how can we justify our hazy picture of a place where we've been? How can we be sentimental about our slavery?

This foolishness, you see, is not quarantined with Israel in the wilderness. It is a diabolical part of our human condition. While you and I have not left Egypt behind, we have been delivered from slavery. Jesus and Paul both speak of sin as slavery (for example, John 8:34; Romans 6:16-20). That is the bondage from which the Lord endeavors to set us free. And that is where you and I run the risk of becoming sentimental slaves.

Peter quotes a proverb to identify the problem: "It has happened to them according to the true proverb, 'The dog turns back to its own vomit,' and, 'The sow is washed only to wallow in the mud' " (2 Peter 2:22).

Lot's wife may be the poster child for this tragic flaw. The stench of Sodom and Gomorrah's wickedness was so great that it evoked a rare and apocalyptic sort of judgment from God. Before the catastrophe hit, however, Lot and his family were forcefully rescued by angels. And yet, as they fled from the place (which perhaps they ought to have left voluntarily years before), Lot's wife looked back, and it proved fatal.

Why look back to a place like that? To Sodom. To Egypt. When God has delivered you, and his best plan for you is ahead rather than behind: Why look back?

Perhaps because it's home. Sodom had become home to Lot and his family. Egypt was home to those Israelite slaves. And we always tend to be sentimental about home.

For us today, we must remember that, at some level, sin is home for us. That is to say, we were born and raised in it. It's where we come from.

When the Jews sit down each year to eat their Passover meal, they include bitter herbs, which symbolize the bitterness of their bondage. That's an important reminder to build into the Passover menu, lest the people's memory grows hazy, and the recollection of Egypt tastes more like fleshpots and bread than bitter herbs.

When Moses said his farewell to the children of Israel in the book of Deuteronomy, one of his great recurring exhortations was, "Remember!" He understood that memory would be key to the people's faith and faithfulness.

And so it is for us, too. We must not let a little discouragement, a little challenge, a little difficulty in our journey send us scurrying back to some memory-mirage of a smorgasbord back in Egypt. Instead, let me ask you to do a little remembering today: to remember clearly the bitterness, the bondage, and the ultimate emptiness of sin.

God provided manna for those hungry souls in the wilderness. A jar of it was kept in the Ark of the Covenant as a constant reminder of God's faithful provision. He responds to the needs of his people, and he shows that he can meet our needs even in the most inhospitable and improbable environments. And in the end, that manna was the foretaste of the real "bread from heaven": the ultimate provision for all sin-sick souls. Amen.

Proper 21
Pentecost 19
Ordinary Time 26
Exodus 17:1-7

The Proof Is In The Pudding

It is an incongruous scene: a multitude in the desert.

The desert is supposed to be desolate, barren, devoid of life. There may be the occasional sturdy breed of plant, animal, or insect that can survive the inhospitable environment, but little else. Rivers and lakes may teem with fish; the forests are full of birds and wildlife; the fields and prairies are home to countless animals; the desert is a mostly unpopulated expanse that lacks almost everything necessary to sustain life.

And yet, as our camera zooms in on one particular portion of the vast wilderness that lies between Egypt and Canaan, we are astonished to see life there. A lot of life. Hundreds of thousands of men, women, children, and animals. Where we expect to see tumbleweed blowing along unimpeded, we see instead a crowded throng of tents, families, and cattle.

It is an incongruous scene: a multitude in the desert. How in the world can they all survive there?

Well, that was their question, too.

They were the children of Israel. Having been slaves in Egypt for centuries, they were now finally free. But their new life of freedom was not to be lived out in the land of their former captivity. No, God had promised to give them a different land — one reputedly flowing with milk and honey.

In between those two locations, however — between the place of their bondage and the place of God's promise — there was a journey to be made. The Bible says that they journeyed by stages,

329

reminding us that this was a process. They could not get from here to there in a sprint, a burst of enthusiasm. Perhaps, as they emerged from the borders of Egypt as freshly freed people, they felt that they could leap broad deserts in a single bound. The reality was that the Israelites would have to endure a lengthier process: They would have to journey by stages.

We almost always do, of course. There is not much of lasting importance that can be had by a single inspired burst of energy and will. We may embark on some journeys with such enthusiasm — marriage, a new job, discipleship, and the like — but the journey always outlasts our initial enthusiasm. Few important destinations in our lives are sprinting distance.

Most of the stages of Israel's particular journey were experienced in the wilderness in and around the Sinai Peninsula. And that wilderness was no place for a group like these Israelites.

The problem, obviously, was the provisions.

Every responsible person who has set out on a trip has made these calculations. Money, food, fuel, clothing — how much will I need? I will need more if the trip is longer. I will need more still if I am taking additional people with me. And I will need still more if I am not guaranteed that such provisions will be available along the way.

See, then, the enormous problem confronting the Israelites.

The journey is a long one, indeed. At a minimum, it was to take several months. (And in the end, it took an entire generation!)

Next, consider the numbers. It was certainly feasible for a caravan to pack enough food and water to cross this wilderness. Likewise, a small, manageable group of nomads could make the journey. But how can you possibly provide for the needs of over a million men, women, and children, plus significant flocks and herds, in the middle of nowhere?

And, finally, consider the dearth of resources along the way.

You and I live in a very plush culture when it comes to travel. Stores, restaurants, motels, and gas stations line our highways. Every need is anticipated and accommodated, right down to high-speed wireless internet access.

But for the Israelites in the wilderness, there were no such resources. Nor were there even the ordinary along-the-way provisions of creeks, lakes, fields, wells, gardens, and fruit trees. They could travel for miles without finding enough food and water for even one person, let alone an entire community of people and animals.

So it is that the community came to camp at a place called Rephidim, where there was no water. There, desperate with their understandable hunger and thirst, they complained.

Parents are well-acquainted with this scene — at least on a small scale. My wife and I have three young children, and we enjoy taking family trips together. Yet, when any of the basic physical needs goes unmet, a certain kind of chaos ensues. The need to eat, drink, sleep, or find a bathroom leads to complaining and whining, which in turn creates an unpleasant environment in the car. There's a growing tension and unhappiness, and the parents try to quell the uprising with a promise: "Only five more miles — just hold on!"

I multiply in my mind our three children by some astronomical figure to imagine the unhappy mob in Moses' backseat. And he had no such reassurance to offer them! There was no green sign promising relief at the next exit, a few miles away. Rather, there was just more of the same — dry, desolate desert — as far as the eye could see in every direction.

Moses and the people snipe at one another.

"We want water," they cry.

"Why are you bugging me about it," he shoots back, suggesting that their real complaint is with God.

But the people do not take their complaint to God. Instead, they fuss at Moses still more: "Why did you bring us and our children and our livestock here just to die of thirst?"

This must have been a galling business for Moses. You remember that, back at the burning bush, he wanted nothing to do with this whole project. He was quite unwilling to take the assignment, but God effectively forced him into it. Now that they were out of Egypt, it was God who was setting the itinerary — leading with cloudy and fiery pillars — as well as setting the menu. But

331

Moses was the one who had to take the heat when the people were discontented.

Moses is the classic middleman. Like the waiter or waitress who gets an earful when it's actually the folks in the kitchen who made a mistake, or like the ticket counter agent who has to put up with the moaning when a flight is delayed; Moses mans the complaint department for what was, beginning to end, God's project.

He takes his own complaint, therefore, to God. "What shall I do with this people? They are almost ready to stone me." And, in response, God directs Moses to a rock that will become for the people a miraculous source of water.

What followed then must have been a sight to behold. The water miracle that gets the most attention in Exodus is the parting of the Red Sea. But this water-from-the-rock event must have been an eyeful, too. After all, no mere trickle, no ordinary faucet was going to suffice for this community of men, women, children, and livestock. The rock must have produced a torrent of water, as though some dam had burst within it.

When the whole episode is all said and done, however, Moses gives the place a pair of unhappy names. "He called the place Massah and Meribah." *Massah* was a Hebrew word meaning "test" or "despair." *Meribah* was a Hebrew word meaning "strife" or "contention."

At some level, the names are disappointing ones, and they probably reflect how cumulatively wounded Moses must have been. Why didn't he name the place "provision"? Why not "need met," "thirst satisfied," or "problem solved"? It is an example that may invite us to look in the mirror and ask how we remember times and places. Will our memory be dominated by the unhappiness and troubles, or will it let God have the final word?

Moses "called the place Massah and Meribah, because the Israelites quarreled and tested the Lord, saying, 'Is the Lord among us or not?' "

There, at the conclusion of the episode, we meet with a detail not disclosed earlier in the narrative. The people tested the Lord, saying, "Is the Lord among us or not?"

Certain questions strike at the heart of our faith and our doubts. When Jesus was sleeping through the storm that had the disciples panicking, they cried out, "Teacher, do you not care that we are perishing?" (Mark 4:38). The suffering psalmist asked, "How long must your servant endure? When will you judge those who persecute me?" (Psalm 119:84). Gideon saw the circumstances of his people, and wondered, "If the Lord is with us, why then has all this happened to us? And where are all his wonderful deeds that our ancestors recounted to us?" (Judges 6:13). And Habakkuk called out in the face of troubles and injustices, "O Lord, how long shall I cry for help, and you will not listen?" (Habakkuk 1:2).

At Rephidim, the people of Israel voiced such a quintessential question of faith: "Is the Lord among us or not?"

We may be instinctively sympathetic with Israel's question, for it may be a question we have asked along the way. In a hospital room, in a financial crisis, in the aftermath of some natural disaster, in the wake of some tragic accident, we have wondered, too: "Is the Lord among us or not?"

On the other hand, look closely at these people and what they have experienced. They have witnessed firsthand the mighty deliverance of God. They have seen the series of plagues that broke Egypt and eventually broke their bonds. They have watched the Red Sea open up before them, and then close behind them at Pharaoh's expense. They have been greeted each morning by the massive cloudy pillar, and gone to sleep each night with the fiery pillar visible outside their tents. They have been abundantly fed with quail, and daily sustained with manna. And yet, when they get a little thirsty, they question the very presence of God: "Is the Lord among us or not?"

It may not be a sympathetic question, at all. It may, instead, be a myopic and faithless question, and an offense to the God who has guided and provided every step along the way.

We human beings are relentlessly physical creatures. When we are confronted with a physical need or problem or pain, therefore, it's hard for us to think about much else.

Satan knew this about us. Skeptical and unimpressed by Job's initial faithfulness, Satan curtly challenged God, "Skin for skin!

All that people have they will give to save their lives. But stretch out your hand now and touch his bone and his flesh, and he will curse you to your face" (Job 2:4-5).

Job did not sink to Satan's expectation, but the Israelites in the wilderness often did. Faced with a physical need, they asked a question that cut to the very core of God's faithfulness.

How shall we determine whether the Lord is among us or not? How does one measure or judge or prove such a thing? For the Israelites, it was a matter of hunger and thirst — whether their needs were met. The proof was in the pudding. For as long as their tummies were full, they were willing to trust and obey. But when the provisions of food or drink were interrupted, it called into question the very presence of God.

It is a vain, self-o-centric way of doing theology and faith. But it is not uncommon. We confuse the goodness of God with the goodness of our circumstances. There in the desert, it made for an incongruous scene: a multitude of people who had been freed, led, and fed by God, wondering aloud whether he was there or not. Amen.

Proper 22
Pentecost 20
Ordinary Time 27
Exodus 20:1-4, 7-9, 12-20

Appointment With Thunder

If you're like me, then you've spent your whole life in the church. And if you've spent your whole life in the church, then you've surely heard about the Ten Commandments before. We grew up with them displayed on the walls of our Sunday school classrooms, and perhaps in the stained-glass windows of our sanctuaries. We have heard sermons, lessons, and devotionals based on them. Perhaps we've even seen a movie or two about them. Why, then, would a preacher want to return to such well-worn material?

First, we need to return to them precisely because the Ten Commandments are so familiar. You see, once something is familiar, we run the risk of no longer paying careful attention to it.

When a place is familiar, we stop exploring it. We may no longer look carefully at the picture that is familiar. We may no longer listen carefully to the song that is familiar. And, we may no longer say thoughtfully the prayers, sing meaningfully the hymns, or read carefully the scriptures that are familiar.

The Ten Commandments are so familiar that it may have been quite some time since some of us read them carefully. Or thought about them carefully. Or perhaps obeyed them carefully.

And then there is this other matter. The Ten Commandments suffer a bit from the fact that we teach them to children. In Sunday school classes, in vacation Bible schools, in children's Bible stories, and in our homes, we teach the Ten Commandments to children.

Please don't misunderstand my meaning: It's not a bad thing to teach the Ten Commandments to children. It's good and it's right.

But in the process of teaching them to children, we may express the commandments in a kind of shorthand that shortchanges their meaning. And so we think of "taking God's name in vain" as, simply, "swearing." Or we think of "bearing false witness" as, simply, "lying." We simplify the commandments for children, and in the process lose the full depth and breadth of their meaning for ourselves.

The law of God contains the wisdom of God and the will of God. You and I will not easily exhaust what there is to be gained from meditating on it. And so we return today to that familiar, well-worn material.

And yet, we're not actually talking about any of the individual commandments today. Before we can study the commandments — or, for that matter, before we can even obey the commandments — we must first receive the commandments.

Perhaps someone will say, "That's a little ridiculous. We don't need to receive them; we already have them. We've had them for 3,000 years!"

Yes, we've had them, but we have not necessarily received them.

In our day-to-day communication, we understand that the message received is more than just the words spoken. In conversation, for example, the tone of voice, the body language, and the eye contact are all part of the message.

Likewise, when you're speaking with a child, whether you stand high above or crouch down face-to-face, becomes part of the message the child receives.

When we hear the national anthem or say the pledge of allegiance, the message exceeds the mere words when they are accompanied by certain actions: When we stand up, take off a hat, and put a hand over our heart.

When the president of the United States addresses the nation from the oval office, the message received is more than just the words spoken. For the formality of the setting and the rareness of the occasion contribute to the weight of the message.

In so much of our communication and experience, the message received is far more than just the words that are spoken. And if that is true in ordinary conversation, in patriotic protocol, and in presidential addresses, then it is a thousand times true of the Ten Commandments. The message received by the people was more than just the words spoken. The message received by the people was also the context, the setting, in which those words were spoken.

I want for us to see that setting this morning.

The scene is Sinai. The Sinai Peninsula was the triangular wilderness that lay between Egypt and Canaan and it was an inevitable part of the Israelites' journey as they traveled from slavery to the promised land.

But Sinai was more than just the wilderness that was in the way. Sinai was also a part of their destination: It was a scheduled stop.

You and I serve and follow a God who has more than one destination for us. The itinerary of his providence has more than one stop, and so we must be careful to guard against either of two obstacles to faithful following: First, that we should be so impatient for some final destination that we try to bypass the stops he has for us along the way; or, second, that we should become so content with some stop along the way that we resist moving on to his next destination for us.

Bethel and Penuel were essential stops for Jacob, yet neither was his home. The Jordan River and the Judean wilderness were both necessary stops along the way for Jesus before he began his Galilean ministry. And for Israel, the promised land was God's ultimate destination for them, but Sinai was an essential, scheduled stop on the way there.

It all began when God had first called Moses at the burning bush. Moses initially hesitated, and then his hesitation developed into a full-fledged resistance. Yet God persisted. And along the way, God spoke this reassuring word to his reluctant, would-not-be servant: "I will be with you; and this shall be the sign for you that it is I who sent you when you have brought the people out of Egypt, you shall worship God on this mountain."

So, you see, from the beginning of the project, Sinai was on the itinerary.

After Moses arrived in Egypt, things actually got worse before they get better. And since we human beings are such slaves to the present, the unfavorable developments prompted both Moses and the people to question whether God was going to guide this process to a successful end. Because the offense lost yardage on the first play from scrimmage, the faithless fans assumed that they were doomed to lose the whole game.

God did win, of course, in the end. Through frogs and flies, through disease and darkness, from blood in the Nile to blood on the doors, God won. And the Israelites marched out of Egypt free, encumbered only with the plunder of the Egyptians.

It turned out, however, that their deliverance was not complete, for they were pursued and trapped by pharaoh at the banks of the Red Sea. Yet, God's saving power and saving grace were not depleted: He rescued them from pharaoh at the Red Sea as decisively as he had rescued them from pharaoh back in Egypt.

And then, from there, it was on to Mount Sinai.

If you look at a map of the ancient Middle East, you'll discover that Mount Sinai is not exactly on a straight line from Egypt to Canaan. In fact, to go to Mount Sinai on the way to the promised land took the Israelites quite a distance out of the way. That may seem a poor strategy on God's part — to detour several hundred thousand men, women, and children several hundred miles on their journey — and yet it is a strategy that we should recognize.

We know what it is, in our human relationships, to take someone aside, or to be taken aside by someone else. Some conversations deserve *not* to happen on the way or in the midst. Some conversations ought to happen when one person takes another aside: just the two of them, away from the rest of whatever the setting may be.

So God took Israel aside. Here was this brief moment when he had them alone; away from the context of Egypt, where they had come from, where the people did not know and did not serve the Lord. Away from the context of Canaan, where they were going to, where the people also did not know and did not serve the Lord.

God made an appointment to meet his people, and he took them aside for this meeting: took them aside to Sinai.

When the people had arrived and set up camp at the foot of Mount Sinai, they were told to prepare themselves for their appointment with God. For two days, they were to purify themselves, and they were told to set up a boundary around the base of the mountain. That boundary was a line not to be crossed — not by priest, not by people, not by animals — not until the trumpet sounded.

Frankly, the whole process and scene there at Sinai may be unappealing to us. For you and I have cultivated a very different understanding of our access to God. We cherish the picture of a God that we can talk to any time and any place; and in this matter we have surely gained much over the ancient Israelites, who trembled at a distance.

But it is not all gain, for we have perhaps also lost some things that those ancient people had. Perhaps, for example, we have lost sight of the privilege: the privilege of the divine appointment called prayer. Perhaps we have lost perspective of the mind-boggling honor of an audience with Almighty God. And perhaps we have lost a recognition of the awesome presence into which we are invited. So far from trembling at a distance are we that we presume to meander in and out of the throne room of the universe, coming and going according to our own convenience. And in the very presence, where the angels themselves veil their sight and cry "Holy," we are often casual and distracted.

For two days, the Israelites purified themselves and kept their distance. And then, on the third day, there was thunder and there was lightning. The top of the mountain was enveloped in a thick cloud, and a loud trumpet blast was heard.

There is no indication in the text, incidentally, that any human being was given the assignment to blow a trumpet.

In the New Testament, the apostle Paul wrote to the Thessalonians that when Christ comes again in glory, His return will be accompanied by two things: the archangel's cry of command and the sound of God's trumpet.

Perhaps it was the sound of God's trumpet that Israel heard that day at Sinai.

Then the Lord came down in fire on the mountain, and the mountain was covered with smoke, and the sound of the trumpet grew louder, and the people shrank back with fear and trembling.

339

The message that is received is more than just the words that are spoken. The message that is received includes the context, the setting, and the scene, in which the words are spoken.

The commandments of God were not issued willy-nilly, at some random place and time. Rather, God made an appointment to meet his people at a specific place, time, and setting. And if we see that setting more clearly, you and I will be in a better position to receive his commandments, too.

A cordoned-off, out-of-the-way mountain. Thunder and lightning. Fire and smoke. A thick cloud and a loud trumpet. That is the scene. It was then and it was there that God gave his people the Ten Commandments.

You and I gather together here in this place. It is not Sinai, but it is a gathering of those who have been saved by him. It is a gathering at an appointed time and place to meet with God. It is a setting of worship, where we pause in reverence, praise, and awe before a holy God. And it is the place where God is able to take us aside, to get us alone with him, apart from the context of the world: the world from which we came; the world to which we will return; and a world where he is largely not known and not served.

And it is here, in this setting, that we are invited to hear his message and to receive his commandments. Amen.

Sermons On The First Readings

For Sundays
After Pentecost
(Last Third)

Forward March

Timothy J. Smith

To my wife, Donna,
and children, now young adults,
Becca and Matt

I thank God each and every day
for bringing all of you into my life!

Introduction

What I have learned after two decades of ministry is that we cannot depend on what we have done in the past. What might have worked well in the past may not work now. God's promises are new each morning. I believe that God continues to be at work in our lives, in our churches, and in our world. God is doing a new thing in our midst — of which we are privileged to be a part.

Late one week, I was still looking for a story to conclude my sermon. I had looked in my usual places and kept coming up empty. I was about to panic when a friend and colleague called. In our conversation, I asked what passage he was preaching on the coming Sunday. When I learned it was the same text, I asked if he had an illustration he might share with me. On the other end of the phone I heard him chuckle and then say, "That went out ten years ago."

"Sorry," I replied, "I disagree." I have seen repeatedly the power of a good story. People become caught up in the story and then go home to ponder it further. I am always amazed and humbled when someone remembers one particular story from a sermon several months ago. They remember because the story spoke to them — offering new insight into their life. Stories inspire us, and fill us with hope. Stories capture our attention in ways that fill-in-the-blank sermons cannot. People are more likely to remember a good story than an outline for a fill-in-the-blank sermon.

On a recent Sunday, I shared with my congregation my struggle with finding applications from biblical texts. Of course some passages are easier than others. I just completed an interesting book that suggests that we need to engulf ourselves in the biblical narrative and not always look for, "Three Steps to Happiness" or some such over-simplified relevance. We are a people of the book — the

Bible. The more we hear the Bible stories, the more they become part of us — they become our story.

I offer this collection of Old Testament sermons in the hope that they will inspire the readers in fresh ways to discover what new thing God is doing in our world today.

— Timothy J. Smith

Proper 23
Pentecost 21
Ordinary Time 28
Exodus 32:1-14

A Change Of Mind

While it has been suggested that idle hands are the playthings of the devil — the same may be true of our minds. Without a clear sense of who we are and whose we are, we have the tendency to wander into some barren wilderness. Sometimes our slip is gradual, we do one small thing that is questionable and before we realize it we are in deep trouble. There are other times when it is obvious that we have strayed in a big way, and whether we like it or not, there are consequences to our actions.

Without a clear sense of vision of who we are and where we are going, we are in danger of wandering off in the wrong direction and becoming lost. We need to be reminded daily of our journey, that we are God's children, that we belong to Jesus, and that something is expected of us.

The ancient Israelites escaped from the pursuing Egyptian army by miraculously crossing the Red Sea. They followed Moses into the wilderness where they would journey to the promised land. However, not everything went well for the people, they complained about being hungry and thirsty. They questioned Moses' authority and motivation. Did he lead them into the wilderness so they could die from starvation? Some suggested returning to Egypt, where life might not have been great living as slaves, but at least they had a warm bed and enough food. God gave the Ten Commandments, hoping to reform and remold the people. Let's just say that they were not too open to changing their ways.

Idle minds are the playthings of the devil. Without a clear sense of who they were and what they were trying to accomplish they

345

were in danger of falling into sin. Moses was up on the mountain communing with God. He was already gone forty days — almost six weeks. The people were beginning to wonder if he was ever coming back. Did something bad happen to him on the mountain? The people were becoming restless and impatient because he had been gone such a long time. The people decided to take matters into their own hands, which was exactly what would get them into trouble. They approached Aaron, Moses' brother and second in command. The people made an outrageous request to "make gods for us."

Aaron should have known better but instead he granted their request. Some suggest that Aaron was trying to challenge Moses' leadership, trying to gain popularity among the people so that they would look to him as their leader at some point. However, Aaron was a weak and ineffective leader because he gave the people exactly what they wanted. There always has been a danger in giving people what they want rather than what they need.

There always has been the temptation to give in to what the people want instead of standing up for what is right. Aaron caved in to the demands of the people, perhaps to gain popularity and status in the eyes of the people. Living out our faith does not always make us popular especially when we stand up for what is right. Sometimes we have been tempted to soften Jesus' demands to make them easier, more appealing. If we relaxed the demands of the gospel, the faulty thinking is that we would gain more people. And that, too, is dangerous.

Aaron must have realized what they demanded was wrong. They were breaking two of the most important and significant of the Ten Commandments, "You shall have no other gods before me," and "You shall not make for yourself an idol." But he gave the people what they wanted apparently without a second thought.

Aaron instructed the people to take all their gold rings and bring them to him. "He took the gold from them, formed it in a mold, and cast an image of a calf." The golden calf or bull was a symbol of pagan religion. The golden image clearly was viewed as a replacement for the absent Moses. In the people's eyes the calf was a visible reassurance of God's presence and activity in their

346

midst as they exclaimed, "These are your gods, O Israel, who brought you up out of the land of Egypt!" And they worshiped the golden image breaking another of the Ten Commandments. "You shall not bow down to them or worship them." The next day they brought sacrifices and offered them to the golden calf. There in the wilderness the people "reveled." How could they do such a thing? How could they have forgotten all that God had done for them in such a short time? Idle minds are the playthings of the devil.

While this reveling was going on at the base of the mountain, God instructed Moses to, "Go down at once!" God knew what was taking place and told Moses, "Your people, whom you brought up out of the land of Egypt, have acted perversely they have been quick to turn aside from the way that I commanded them; they have cast for themselves an image of a calf, and have worshiped it and sacrificed to it." God was angry and upset with the people. Notice that God referred to the people as "your" people and not "my people." It was as if the Lord God was so mad that God was ready to disown the people and have nothing more to do with them after this outrageous act.

The word translated as "perverse" is the same word used to describe the peoples' activity at the time of Noah and the great flood. Just like in Noah's day, God was ready to destroy the people for what they had done. God was ready to write them off and start fresh with Moses, "and of you I will make a great nation," God informed him. At the moment, it did not look good for the people. "I have seen this people, how stiff-necked they are," God told Moses, "Now let me alone, so that my wrath may burn hot against them." "Stiff-necked" referred to animals refusing to be steered in a direction they did not want to go, even when it would be beneficial to them. The people in their willfulness were like a stubborn ox that refused to move forward.

Courageously, Moses implored and pleaded with God on behalf of the people. Moses did not leave God alone but reminded God that the people were God's own people. They were the very people God "brought out of the land of Egypt with great power and with a mighty hand." Even though the people complained and grumbled against him, Moses had the people's best interest in mind, which reveals much about his character and leadership. He certainly had the best interests of the people, God's own people in mind.

In spite of great risk, Moses stood before God pleading on behalf of the people who obviously were sinning at that very moment. In addition Moses asked God, "What would the Egyptians think, that God led them to freedom just to kill them out in the desert?" In a passionate appeal, "Turn from your fierce wrath," Moses told God, "change your mind and do not bring disaster on your people." Moses wanted God to remember the covenant established with Abraham, Isaac, and Israel, the promise of "descendants like the stars of heaven" as well as the promised land. As a result, the most amazing thing happened; God did indeed change his mind and did not send destruction on the people.

For some reason we think that God never changes his mind. We view God as unmovable and unchangeable. Moses the prophet par excellence made an emotional, logical plea and God had a change of heart and did not send destruction on the people. We pray that God will intervene on our behalf to change our current circumstances. God hears our prayers and is able to change the outcome. Isn't that one reason why we pray? Moses appealed to the graceful side of God.

Thanks to Moses, God had a change of heart and allowed the people to live and continue their journey to the promised land. Moses descended from the mountain once again carrying the two tablets containing the Ten Commandments written in God's own hand. When Moses saw what the people had been doing he became angry. "Moses' anger burned hot, and he threw the tablets from his hands and broke them at the foot of the mountain." Moses was upset with Aaron who gave the people what they wanted. It was time for the people to repent of their sin and wrongdoing and return to the Lord God.

Martha Byrne was living her dream of becoming an actress. She said good-bye to the house and church where she'd grown up and moved to Hollywood, California. At first she had small roles in made-for-television movies and, in time, landed a minor role in a feature movie where she played someone's girlfriend. She auditioned for commercials and even made a pilot for a television show. However, her big break never came which left her feeling discouraged.

Soon Martha wondered why she wasn't having fun anymore auditioning for various roles. She waited for her telephone to ring with news that she had gotten the part — her big break. However the call never came. Her agent would call to inform her that the part she was hoping for went to another actress; the pilot television program would not be produced. She was discouraged, losing sight of herself.

A conversation with a pastor of a church she had been attending in California revealed her deep longing. "You miss your family," he told her. She admitted that it was true as tears rolled down her cheeks. She said she knew that all along but needed someone to tell her. "God has a way of bringing us what we truly need, when we follow our hearts desires," he told her.

A month later, Martha moved home, returning to her old church, catching up with her brother and sisters. "It was like my life went from black and white to color again," was how she described what she was feeling as she reaffirmed her faith.[1]

Yes, idle minds are the playthings of the devil. That is why it is important for us to keep our focus on our destination and not be sidetracked. Moses intervened on behalf of the people and God had a change of heart. Centuries later, Jesus Christ would intercede on our behalf restoring our relationship with God. Amen.

---

1. Martha Byrne, "Closer to Home," *Guidepost* magazine, April 2005, pp. 34-38.

Proper 24
Pentecost 22
Ordinary Time 29
Exodus 33:12-23

Show Me What's Real

Have you ever found yourself in a position or place where you would rather not be? Sometimes it is our own doing, our own poor choices that bring us to a place we would not choose. At other times it is a series of circumstances that carries us to that place.

A church near campus has a chapel for university students to meditate and pray. Students have the opportunity to reflect and share their thoughts in a notebook. The entries sometimes reveal an inner struggle. One young woman candidly shared, "My thoughts, ideas, beliefs, preconceptions; my ways and feelings of what is right or wrong are being challenged." We can probably all identify with her at some point in our lives. Other people sometimes challenge what we believe.

We wrestle with how we can live in the world while maintaining our faith. This same young woman writes, "I do not want to live a secluded lifestyle from the rest of the world." We can sense her pain when she writes, "I'm frustrated with some of the Christians I know whom I feel I have to hide some things from." She then pleads, "From the small details of my life to the big — show me truth in how you desire this life of mine to be lived." Then in despair she concludes, "All I see is fakeness in me, in him, in her, in all." She cries out, "I want to know what is real." Have you ever felt that way? Perhaps it was peer pressure that thrust this young woman into a place where she was uncomfortable and clearly did not want to be.

Moses was in a position he did not want to be in. It was a position that Moses probably would not have chosen for himself.

God had called Moses to lead the people out of Egypt to the promised land. The journey into the wilderness had not been without incident. The Israelites dramatically escaped from the powerful pursuing Egyptian army through the Red Sea. Soon after that, the people began complaining and wondering why they were in the wilderness in the first place, with some expressing a desire to return to familiar surroundings in Egypt. They grumbled about food being scarce. God heard their cries and provided manna, bread from heaven, each morning. Later, quail was added to their menu. They griped about the lack of water and again God responded instructing Moses to strike his staff on a rock. The result was plenty of water, enough for all the people along with their livestock. You might have thought that the people would have trusted God, knowing that God was present and would continue to provide for them, but they did not.

While Moses was on the mountain communing with God, the people down below made a golden calf and began worshiping it. This was a serious sin that broke several of the Ten Commandments. God was angry; threatening certain destruction and desiring to start all over with Moses. However, Moses interceded pleading on behalf of the people. The result of that conversation was that the people would live. Moses would continue to lead the people to the promised land. When Moses descended from the mountain and saw with his own eyes what the people had done he, too, burned with anger. How could the people have done such a thing, especially after all that God had done for them? There would be consequences from their sinful rebellion.

Moses was in a place he really did not want to be — out in the middle of nowhere with God threatening to abandon them. It has been said that when we are at the lowest point in our lives, we are the closest to God. At such times, we turn to God knowing deep within our hearts that God is with us and will somehow see us through our trials. Our descent to the depths does not usually occur all at once, but gradually. One misstep is followed by another and before we know it we are in a place we did not intend to be. It frequently takes much more effort to climb out of that place, and rebuild our lives than to fall into such a place. But God remains with us and will never desert us as the ancient Israelites would discover.

The present situation would build Moses' character. In spite of their complaining, the people looked to Moses as their spiritual leader. Moses spoke directly with God, telling God what he thought at a considerable risk to his own safety. Again, he had the best interests of the people under his charge in mind. Moses would gain confidence from his experience and would be an effective leader.

When God informed Moses that an angel would lead the people from that moment until they arrived at the promised land, Moses took exception. He knew that God was still angry with the people and wanted God to continue to take an active a part in their sojourn. Moses would not stand for the notion that God would be absent but insisted that the Lord God resume God's role. Where in the previous chapter God referred to the people as Moses' people, in our lesson Moses subtly reminded God that the people were in fact God's own people. "Now if I have found favor in your sight," Moses told God, "show me your ways, so that I may know you and find favor in your sight." Moses was seeking a sense of assurance that he and the people would not be abandoned in the middle of the desert where sand was the only thing that all anyone could see for miles and miles in every direction.

It was at that moment that Moses realized that he could not continue without the daily presence of God. Left to his own devices many things could go wrong. The people could very easily rebel against him, thus ruining God's plan. Moses shuddered to think what their sojourn would be like if God were absent. Deep within himself, Moses realized how much he needed God. This was another important turning point in his life. Moses drew on his personal relationship with God when he asked, "For how shall it be known that I have found favor in your sight, I and your people, unless you go with us?"

The people Moses was leading were not just ordinary people but were God's own people. Moses continued his persuasive argument, "In this way, we shall be distinct, I and your people, from every people on the face of the earth." What made these people "distinct" was that they were God's own and that God was with them, truly dwelling in their midst. God's constant presence protected the people in the face of danger and allowed Moses as well as the people to continue their journey.

God knew Moses and Moses had found favor with God. Moses realized how much he needed God and it seemed at that moment that God recognized the need for Moses. It was a moment of divine grace when God replied, "I will do the very thing that you have asked, for you have found favor in my sight, and I know you by name." God would be present once again with the people as they continued their journey to the promised land.

One might have thought that this victory would be enough for Moses, but it was not. He appealed to God's gracious side and God responded favorably. Moses made one more request of God, "Show me your glory." What more does Moses want? You could argue that God had already shown Moses glory — what else did anyone need? Perhaps Moses wanted to make sure that the breach opened up by the idolatry of the golden calf was now completely healed so that it would not negatively affect the people any longer. Moses had committed his life to God and would continue with the people knowing that it would not always be easy. He needed another sign and assurance that God was truly with him and all the people. Moses did not make his request lightly when he requested, "Show me your glory."

If God would once again allow Moses to see God's glory, then Moses would know that everything would be all right. "I will make all my goodness pass before you," God told Moses, "and will proclaim before you the name, 'The Lord.'" However, this time Moses asked for more than was possible. Given the gravity of Israel's sin God explained, "You cannot see my face; for no one shall see me and live."

In spite of the hurt and anger that the betrayal stirred in the heart of God, God did not seek the death of the people but rather that they would continue forward, "I will be gracious to whom I will be gracious, and will show mercy on whom I will show mercy," God told Moses. While God remains loyal to past promises God is always free to be whoever God needs to be in any new situation.

Then God directs Moses to a "cleft of the rock" where he could safely observe the glory of God. Moses would see the glory of God pass and for a brief second see the "back" of God. Moses would experience the glory of God both by sight and sound. With this sign revealed, Moses would be able to go back down the mountain to lead the people. Moses would again descend the mountain after spending forty days and forty nights with freshly engraved commandments for all the people.

Eleanor Josaitis was sitting at home watching television one evening in 1962 when she was thrust into a place she did not want to be. She was watching a program about the Nuremberg Trials that caused her to ask herself what she would have done if such atrocities were taking place in her own backyard. "I sat there and cried my eyes out," she remembered of that night. The program was interrupted with a breaking news bulletin. There were pictures of Mississippi police turning dogs and fire hoses on Civil Rights protestors. Eleanor knew that this was her moment of truth.

She began supporting the work of Dr. Martin Luther King Jr. as riots burned parts of her hometown of Detroit in 1967. She quickly learned that hunger was merely a symptom of a much larger problem. "You end racism," she claimed, "by making sure people enter the economic mainstream and ensuring that they can support their own families."

"Focus: HOPE" was founded the following year as a food program serving pregnant women, new mothers, and their children. The food distribution program would eventually expand to include the elderly. "Hunger is still a reality," Eleanor said, "do not pretend we have solved the problem of hunger," because we have not.

Eleanor, the housewife who got off the couch, built an organization from a basement operation run by a handful of friends into a sprawling forty-acre campus in downtown Detroit. Today, Focus: HOPE employs over 500 people, boasts of more than 50,000 volunteers, and has helped over 4,000 people become gainfully employed through job-training programs, and teaching skills for the twenty-first century.

"You will not change a thing," Eleanor claims, "by sitting in front of the television with the clicker in your hand."[1]

This incident from Exodus reminds us to trust in God at all times especially when everything around us seems to be crumbling before our very eyes, at those times when we sink into the depths of despair, and we are not sure of anything. Trust in God when we find ourselves in places we do not wish to be. And do not be afraid to step out in faith at times going against the popular current. It is at such moments that we trust in the God who loves us — the God who is with us and will continue to be with us.

While Moses might not have seen as much of God as he would have liked, he did see God's glory. Martin Luther commenting on this passage claimed that we did see God — when Jesus died upon the cross. Amen.

---

1. Willow Creek Leadership Summit, 2005.

Living On The Edge

The long journey was finally nearing its conclusion. Forty years wandering around the hot desert must have been physically as well as emotionally exhausting. It had not always been pleasant living like nomads for so long. As Moses climbed the mountain for what would be the last time, he must have felt a clear sense that his life was not lived in vain. All of his struggles had been worth it as he sought to communicate once again with God on the mountain. He could look back over his long life and realize that God had a plan for him and more importantly, that God was with him every step of the way.

What was going through Moses' mind as he neared the promised land? Like a movie flashback, did he remember the time many years before when God first called him through the burning bush? He was just minding his own business tending his father-in-law's sheep when God broke into his life. Maybe he recalled the dramatic escape from Egypt through the Red Sea with the Egyptian army in hot pursuit. Then there were all the times the people griped and complained getting themselves into trouble. While Moses was on another mountain receiving the Ten Commandments, the people were melting all their gold jewelry to make a golden calf to worship. This might have been a decisive moment in his journey. Maybe Moses was feeling a sense of relief with his sojourn coming to an end. He had done what God wanted him to do.

Maybe Moses felt a sense of relief — after all he spent the better part of his life to get to this moment at the edge of the promised land. He might have been thinking, "This is it — the moment

357

I've waited for all my life." And indeed it was. At that moment, Moses was feeling the joy of accomplishment. His goal had seemed so far off that at times he might have wondered if he would ever make it. Yet, here he was at the foot of the promised land. No one would think ill of him if he paused to enjoy the moment.

Moses might have also felt a sense of disappointment. He had spent the last forty years of his life leading the people to this place, the promised land, and now at the very edge he knew he could not go any further. God told Moses, "Go up to the top of Pisgah and look around you to the west, to the north, to the south, and to the east. Look well, for you shall not cross over this Jordan" (Deuteronomy 3:27). It might not have seemed fair to have gone all that way, endured many hardships, and then not be permitted to set foot on the land. Earlier, Moses had disobeyed God and as a result was told that he would not be allowed to enter the promised land. He could see it, but not enter it. It was wonderful to finally have arrived but also disappointing to not enter the land God had promised to his ancestors.

Maybe at that moment Moses wasn't feeling any one of those emotions, but rather a combination of relief, joy, and disappointment. For the last time he would climb the mountain to speak with God. From the top of the mountain, Moses could see a panoramic view he could never have imagined. On one side, as far as his eye could see was sand, the desert where he had spent the last forty years of his life. But on the other side, as far as he could see were palm trees with green grass, animals grazing in lush pastures. He could see everything that God promised. It might have been like seeing only black and white and then as in the movie, *The Wizard of Oz*, suddenly everything turns to color. There, on the mountaintop, God spoke to Moses once more, reminding him of the covenant, "This is the land of which I swore to Abraham, to Isaac, and to Jacob, saying, 'I will give it to your descendants.' " This was another sign that God keeps God's promises. Nearing the end of his life someone might have asked Moses how he was feeling having experienced so much. "This is my crowning achievement," Moses might have replied. "I've been asked time and again was it worth it — well here is my answer — yes, most definitely!"

There, on the mountain, having seen the promised land, Moses died. We are told that even though he was 120 years old when he died, "His sight was unimpaired and his vigor had not abated." This was a fitting end for Moses. It was the end of an era. There would never be another leader like Moses, "For all the mighty deeds and all the terrifying displays of power that Moses performed in the sight of Israel." Fittingly, the people mourned their fallen leader for thirty days.

While it was the end of an era, it was not the end of the story. From among the people another leader had already been chosen — Joshua. God had chosen Joshua to lead the people into the long awaited promised land. However, Joshua was not Moses; he would lead the people in a different way and in new directions that hopefully would honor God. Moses led the people through the wilderness and now Joshua would have the privilege to actually cross the border into the promised land. Joshua was "full of the spirit of wisdom, because Moses had laid his hands on him."

Moses died knowing that the people were in good hands; they had a new leader — Joshua — and they also had the Torah to guide them. It would be a new day for God's people. Joshua would face different challenges than Moses did, but with God's help he would work through them.

Jackie Spinner spent nearly a year covering the war in Iraq for the *Washington Post*. During that time, she had several dangerous encounters. Once, when she was interviewing detainees behind the Abu Ghraib prison fence, she felt a tug on her wrist. Strange men began pulling her toward a car all the while she was shouting "La la rajan" (no, no, please). Jackie says, "Not until a helicopter flashed overhead and a curious contingent of Marines approached did my kidnappers scatter." The ensuing months brought more close calls.

Like many others, when Jackie returned to the United States she had a difficult time readjusting. "I tried to reconnect to my old life," she said but admitted, "nothing about me worked like it once did." Her editor at the newspaper suggested that she take some time off. She had a fight with her twin sister. And she was having difficulty sleeping, "I knew the nightmares would come ..." she explained.

Several weeks later, Jackie and her sister traveled back to their hometown in Illinois. She felt comfortable back in the familiar neighborhood, driving past her old high school. That Sunday she attended the church she had grown up in. Suddenly, she realized that the way to make peace with what she had experienced was to trust God. "God will be present for me — just as God was in Iraq." It was at that moment that she realized God had not deserted her and that in time she would be all right.[1]

God calls and inspires people at just the right time, a time she or he can advance God's mission. Moses was the right person for the right time. But his time had come to an end. Now it was Joshua's turn. Joshua would lead the people triumphantly into the promised land.

No one else could have led the people like Moses had; no one could do what Joshua would do, and no one can reach the people like we can as we share our unique life experiences.

In that moment, as Joshua assumed leadership he too might have felt uncertain about what the future held for him, but "full of the Spirit" he knew that God would be with him and the people he would lead. Joshua would face some tremendous challenges as the people took possession of the land God promised to their ancestors, but through it all God would not desert them. He would learn to trust God.

We do not know what the future holds for us but we know the one who holds the future — we live our lives trusting God for all of our tomorrows.

God continues to call people today, often for a particular task at a time when they are most needed. God calls Moses, Joshua, and each one of us along with millions of other people around the world. God continues to call people, away from self-centered concerns and more toward God.

Ruby Jones decided to stay as Hurricane Katrina churned menacingly toward New Orleans in late August 2005. Her children urged her to leave, begging her not to report for her Sunday nursing shift at Lindy Boggs Medical Center. Ruby Jones, then 67, chose to ride out the storm with her patients in the hospice unit of the hospital. On Monday, the raging winds shattered the hospital's windows and burst open doors. By Tuesday, the power was out, the water supply was cut off, and the hospital was flooding. Ruby continued to take care of her patients — bathing them, feeding them, and dressing their wounds. When help arrived on Wednesday, Ruby assisted in the evacuation. She finally left the hospital on Thursday, having kept her promise to care for her patients.

Her faith sustained her through those dark days. During the most harrowing moments of Katrina, Ruby would recite Bible verses for guidance and strength. She believed that God would see her through the ordeal.

Quite simply she said she was just doing her job — one she has carried out with boundless compassion for over 45 years. Ruby was a model of caregiving at a time when some health care providers abandoned their posts.[2]

God is at work in our world. Just when you are about to give up all hope, there are subtle signs that God is at work, through people like you and me who are able to accomplish God's own purposes. What glimpse of the future is God giving us? Working together with God we can make that glimpse come true.

If you look closely enough, you just might see the hand of God at work in our world today. We have all done enough wrong in our lives to merit God's judgment. Jesus Christ took our sins to the cross. Here is the good news — our punishment has been paid in full. Thanks be to God. Amen.

---

1. Jackie Spinner as told to Jim Hinch, "Back from Baghdad," *Guideposts* magazine, June 2006, pp. 53-57.

2. Catharine Skipp and Arian Campo-Flores, "Beyond the Call," *Newsweek* magazine, July 3/July 10, 2006, p. 71.

Hearts On Fire

Writer, Anne Lamott, tells of her struggle in getting her teen-age son, Sam, to go to church with her. "Why do I make him go?" she reflects and then writes, "We live in bewildering, drastic times, and a little spiritual guidance never killed anyone. I think it's a fair compromise that every other week he has to come to the place that has been the tap for me: I want him to see the people who loved me when I felt most unlovable, who have loved him since I first told them that I was pregnant, even though he might not want to be with them. I want him to see their faces."[1] The church is the place where we feel loved and accepted as God in Christ loves each one of us. The church is where we are held accountable for our actions in love. And the church is the place where we experience a new sense of community.

The church continues to evolve to reach new generations of believers. What is burning in your hearts this Reformation Sunday? William Sloane Coffin once suggested that the problem plaguing the modern church is our sense of complacency. We come to church not expecting anything out of the ordinary to happen to us, let alone change us. We go with the flow, not wanting to upset anyone. We in the church lose focus on important issues and instead disagree over lesser matters. Instead of devising a plan to take the gospel to our community, we fight over what color to paint the fellowship hall. There might be some that do not even think it should be painted in the first place. Instead of taking a stand on peace and justice issues, we simply take a seat questioning whether the church should involve itself in such matters.

From time to time, God places a fire in someone's heart. The fire burns so brightly that they are compelled to act and are not able to stay quiet any longer. Martin Luther was one such individual. Luther challenged the church with what he believed was wrong. In a moving scene from the movie, *Martin Luther*, someone exclaims, "You are tearing the world apart!" Luther replies, "Did you really think there wouldn't be a cost?" Luther turned the world upside down setting the world on fire — a fire that is still burning over 500 years later. Among his bold steps, Luther translated the New Testament into the language of the people — German. Luther placed his own life at risk on several occasions. However, it was time for the world to hear what Luther had to say. What we sometimes overlook is that the Reformation that Luther began led to great revival and renewal both within Protestant and Catholic churches.

What is burning in your hearts this morning? When we step out in faith and take a stand, God will bless our effort. We discover this principle throughout the pages of the Bible as well in the lives of the reformers and millions of Christians.

It was often dangerous for the prophets of old to speak the word of God. No one wants to be told they are doing something wrong in the sight of God and must change their ways. As a result, prophets were not always popular. Jeremiah was a case in point.

Jeremiah criticized just about everyone including the king and the priests. At the gates of the temple, Jeremiah said that if the priests thought God was impressed by their words, they were wrong. He condemned the rich for exploiting the poor and the poor for deserving no better. The people grew tired of his messages of doom and gloom.

When he predicted that the Babylonians were about to attack and the people deserved it, the people beat him up and threw him in jail. On more than one occasion, Jeremiah complained to God about his role and the people's lack of response. The people had grown complacent, no longer placing their trust in God. As a result, life was going from bad to worse. The people were living in exile in incredible pain and despair. Almost in the middle of the book of Jeremiah, the prophet offered words of comfort and hope to the people who had suffered so much. The people were in need of a word of hope and chance for a new beginning.

The prophet Jeremiah was convinced that God was about to do something radical in order to effect the redemption and restoration of God's own people. The day was coming, Jeremiah told them, when God would again establish a new covenant. God would place the Torah within them and write it on their hearts. Previously, God had established covenants with Abraham and later with Moses, but the people had difficulty keeping those covenants, frequently straying from God's path. The old covenants had been broken so decisively as to nullify them. The message that God was about to establish a new covenant in the midst of incredible pain gave the people a fresh sense of hope.

"The days are surely coming, says the Lord, when I will make a new covenant with the house of Israel and the house of Judah." Like all covenants, this one is initiated by God. God wills an enduring relationship among the people. With this new covenant the people will not stray.

The new covenant will not resemble the ones the people had previously broken. God would forgive the people for their prior shortcomings as well as the times when they had broken preceding covenants. This covenant would be between God and the people.

What would make this covenant unique, God claims, "I will put my law within them, and I will write it on their hearts; and I will be their God, and they shall be my people." This covenant could not be broken; it would become an integral part of their identity, written on their hearts. The new covenant will affect both the minds and hearts of the people. This new covenant will bring forth a newfound sense of wholeness and joy. This was clearly good news for the people.

When we are forced to do something, often we feel some resentment. At the least, our hearts are not interested in whatever we are asked to do. While we might think we are fooling others with our half-hearted effort, we are not. Certainly, God is not fooled. The situation is a familiar one. A church that was once vital had fallen onto hard times. There were reasons for the decline in membership. Unable to accept the diminished position the members of the congregation began fighting with each other as well as the pastor. They purchased several growth producing programs but were disappointed with the poor results. People serving on committees began complaining about having to do anything.

The culture of that church began to change, starting with one person's vision of what the church could become in the future. Gradually, sometimes painfully, the culture of the church began to change. And when it did, they discovered that they found meaning in what they were doing. It was their own program utilizing the people's spiritual gifts and not something passed down from on high. "Reformations always start with the peasants; they don't start with the elites" states Rick Warren, pastor of Saddleback Church in California and author of the best-selling, *The Purpose-Driven Life*.[2]

A layperson describes the transformation that both their church and individuals experienced: "People were giving four or five hours a week to the church and complaining that it was way too much. After we expanded our program, there were some people spending twenty hours at the church and loving every minute of it. When we were trying to be something we weren't, everyone was exhausted, but when we began living out of our gifts it was like we had energy to burn. You have never seen such passion."[3]

God was about to do a new thing, giving the people a new covenant, one written upon their hearts. The people will "know the Lord" acknowledging a deep trust. The new covenant will be one of radical obedience to God's commands written on the people's hearts.

People will no longer have to look up paragraphs in books of rules and regulations but will instinctively know what God requires of them. When laws are external we obey because we are told we must. However, the new covenant, written on our hearts will be different. The old ways, like scolding and lecturing, even fire and brimstone preaching, will no longer be necessary. The new covenant will be written on our hearts, it will be a part of us.

We cannot read this passage without thinking of Jesus. This passage helps us in our understanding of what God has done for us

366

in Jesus Christ. Jesus is the new covenant who by his life, death, and resurrection models for us what it means to belong to God.

What is burning in your heart today? What new thing is God calling you to do in our church or community? You may be the only person who is able to win others over and complete the task. God continues to do new things in our lives, in our church, and in our world. Today, we remember the sixteenth-century Reformation, thankful for the faithful witness of Martin Luther ... and others through the centuries. Yet we also realize that the work of God continues to evolve in our day as well through us.

May we go forth believing that God has touched our lives, has written God's law on our hearts, living out our faith. As we leave this place of worship may we do so knowing we can make a difference and cannot remain silent any longer. May we take our stand and speak out against injustices knowing that Jesus is with us always. The church remains the world's great hope! Amen.

1. Anne Lamott, *Plan B: Further Thoughts of Faith* (New York: Riverhead Books, 2005), p. 195.

2. Lisa Miller, "The Innovator," *Newsweek* magazine, July 3/July 10, 2006, p. 66.

3. Dan R. Dick and Barbara Miller, *Equipped for Every Good Work: Building a Gifts-Based Church* (Nashville: Discipleship Resources, 2001), p. 96.

The Victory Is Ours

All Saints provides an opportunity to remember and give thanks for all the believers who have lived before us. Some of the saints are people we might have known quite well, we might recognize the names of others, and still there are many more numbering in the millions whose names and lives are known only to God.

There are people we knew personally who impact our faith in profound ways: our parents, grandparents, other relatives, good friends, fellow church members, or neighbors who now reside in heaven. We thank God for the privilege of knowing them, of walking beside them, and for the influence of their lives on our own.

It was a life-lesson Jon would never forget. One day, when Jon was about seven, he remembered having a fight with his best friend, Jimmy. "Sparks flew," Jon fondly recalled, "names were called, and off we stomped — separately — to mourn the loss of our friendship." That day, Jon was certain he would never speak to Jimmy again.

His mother tried her best to comfort him, "These things happen in life," she said. Jon thought his father would have a better grasp on the situation. After telling his dad everything that happened and how he never wanted to see Jimmy again, his father said something he would never forget.

"I know you're angry with Jimmy" his dad said, "but he's your best friend. You should forgive him." Then, with a long stick that he'd been using to clean the chicken coop, his dad drew three circles in the dirt. In the right circle, he wrote, "God." In the left circle, he wrote "Jon." And in the center he wrote "Jimmy."

"When you don't forgive someone," he told him, "you let that person get between you and God." Jon and his dad talked at length that day about forgiveness. He told him that every relationship hit bumps in the road, even with our closest friends, but that should not spoil the ride. By the next morning the two boys were best of friends again.

"My father's lesson has served me well through 38 years of marriage," Jon claimed. His father's words spoken over fifty years ago "taught me everything I ever needed to know about selflessness and generosity," he wrote. "And I feel all the closer to God for it."[1]

Today we give thanks to God for those special people in our lives and the lessons they have taught us.

We know from our own experience that it is not always easy to live out our faith as modern-day disciples of Jesus Christ. We try our best to obey Jesus' commands of loving God and neighbor while paying attention to "the least of these who are members of my family." There is a cost to our discipleship.

If we have not ruffled some feathers now and then, perhaps we were not living out our faith in the way Jesus instructed us. As we discovered, in Jesus' ministry there were times when those in positions of power took exception to his teachings. The religious leaders who should have been supportive of Jesus and his ministry were the very ones who plotted against him. The apostles experienced personal hardship as they told others about Jesus, as did many early Christians. It is not easy following Jesus, whose teachings and way of life seem to run counter to what our culture defines as important.

A frequent question we ask after we have gone through a rather difficult time is, "Was it worth it?" How does what we experienced benefit other believers? The apostle John may very well have asked himself that same question while living in exile on the island of Patmos. John had accompanied Jesus all through his earthy ministry. Following Easter, John obeyed Jesus' command: "Go therefore and make disciples of all nations, baptizing them in the name of the Father and of the Son and of the Holy Spirit, and teaching them to obey everything that I have commanded you." Doing those very things was what got John into trouble. As a result, those in power shipped him off thinking that would be the last they would hear from John. There on that tiny Greek island John had a powerful vision of the end time. While some may shy away from the book of Revelation, it actually is a word of hope proclaiming that no matter what happens to us we will be with God and Jesus. Therefore, in the end, all of our struggles and suffering will be worth it.

In that powerful vision, there was a large crowd gathered, "a great multitude that no one could count," John wrote, "from every nation, from all tribes and peoples and languages, standing before the throne and before the Lamb." There were so many people, not only from all over the earth but from every time as well. Picture a large football stadium that holds 100,000 fans and then multiply the crowd several times. There would be nothing but people as far as the eye could see in all directions. It must have been an awesome sight.

All of these people had one thing in common. They had all suffered in some way for their faith. Some were persecuted and harassed while others might have been tortured or even killed for the faith they professed. Others resisted the pressures of the day, the allure of Babylon. They experienced so much hardship. They were gathered near the very throne of God and Jesus, "with palm branches in their hands." In spite of what they endured, the mood was one of celebration since they were now in the very presence of both God and Jesus.

"With palm branches in their hands" was reminiscent of another celebration — Palm Sunday as Jesus made his triumphal entry into Jerusalem. On that occasion, people were shouting and singing, "Hosanna! Blessed is the one who comes in the name of the Lord." The religious leaders were uncomfortable with all the attention Jesus received. On that day they said to one another in frustration, "You see, you can do nothing. Look, the world has gone after him!" It was an ironic foreshadowing of John's vision because the whole world has gone after Jesus.

According to John, in that victory celebration the people were shouting "in a loud voice ... Salvation belongs to our God who is seated on the throne, and to the Lamb!" The reference to the Lamb, of course, was to Jesus who gave his life that all who believe in him may receive eternal life. We were reminded that salvation rests with God alone. We did not earn it or even deserve it; rather salvation came as a gift from God, as part of God's amazing grace. While others might boast and made promises they could not possibly fulfill, only God was the ultimate source of total well-being and peace. Salvation came from God.

John was caught up in this incredible scene watching angels surrounding the throne of God. Then one of the elders asked John about the people wearing white robes. Unsure what to say, John replied that the elder should know the answer. "These are they who have come out of the great ordeal," the elder told John. "They have washed their robes and made them white in the blood of the Lamb." The people wearing the white robes were those who suffered and who were now with God. They were the saints whose devotion and loyalty to God and Jesus were both deliberate and costly. They had made it and now were present with God and the Lamb. They stand before God's throne where they serve God day and night.

Their time of suffering is over, "They will hunger no more, and thirst no more; the sun will not strike them, nor any scorching heat; for the Lamb at the center of the throne will be their shepherd, and he will guide them to springs of the water of life, and God will wipe away every tear from their eyes." Those wearing the white robes are no longer victims but rather victors. Thanks to Jesus the battle has already been fought and won. In the end the people will answer the question yes — everything they endured was worth it.

John's vision has brought hope to millions of believers. When we feel like giving up, falling prey to the allure of Babylon, when the cost of discipleship seems too great, we need to remember that the victory is already ours — thanks be to Jesus. One day we shall join those who have gone before us, we will join in the grand celebration before the throne of God and Jesus.

God's ongoing work of salvation continues in our day and time. The saving work of God continues through us as we seek to live out our faith as modern-day disciples of Jesus Christ. We share our faith with others, hoping and praying that the seeds of faith that we plant will take hold.

LaChanze's husband had been killed in the World Trade Center on September 11. She was devastated at her loss; she questioned God, seeking answers to this terrible tragedy and her personal lost. She wrote about her feelings in a journal she kept. She had begun journaling as a young girl. She wrote about things that happened as well as her dreams of seeing the world. "All my journal entries ended with a prayer for God to help or teach me."

Her love for the theater led her to college to pursue her dream. That year the movie, *The Color Purple*, was released, with Whoopi Goldberg in the lead role. "I was blown away by its story of a girl who overcomes adversity to learn to love herself," LaChanze reflects, "I felt a special connection with her because she too kept a journal in which she wrote to God." This soon became her favorite movie.

By September 2001, life was good for LaChanze and her husband, Calvin, and toddler, Celia. LaChanze was expecting their second child that fall. "It was a happy, busy time and my journal entries were full of hope and gratitude for the future Calvin and I were building together," she says. However, all that changed on the morning of September 11.

Months passed as LaChanze continued to struggle and come to terms with her husband's death. During that time, her second daughter was born. She realized that she would need to take care of her girls. "So I pushed myself daily," she explains of that time.

One day, a playwright called offering her a role in a play. He told her it would do her good. She prayed, "Dear God, please help me to forgive. Take my hand. Guide me into a new life." She later landed her dream role in the Broadway production of *The Color Purple*. "I'm filled with wonder now at God," she writes, "I believe God's inside us and all around us.... I know the audience is cheering not for me but for God working through me, turning my pain and struggle into something beautiful."[2]

Today we remember and give thanks to God for all the saints who have lived before us, especially celebrating the lives of those who impacted our own lives. As the hymn states, "They are saints of God ... and I mean to be one, too."[3] May we live in such a way that our words and actions will point others toward Jesus Christ. Amen.

1. Jon B. Fisher, "Circles in the Dirt," Marlo Thomas, *The Right Words at the Right Time, Volume 2: Your Turn* (New York: Atria Books, 2006), pp. 286-287.

2. LaChanze, "Words of Love," *Guidepost* magazine, September 2006, pp. 38-42.

3. Lesbia Scott, "I Sing A Song Of The Saints Of God," *United Methodist Hymnal*, #712.

**Proper 26
Pentecost 24
Ordinary Time 31
Joshua 3:7-17**

Forward March

It was truly a day of new beginnings as the people prepared to make the long-anticipated entry into the promised land. After the Israelites had spent forty years journeying through the desert, they had finally arrived at this pivotal point in time. To say that there were problems or even setbacks along the way would be an understatement. The people complained about not having enough food and water. Along the way there were some who desired to return to the land of slavery — where life was not great but at least they had daily meals and a bed to sleep in at night. All that was behind them as they prepared to set foot on the land God had promised to Abraham centuries before.

Joshua became the new leader and would actually lead the people into the promised land. The people mourned the death of Moses who had led them all those years. No one could ever replace Moses. The transition from traveling to actually arriving and settling can be stressful. Recent graduates frequently feel that way after having completed years of study and then are thrust into the workforce where the expectations are quite different. The first day on a new job can bring about that same sense of foreboding, not knowing what is required of them. During those first days some might even feel that they should have stayed where they were and not have accepted the new position. The people of old might have felt that way as they prepared to step over the threshold to a new beginning.

The Israelites were about to occupy the land after a long, hard journey filled with anticipation, unsure of what would happen to them once they settled in and did not have to live out of their suitcases any longer. It would certainly be a new experience for them. Understandably the people experienced some dread and apprehension.

Our faith always calls us forward — into the future. There are times when we reminisce about the good old days when the church was filled with people, including plenty of children and youth. We view pictures of the past almost in disbelief seeing all the children and youth. It is sad walking past empty classrooms Sunday after Sunday that were once filled with children. Still, we cannot rest on our past accomplishments because our faith leads us forward into the present and beckons us to the future. We have to continue to develop creative programs that will attract people of all ages into our church. The gospel message does not change — only the way we present it. The temptation is to continue doing ministry the way we always have instead of seeking new, creative ways to engage people living in our community.

A visitor to California's Garden Grove Community Church, popularly known as the Crystal Cathedral, was taken in by the many buildings on the beautiful campus. What impressed him the most was the number of well-trained laity serving in various phases of ministry. There were hundreds of lay ministers making hospital visits, following up on first time visitors to the church, and manning the telephone ministry. There were nearly a thousand people in total.

In meeting with some of the lay ministers, the visitor asked what would happen to the church when its founding pastor, Dr. Robert Schuller, retired. "We have a lot more going here than Bob Schuller," one of the ministers replied. "He has seen that we have been discipled in the way of Jesus and trained to do his ministry! When he is gone," the pastor continued, "we will continue to do ministry as we are now."[1] Our faith beckons us forward to the future.

It would only be natural for Joshua to feel a sense of trepidation. After all, he was now the leader and he knew that at least for a while people would be comparing him to Moses. God would be with Joshua as God had been with Moses in the past. God summoned Joshua, "This day I will begin to exalt you in the sight of all Israel, so that they may know that I will be with you as I was with Moses." The people would trust Joshua as they and their ancestors had Moses.

Forty years before, the people dramatically crossed the Red Sea, escaping from the pursuing Egyptian army to freedom. It was a defining moment for the people that they told and retold to their children and grandchildren throughout their long journey. Most of the people who crossed the Red Sea decades before had died by this time. When the people crossed the Jordan River into the promised land, their entrance would be just as dramatic and significant.

Crossing the Red Sea led to freedom from oppression; with the crossing of the Jordan River they would become a people and a nation. Their long journey was finally complete. At that significant moment, the priests were instructed to carry the sacred Ark of the Covenant into the new land. The Ark contained the Ten Commandments and represented the throne of God. The Ark would serve as a daily reminder to the people that God would be with them as they settled in the new land.

Joshua called out to the people, who were anxiously awaiting his direction. He spoke the word of the Lord God, "By this you shall know that among you is the living God who without fail will drive out from before you" all the people currently living on the land. Crossing the river would not be easy as is often the case with most major transitions in our lives. The people had spent forty years in the desert, dealing with sandstorms and scorpions. They were frightened at the notion that they would have to cross the river. The Jordan was neither deep nor wide, except when it floods. The river was only ninety to 100 feet wide and about three to twelve feet deep. However, when the river flooded, it expanded considerably — anywhere from 200 yards to a mile wide. The current was swifter than it appeared making the crossing all the more dangerous. The river also descended about nine feet a mile as the water flowed from the Sea of Galilee to the Dead Sea. To cross the river the people would have to first climb steep hills and then go down and across the badlands, and finally push through the jungle of the flood-plain. It would not be easy, but with God's help they could make it.

The people would follow the Ark of the Covenant "of the Lord of all the earth" as they crossed the river. The procession must have been impressive, again instilling the people with the sense that they were at the start of a new era, a new beginning. The river would not part until the priests actually stepped into the river. We can talk and make all the plans we want, but nothing will happen until we actually take the first steps in faith.

The people were thrust into the future — into the land that had been promised to them generations before — the land that they had spent considerable effort to reach. They were now about to enter and take possession of the land. For the people it was a matter of faith, trusting in the living God who had seen them this far, believing that God would not let them down. They put their fears behind them and then took those first, bold steps. They had finally arrived.

Generations come and go, however, the nature and purposes of God's saving action remains the same. Recent decades have seen many churches decline in worship attendance and membership. Many churches keep doing the same thing hoping that the result will be different somehow, but the church continues down the path of decline. However, there are some churches that are willing to try new and creative ideas to strengthen their ministry.

Pastor Jessica was appointed to a small membership church, having served on the staff of a large church. She wisely realized that what worked at the larger church would not work in her new setting. She began emphasizing the principle of "different functions, equal importance." She led Bible studies as the congregation studied scripture together to discern God's design for the church and each person's role in that plan. This was a break from the past where the pastor dictated whatever direction for the church she or he thought was right. This new approach would involve all the members in every aspect of ministry. This style was different and surprised some in her new church. She continued to model that each member was of equal importance in the body. Together they forged on ahead.

There were roadblocks along the way involving traditional expectations of the pastor as well as some people's resistance to seeing themselves as ministers. The church continued to march forward hoping in time that some of the skeptics would change their minds when they saw the desired results. A new energy and enthusiasm was born in that small church.[2]

In what new direction is God leading *us*? New beginnings bring new opportunities to live out our faith. Our faith always beckons us to the future — to the new thing that God is doing in our lives, in our church, and in our world. We march forward with the knowledge that God is with us as God was with the Israelites when they took their first steps into the promised land. Amen.

---

1. Robert D. Schieler, *Revive Your Mainline Congregation* (Cleveland: The Pilgrim Press, 2003), p. 103.

2. Sue Mallory, *The Equipping Church* (Grand Rapids: Zondervan, 2001), pp. 33-34.

Proper 27
Pentecost 25
Ordinary Time 32
Joshua 24:1-3a, 14-25

A Question Of Loyalty

Lookout Mountain is a popular tourist destination located in the northwest corner of Georgia, just six miles from Chattanooga, Tennessee. From high atop the mountain, on a clear day seven states are visible with the naked eye. Most photographs fail to capture the beauty of this panoramic view. Information boasts of an unforgettable journey ... "where each step reveals natural beauty and wonders." Lookout Mountain also played a role in the American Civil War.

Nearing the end of his life, Joshua called a summit on the mountain. The call was heard both near and far with everyone who was anyone traveling to the historically significant site. Joshua, as you recall, led the people into the promised land after Moses had died. The people had lived in the promised land for quite sometime when our lesson unfolds.

The view from the mountaintop was spectacular. On a clear day, from the top of Ebal, the people could see almost all the way to Jerusalem some forty miles to the south. To the north, the snowcapped Mount Hermon was visible. Looking westward was the great sea and the long ridge of Mount Carmel. To the east was the cavity exposing the Jordan valley. There on the mountain most of the promised land would be visible. It must have been a breathtaking view.

Besides being strategically important as a trade route, Shechem also held historical significance as well. It is the place where Abraham migrated and where God first told him that all the land in his sight would one day belong to his numerous descendents. It

381

is believed that Shechem is where Jacob built an altar. It was there that Jacob saw a vision of angels descending a ladder from heaven. And centuries later, Jesus would converse with a Samaritan woman at Jacob's well in that same general vicinity.

There was one thing Joshua wanted to be absolutely certain about before he died, and that was if the people would remain loyal to the Lord God. In the role of a prophet Joshua tells the people, "Now therefore revere the Lord, and serve him in sincerity and in faithfulness; put away the gods that your ancestors served beyond the River and in Egypt, and serve the Lord." Perhaps it was easier for the people to trust God when they were traveling out in the desert, depending on God to meet their every need during their long journey, than it was once they settled in the promised land where they were more self-sufficient. Once there, they became distracted with other things that began to crowd God out of their lives.

Joshua knew how difficult it would be for the people of Israel to devote themselves totally to God. He knew that their ancestors before them had made similar promises that they failed to keep. There on the mountain Joshua wanted the people to remember all that God had done for them in their recent past. He wanted them to commit themselves to God.

Joshua called for the people to put aside all the objects that got in the way of their relationship with God, including foreign gods. He wanted them to remain loyal to the God who loved them and had led them to the promised land. Today there continues to be many voices as well as activities that seem to constantly draw us away from our relationship with the Lord Jesus. Many of us have good intentions and do not purposely allow other things to crowd out our devotional life but eventually they do nonetheless. There was one question Joshua wanted the people to answer before he was gone: Will the people remain loyal to the Lord God? That is a question that all of us need to ask ourselves. Will we remain loyal, committed Christians or will we unintentionally stray in some other direction?

This passage reminds us that something is expected from each one of us. We are not mere spectators or pew potatoes. Notice how many times Joshua uses the word "serve" in this passage — a total of fifteen times in eleven verses. To serve the Lord is more than just paying lip service.

In Joshua's mind it was all or nothing. Just as there is no such thing as a part-time believer, Joshua urged the people to commit to the Lord God. Joshua challenged the people, "Now if you are unwilling to serve the Lord, choose this day whom you will serve." At the same time, Joshua was clear about his own priorities, "as for me and my household, we will serve the Lord." Joshua wanted the people to follow his example. We all need role models whose positive example we can follow.

A young woman, Allison, had just returned to her hometown where she was greeted by her younger sister whom she had babysat when her sister was only three to five years old. Allison had become the state tennis champion at her high school, set a number of athletic records, then unfortunately fell into drug use and scuffles with the law before giving her life to Jesus Christ. Her young sister looked to Allison as a role model. "I decided that I was going to become just like you," she told her older sister. "I, too, became the state tennis champion, and wherever there was an athletic record posted with your name on it," she said, "I either matched or beat it. I figured it was in my genes."

Then Allison was astonished to learn that her sister had also drifted into drugs and trouble with the law, "just like you did," said the young woman. Allison then took her aside and shared with her a new story, about her new life in Christ. In retelling this story, Allison was amazed how her sister had literally walked in her footsteps, believing that her story was Allison's story, and vice versa. Allison hoped her younger sister would continue to follow in her footsteps and accept Jesus Christ as her Lord and Savior.[1]

Joshua wanted the people to follow his example and "serve the Lord." There was good reason for the people to respond and serve the Lord God. God was responsible for bringing the people to the promised land as Joshua reminded them, "for it is the Lord our God who brought us and our ancestors up from the land of Egypt, out of the house of slavery ..." And further, the Lord God, "protected us along all the way that we went."

The people had entered into a covenant relationship with God. One thing we have learned about covenants is that God always takes them seriously. They could not and would not be broken. The people were required to serve the Lord God and in return God would continue to be their God.

Kathleen Kolar was an experienced hiker, having hiked in several popular west coast locations. When visiting Hawaii, she decided to hike a trail that was a grueling eleven miles long. The trail has stream crossings, lava ridges, lush valleys, and 100-foot drop-offs to rocky beaches below.

The trek was everything Kathleen had heard — "difficult but spectacular." On her way back, she found herself a "little off trail." She wasn't concerned, all she would have to do is retrace her steps and she would be fine. She was sure the trail would loop around. She continued for a while before realizing that she was well off the trail — in other words, lost. She climbed a steep wall, which used to be a waterfall, hoping to once again find the trail. "It's just you and me, Lord," she prayed. "You alone can get me out of this mess."

Things went from bad to worse. She found herself on a small foot-and-a-half perch. She was horrified. It was then that Kathleen realized that she needed to stop so rescuers could find her. It was getting dark; she would have to spend the night on the perch. "I cried and was angry at myself for being so stupid."

The next morning, she felt God show her that this hike was similar to her life. She realized how at times her choices had led her away from God. And how those choices would affect her "further down life's path." "On that tiny ledge, I realized that if I were to truly live for God," she explains, "I would have to get to know him better." It took most of the day before anyone found her because of where she was. Unfortunately, the rescuers could not reach her. She would have to spend a second night on that ledge. "I was tired, thirsty, very sunburned and spent," she recalled.

Before she was rescued by a helicopter the next day, she felt God remind her of the two greatest commandments, love of God and love of neighbor. "I'd loved Jesus since I was eleven," she said, "but I hadn't yet surrendered my claim on my life. I was still going my own way. Those nights on the ledge, I determined to make knowing God's heart, thoughts, and purposes my passion in life." Another lesson she learned from her experience was that you cannot continue down a wrong path and remain untouched by the consequences. From now on Kathleen says, "I'm letting God lead — and following his path for my life."[2]

Joshua challenges us today asking what kind of people will we be and to whom will we commit ourselves? Commitment is one of those words that either makes us feel uncomfortable or something that we can easily dismiss as not all that important. While Jesus calls us to be faithful, the choice remains with us this day. In a sense it is a daily choice, a daily commitment, because there are so many things that deceive us, tempt us, and lead us astray. Choose the Lord. Amen.

---

1. Laurie Beth Jones, *Jesus Life Coach* (Nashville: Thomas Nelson Publishers, 2004), p. 260.

2. *Today's Christian Woman* magazine, July/August 2005, Vol. 27, No. 4, p. 22.

Proper 28
Pentecost 26
Ordinary Time 33
Judges 4:1-7

Reversal And Victory

"When God is going to do something wonderful," author Anne Lamott claims, "God always starts with a hardship; when God is going to do something amazing, God starts with an impossibility."[1] All of those ingredients are present in our lesson from the book of Judges. The people were experiencing a crisis, a time of great stress thinking doom was all but inevitable. The situation appeared hopeless and impossible until God raised up the right person to meet the challenge head on.

Time and time again, the ancient Israelites failed when they turned their backs against God. We see this pattern repeated throughout the books of Joshua and Judges. The people of old just did not seem to "get it" succumbing to the same mistakes over and over again. As our lesson opens we find that, "The Israelites again did what was evil in the sight of the Lord." We might ask why were the people doing what they knew was wrong. Why were they so susceptible to sin? Were the people so dense that they just did not understand that there were always consequences to our sins? God had done so much for the people leading them into the promised land. And the people repaid God by repeatedly doing what was "evil in the sight of the Lord."

The natural tendency for us is to frown upon the ancient Israelites who kept falling into the same old trap. It is easy to see this pattern when we look back, however it is more difficult to realize the problem when we are in the midst of a troubling situation. While we may not want to admit it, there are times when we, too, fail the Lord, and do what is evil in God's sight. We may have the best intentions but for some reason we sometimes fall short of what God requires from us.

Sisera was the man responsible for bringing stress and uncertainty. He had assembled quite an army including a seemingly invincible, "nine hundred chariots of iron." Sisera "had oppressed the Israelites cruelly for twenty years." It was a time of crisis, of uncertainty, which apparently brought out the worst in the people. Imagine for a moment what it must have felt like, waking up every morning knowing that a large army was waiting to attack you. Apparently, this stress led the people to do what was wrong in the sight of God. It might have been nothing more than a convenient excuse for sinning.

The people did what was evil and then cried out for divine help. And God in turn responded. Have you ever noticed that God has a way of choosing people that we might never pick? Throughout the pages of the Bible, we have discovered that God never called the qualified but rather qualified the called. God knew exactly what or in this case who was needed at any given moment.

Deborah was a judge in this time before the monarchy was established. She was the first woman judge. Her task was to settle disputes for the people. On most days, Deborah could be found under a palm tree "in the hill country" and it was there that "the Israelites came to her for judgment." The cultural mores of the time prohibited women from meeting with men indoors so Deborah had to move her office out under a palm tree to conduct business. Deborah was also a prophet transmitting the word of God. She held a unique position as both judge and prophet.

Out of her great love for God, Deborah was driven to do what was pleasing in God's sight. There is no telling how God might use our lives when we open ourselves to God. When we pray the Lord's Prayer we pray, "Thy will be done." The problem is that frequently we insist on doing things our own way, and when we do, we close ourselves off to God. Deborah's desire was to please God and allow God to use her in a mighty way. People respected this independent-minded, spirit-filled woman who spoke the word of the Lord.

The ranking military commander of the time was a man named Barak. Evidently, Barak did not have a problem with a woman judge or taking orders from one, for he went immediately to see Deborah after she sent for him. Deborah instructed him, "The Lord, the God of Israel, commands you, 'Go, take position at Mount Tabor, bringing ten thousand from the tribe of Naphtali and the tribe of Zebulun.' " The Lord God was about to act once again on behalf of the people. God was clearly in control of the situation. Deborah explained how God would draw out the enemy, Sisera, and promised, "I will give him into your hand." God promised to lure Sisera into a ravine thus giving the victory to the Israelites.

With such clear direction and promise of victory, one might have thought that Barak would set out without hesitation. And perhaps he might have. However, he had one request for Deborah. He asked that she accompany him and the troops. This was an unusual request. Some have suggested that maybe Barak was weak or unsure of himself. Others have maintained that Deborah's charismatic personality would inspire the soldiers in battle or maybe Barak was simply testing her commitment. Without faltering, Deborah agreed to go with him, assuring him of the victory, but noting that it would come at the hand of another woman, Jael. So much for Barak's male ego!

Deborah was not afraid to lead by example. She teaches us that leaders should be on the frontline, getting their hands dirty, not secluded in a safe location. Her love and trust of God was so great that she was willing to place her life on the line when needed.

Ronald Sisk remembers his first pastorate in rural Kentucky. The church possessed an old-fashioned belfry with a bell that could be rung by pulling on a rope. This fascinated him. In his mind, he envisioned ringing that bell every Sunday morning, calling the faithful to worship, and announcing faithful witness to the community at large. However, when he asked about the bell, he was told the sad tale that the bell had not been rung in years. "That bell keeps rusting, pastor," one of the men of the church explained, "the roof is high and steep and we can't get anybody to crawl up there and grease it."

Ron admits that he was both "young and stupid." One Saturday morning, he climbed the roof, crab crawling his way to the belfry with a can of grease. His wife stood on the ground thirty feet below holding a safety rope.

He got it greased and made it down safely. Several church members saw their new, young pastor on the roof of the church that day. By the next day, the new pastor's stunt was the talk of the congregation. Before church was over that morning, at least two members of the building and grounds committee made a point of telling their pastor, "You don't have to worry about that bell next time, pastor. That's our job." Ron proudly claimed, "We rang the bell every Sunday for the rest of my tenure with that congregation."[2]

Deborah's presence inspired the soldiers and the victory played out exactly as she had foretold. The menacing enemy was soundly defeated. Deborah composed and sang a hymn telling of this significant victory that is found in the next chapter, Judges 5. It is a poetic song of celebration commemorating this victory in rather graphic detail. Deborah, the Israelites' first woman judge, remained in her position for forty years and according to scripture, "The land had rest forty years." Deborah had accomplished the seemingly impossible.

God has an uncanny way of choosing the right person at the right time to bring about God's desires. When we surrender ourselves to God, we will find both meaning and purpose. Henrietta Mears taught college-age, single, young adults for decades at Hollywood Presbyterian Church. She became increasingly frustrated at not being able to give her students first-rate material, so she began a small publishing enterprise out of a garage. "The lessons were to be bold, challenging, and captivating as they underscored the principles of God's Word," Henrietta explained. Soon her venture grew into Gospel Light Publishers.

She searched for a retreat area where she could take her high school and college-aged students. "If you place people in an atmosphere where they feel close to God and then challenge them with His Word," she said, then "they will make decisions." She founded a retreat center where people could go to speak with God.

Frustrated at not having a good, single volume introduction to the Bible, Henrietta wrote one that sold hundreds of thousands of copies and continues to sell today decades after her death. Her words are still timely today, "God doesn't call us to sit on the sidelines and watch. He calls us to be on the field, playing the games." This remarkable, God-filled woman accomplished these things at a time when many people thought a woman had no business doing such things.[3]

God is at work in our lives and in our world, working with ordinary people to accomplish the seemingly impossible. God is at work even at those times when we are unaware of God's presence.

If only we knew in times of uncertainty which direction we should take. Unfortunately, we do not always know, but we do know that God is with us. God has an uncanny way of calling people we would never expect, and through these people, God's plan is accomplished. God does not call the qualified but rather qualifies the called. The book of Judges challenges our stereotypes and reverses our expectations. Our Lord Jesus calls us to follow him. At times we may not have a clear sense of where we are going, but we follow trusting the Lord to show us the right way. We follow knowing that there are times when we have to step out in faith into the unknown. We do so knowing that we do not go alone. Amen.

1. Anne Lamott, *Plan B: Further Thoughts on Faith* (New York: Riverhead Books, 2005), pp. 33-34.

2. Ronald Sisk, *The Competent Pastor* (Herndon, Virginia: The Alban Institute, 2005), p. 133.

3. John Ortberg, *If You Want to Walk on Water, You've got to Get Out of the Boat* (Grand Rapids: Zondervan, 2001), p. 88.

Christ The King
Proper 29
Ezekiel 34:11-16, 20-24

A Vision Of Hope

Difficult times not only try a person's soul but frequently force a person to step up to a new challenge. Perhaps this has been your experience: You are at a crossroad unsure of which direction to head, so you venture out blazing a new path. Later, when you look back you realize that particular experience was a turning point in your life. There may even be times when something unexpected happens that thrusts you in some new uncharted course. The people living in Ezekiel's day were living in exile, taken against their will living in a foreign land, Babylon. Hope was beginning to fade as a sense of doom overshadowed them. Ezekiel stepped up to the task and became a powerful voice offering the people a vision of hope. He emerged as one of the leaders of the exile and, like the prophets of old, told it as he saw it, which from time to time involved him in conflict but he persisted.

Imagine for a moment what it would have felt like to be taken from your home, to a foreign land against your will. You might have felt lost in the new place, the customs seemed so foreign. There were unfamiliar practices making it increasingly tough to hold on to your long-held beliefs. Parents would have a difficult task teaching their children what they believed when the alien culture kept creeping into their lives. The danger would be that people would lose sight of who they were amid all the outside influences. In such a situation you would look for someone who would assure you with words of comfort and hope that life would one day be better. That was exactly what Ezekiel did — he offered a word of hope. God heard the people's cries and was about to intervene in a dramatic way.

People living in the Sudan know firsthand what it feels like to live with the uncertainty of war. The country has been in a civil war for over twenty years with more than two million people killed. Yet, surprisingly, through this period the church has experienced phenomenal growth.

Bishop Daniel Bul of the Episcopal Church of Sudan claims that because people had nowhere to turn in that war-torn country, they turned to God. "This hard situation has really sharpened the eyes of the people, and the only place to turn is God," the bishop explains. He believes that, in spite of the war, God has been active. People gather outdoors to pray for those who are sick. "There is no food, there is no medicine, but when people gather and pray for a person who is sick, he gets healed," the bishop states. The result is that people turn to Christ. "There is no medicine, no anything at all. So you can see that it is only God who protects his church in the Sudan." The result is revival as the Holy Spirit moves among the people throughout the land.

No one living in Sudan could escape the threat of war. "But by the grace of God," Bishop Bul boldly claims, "we are alive. You don't know whether tomorrow you will be alive or not. So the threatening of physical (harm) is there because danger is everywhere in the southern Sudan. But we have a hope always that whether we die or we're alive, we glorify God. So we are not worried about what is going to happen, but we know that we are going to die like our brothers and sisters who have already gone before us."[1]

Living under such dangerous conditions is hard for most of us to comprehend. Perhaps what is most amazing is that the people feel a powerful sense of hope. God had not forgotten them.

The prophet Ezekiel tried to instill a similar sense of hope in the people living in exile. God had not forgotten them and would act in a dramatic fashion. God would lead the people like a shepherd caring for sheep. Ezekiel, speaking for the Lord God, assured the people, "I myself will search for my sheep, and will seek them out." Like a shepherd, God will actively search for the missing sheep. Even though the people felt as though they were forgotten, living in a foreign land, God still loved and cared for each one of them, like the good shepherd. "As shepherds seek out their flocks when they are among their scattered sheep, so I will seek out my sheep," was the word from God with the promise, "I will rescue them from all the places to which they have been scattered on a day of clouds and thick darkness." You can understand how these words gave the people a new sense of hope — God will "rescue them."

Within the people's collective memory was the story of the exodus, how God heard the cries of the oppressed people and intervened by leading them out of Egypt to the promised land. Ezekiel employed the same imagery. The time had come for God to act in a decisive way, "I will bring them out from the peoples and gather them from the countries, and will bring them into their own land...." What God was about to do would be greater than the first exodus. The people longed for a new day, when they could return to their home country. They would live with that sense of expectant hope.

Connie was going through a trying time in her life. The stress of unexpectedly losing her job while living in a rural community with limited opportunities added to her troubles. Friends expressed concern trying their best to comfort her but nothing seemed to help. "I felt an unshakable aloneness," Connie recalled, "even though I was trusting God as never before." She kept sinking deeper and deeper into despair.

One day while driving, an idea popped into her head. She needed a prayer partner to pray for her every day. She was uncertain which friend to ask — they were all busy with their lives. Then she remembered her college roommate. Though they lived in different parts of the country, they had kept in touch over the years via letters and email. Connie emailed Linda asking if she would be her prayer partner. "Yes," Linda replied, "I'll pray with you. Your message was timely. I've been thinking about you and how much I need you." Linda was going through a difficult time in her own life and needed someone outside of her immediate family and circle of friends to confide in. Linda would be glad to pray for her every day asking her old friend to also pray for her.

395

These two women connected, sending each other simple, heart-felt prayer requests each day. Each day they would pray for each other. "Though my circumstances remained unchanged," Connie shared, "it wasn't long before my burden began to feel lighter. Instead of turmoil, I now felt comfort and peace. My prayers began to reflect quiet rest in God's presence rather than preoccupation with my concerns."

After one month, Connie realized that "walking with God in the middle of the woods is more vital than finding a way out." With God she said, "We find stability, rest, and hope, no matter what path we're on." What seemed like a hopeless situation for Connie had turned into a blessing, a new sense of hope.[2]

There is more. The Lord God would pronounce judgment. Some previous leaders took unfair advantage of the people. Again, through the prophet Ezekiel, God tells the people, "I myself will judge between the fat sheep and the lean sheep." The leaders entrusted to care for the people did not pay attention to the "lean sheep," the weak and powerless. Apparently, their only concern was for themselves ignoring the pressing needs of widows and the poor. Israel's past shepherds failed; they exploited the people in order to care for themselves. With restoration those "fat sheep" will be held accountable for their actions or inactions. God will sort out those who disrupted the peace of the community. Justice would prevail one day soon.

God had not forgotten about the people living in exile. Like a shepherd, God would act to save the flock and bring about justice. Only God is able to save, we cannot save ourselves. For the first time in a long while the people regained a sense of hope — that their lives would soon improve.

Prophets spoke from the heart, telling of future events that would instill a deep sense of hope in the people. Our lesson ends with the promise, "I will set up over them one shepherd, my servant David and he shall feed them: he shall feed them and be their shepherd." The people fondly remembered the reign of King David as the good old days to which they longed to return. David's reign brought about many positive changes and was viewed by many as an almost idyllic time. It had been nearly 400 years since the time of David. The promise that God would send a new leader, a new shepherd in the line of David, filled the people with expectant hope. The new shepherd would love and care for the sheep and would not desert them in the face of danger.

Even though the people living in exile were scattered, the day would come when God would act, and they would return to their home together. The appeal of returning home struck a cord with the people living in exile. There under the care of a shepherd they would feel safe and secure. Ezekiel gave the people a much needed dose of hope, but he wanted them to know that it was God who would ultimately save them.

One of the most enduring images of our Christian faith is of Jesus as the Good Shepherd. Many churches have beautiful stained-glass windows portraying Jesus as the Good Shepherd caring for the sheep. In addition, there are works of art depicting Jesus caring for a lost sheep. Such images are comforting to us, especially in times of stress. Jesus loves the sheep so much that he is willing to lay down his life.

Could it be the hectic pace of our modern lives that makes the notion of sheep and shepherds so appealing to us? Maybe deep down we long for the simpler days of green pastures and sheep although most of us no longer have direct contact with either sheep or shepherds.

Jesus defines his mission as one of a shepherd, "I am the good shepherd," Jesus teaches. "The good shepherd lays down his life for the sheep" (John 10:11). Jesus rejects the notion of being a political ruler but instead repeatedly employs the gentle image of a caring shepherd. The relationship between sheep and shepherd is so strong and personal that, "the sheep follow him because they know his voice," Jesus claims. The sheep respond to the voice of the shepherd and follow. "I am the good shepherd. I know my own and my own know me," Jesus says (John 10:14).

Today we celebrate Christ the King Sunday as we conclude the Christian year. We look to Jesus as the Good Shepherd who loves and cares for us and who will one day return in glory. Amen.

1. Stan Guthrie, "Hope Amid the Ruins," *Christianity Today*, January 2004.

2. Constance Fink, "You've Got Prayer," *Today's Christian Woman*, July/August 2005, Vol. 27, No. 4, p. 34.

Not All Of This Is Me

It was certainly a treat for four-year-old Tara to go shopping with her grandfather one day at the mall. Tara had many things to tell her grandfather as they went from store to store. At one point, as Tara was high upon her grandfather's shoulders, a family friend stopped to talk with them. "My, you are getting to be such a big girl," the friend remarked. With the innocence that only a child can muster she replied, "Not all of this is me!" Sometimes children are our greatest teachers without even knowing it.

Every Thanksgiving provides us an opportunity to reflect on the many blessings God has given us realizing that "not all of this is me." We pause to count our many blessings "one by one" as the hymn suggests. We could never have come this far without the grace and love of God.

"Not all of this is me" becomes a statement of faith. God is the source of life and everything we have. Without the love of God we would be nothing and have nothing. The constant temptation is to look around and think that everything we are and everything we have is a result of our own doing, our own smarts, or ingenuity. We live in a world where people live as though they are the only ones who are responsible for their achievements. It is easy to get puffed up, highlighting our jobs and promotions, the neighborhoods where we live, the cars we drive, the vacations we take and many, many other things. Do not fall into that trap this Thanksgiving as we acknowledge that God is behind all that we are and have. We are a people of faith. We belong to God. We depend on God's grace for all that we are and all that we have.

The ancient Israelites were nearing the end of their forty-year sojourn through the wilderness. There had been some anxious moments as the people fled the Egyptians and journeyed into the unknown. The forty-year journey was at times extremely difficult. Early on, the people complained about not having enough food to eat. God provided for their needs, as manna, or bread, showered down from heaven. Each morning, the people ate their fill of the bread from heaven. When the people grumbled about not having meat to eat, God sent quail for them to feast on. At another point, the people were thirsty and God instructed Moses to strike a rock with his rod. The result was that enough water flowed for all the people and even their livestock to drink. These experiences taught the people to trust God, God would continue to provide for all their needs. Imagine wearing the same garments for forty years without them wearing out. Never once did the people have blisters on their feet. God would see them through to the promised land.

As our lesson from Deuteronomy opens, the people were on the boundary about to cross over to the promised land. This was the end of the journey for Moses who would not cross over into the land, "a good land, a land with flowing streams, with springs and underground waters welling up in valleys and hills, a land of wheat and barley, of vines and fig trees and pomegranates, a land of olive trees and honey...." Earlier, Moses had disobeyed God and was told he would see the promised land but not enter it. On this occasion, Moses was reminding the people of their long journey and all that they learned along the way. He contrasted the barren wilderness where they had just spent forty years with where they were going, "A land where you may eat bread without scarcity, where you will lack nothing." Not only would there be plenty of food to eat, but also the ground was rich in mineral deposits. The people would have everything they would need to live prosperous lives.

Since Moses would not enter the promised land with them he wanted to be certain that the people understood where these blessings had come from — the Lord God. They were about to enter the promised land not because of their own abilities, but as a direct result of God fulfilling past promises.

Moses wanted the people to remember and never forget their journey through the wilderness and how God provided for all their needs. "Take care that you do not forget the Lord your God, by failing to keep his commandments, his ordinances, and his statutes, which I am commanding you today." The message Moses wanted them to grasp was not to forget God and assume that they had brought themselves into the promised land.

It is a natural human response to look to God for help in times of trouble. It is easy to forget or neglect God when everything is going well. The temptation is to assume that when everything is going fine, we do not need God or that God can do nothing for us. We erroneously tell ourselves we are the ones who provide for our needs; we no longer need God because we can do it all ourselves. This simply is not true. God is the source of all life and all blessings.

God would provide for the people and they would have abundance. Having surplus always seems to get people into trouble. Dot Jackson is a newspaper columnist who wrote one Thanksgiving, "Enough was a roof that didn't leak. Plenty of chairs on the porch, and at the table ... Enough was food and safety from the elements ... enough was a little help for a friend in need and debt to no one. There is something perverse about more than enough. When we have more, we never have enough. It's always somewhere out there, just out of reach. The more we acquire, the more elusive enough becomes." In our materialistic world, we never seem to have enough, we always want more, we never seem to be satisfied.

The question for us to ponder this Thanksgiving is, "How can we remain faithful when we have so much?" Most of us do not live in life-threatening situations; we never go to bed hungry, and there is plenty of food in our refrigerator. We have fresh fruits and vegetables in the middle of winter. Our closets are overflowing with clothing and all sorts of other stuff. Prosperous people might forget the gift giver and think everything they have is a direct result of their labor. Moses was aware of this problem as he addressed the people, "When you have eaten your fill and have built fine houses and live in them, and when your herds and flocks have multiplied, and your silver and gold is multiplied, and all that you have is multiplied, then do not exalt yourself, forgetting the Lord your God, who brought you out of the land of Egypt...." Remember, do not forget.

The ancient Israelites were instructed to remember their forty-year trek and never forget their experience. We remember past Thanksgivings, perhaps when we did not have as many blessings as we do today. Have you ever noticed that we often learn the most enduring lessons from periods of struggle?

One day, Tom Maddox was cleaning out his desk when he came across a picture he had not seen for a long time. The picture showed a family Thanksgiving when he was a child. In the picture, his grandfather was about to say the blessing. Tom noticed all his cousins had folded their hands just like their grandfather. Looking at the picture, Tom recalled all the wonderful Thanksgivings he spent at his grandparents' home. "Never in my life," Tom said, "have I ever tasted such wonderful food!"

He remembered the faith of his grandparents. There was more to Thanksgiving than physical food. There was a spiritual food as well. Before the family ate, his grandfather always read from the Bible. He would discuss the passage of scripture with his children and grandchildren at the table, and then he would fold his hands to pray. His prayer was a reverent, "God, thank you for the food." "Grandfather never said a long blessing," Tom reflected, "but somehow I always felt the sincerity of his thankfulness."

"Looking at this picture of my cousins with their hands folded and heads bowed," Tom said, "I realized the importance of passing down a tradition of thankfulness to God expressed in simple, reverent ways."

What is the message we are passing down to our children and grandchildren this Thanksgiving? Sometimes we need reminders of our many blessings. Linda tells of one Thanksgiving day, when she was 3,000 miles away from home without any family or friends to share the holiday. Linda called a downtown soup kitchen to volunteer her time to help serve Thanksgiving meals for struggling families as well as area homeless. She was pleased. She had something important and useful to do.

On Thanksgiving day, when Linda arrived at the soup kitchen there was already a long line of helpers. The gentleman in charge of the volunteers told her that they had far too many volunteers and did not need her. It never happened before, he explained, but with an ad on the radio, over 200 people volunteered. The gentleman invited Linda to stay for the meal. Linda, by her own admission, had very little contact with homeless people and truthfully had no desire to eat with them. She got in line to eat, still feeling that she did not belong. "Happy Thanksgiving, and God bless you, darling," a man told her as he handed her a plastic cup of apple juice and a corn muffin.

Linda found a seat. A man introduced himself, telling her he was an alcoholic "on the road back." "That's nice," Linda politely answered. Then a pregnant woman, somehow managing to hold a toddler as well as two plates of food, slid into the end seat. "It's nice to sit down," she said. "You know how it is — this is the first time I've been able to eat in peace in days!" Linda offered to feed her toddler so the woman could enjoy her meal. There was a father and son further down the table. She overheard the boy say, "Daddy! Mmmmm! I like this food!" The father explained that they hadn't had much to eat for several days.

The more Linda spoke with these people the more she realized they were not all that different from her. "The only barrier separating us had been the one I erected myself — my unwillingness to see these people as what they were: people." Linda realized how many blessings she had taken for granted. This experience opened new doors for Linda.

May the words from scripture be words for us as we celebrate Thanksgiving day. "Do not say to yourself, 'My power and the might of my own hand have gotten me this wealth.' But remember the Lord your God, for it is he who gives you power...." We give thanks remembering, "Not all of this is me." God has had and continues to have a hand in our lives. Amen.

403

Lectionary Preaching After Pentecost

The following index will aid the user of this book in matching the correct Sunday with the appropriate text during Pentecost. All texts in this book are from the series for the first readings, Revised Common Lectionary. (Note that the ELCA division of Lutheranism is now following the Revised Common Lectionary.) The Lutheran designations indicate days comparable to Sundays on which Revised Common Lectionary Propers or Ordinary Time designations are used.

(Fixed dates do not pertain to Lutheran Lectionary)

Fixed Date Lectionaries *Revised Common (including ELCA)* *and Roman Catholic*	**Lutheran Lectionary** *Lutheran*
The Day Of Pentecost	The Day Of Pentecost
The Holy Trinity	The Holy Trinity
May 29-June 4 — Proper 4, Ordinary Time 9	Pentecost 2
June 5-11 — Proper 5, Ordinary Time 10	Pentecost 3
June 12-18 — Proper 6, Ordinary Time 11	Pentecost 4
June 19-25 — Proper 7, Ordinary Time 12	Pentecost 5
June 26-July 2 — Proper 8, Ordinary Time 13	Pentecost 6
July 3-9 — Proper 9, Ordinary Time 14	Pentecost 7
July 10-16 — Proper 10, Ordinary Time 15	Pentecost 8
July 17-23 — Proper 11, Ordinary Time 16	Pentecost 9
July 24-30 — Proper 12, Ordinary Time 17	Pentecost 10
July 31-Aug. 6 — Proper 13, Ordinary Time 18	Pentecost 11
Aug. 7-13 — Proper 14, Ordinary Time 19	Pentecost 12
Aug. 14-20 — Proper 15, Ordinary Time 20	Pentecost 13
Aug. 21-27 — Proper 16, Ordinary Time 21	Pentecost 14
Aug. 28-Sept. 3 — Proper 17, Ordinary Time 22	Pentecost 15
Sept. 4-10 — Proper 18, Ordinary Time 23	Pentecost 16
Sept. 11-17 — Proper 19, Ordinary Time 24	Pentecost 17
Sept. 18-24 — Proper 20, Ordinary Time 25	Pentecost 18

Sept. 25-Oct. 1 — Proper 21, Ordinary Time 26	Pentecost 19
Oct. 2-8 — Proper 22, Ordinary Time 27	Pentecost 20
Oct. 9-15 — Proper 23, Ordinary Time 28	Pentecost 21
Oct. 16-22 — Proper 24, Ordinary Time 29	Pentecost 22
Oct. 23-29 — Proper 25, Ordinary Time 30	Pentecost 23
Oct. 30-Nov. 5 — Proper 26, Ordinary Time 31	Pentecost 24
Nov. 6-12 — Proper 27, Ordinary Time 32	Pentecost 25
Nov. 13-19 — Proper 28, Ordinary Time 33	Pentecost 26
	Pentecost 27
Nov. 20-26 — Christ The King	Christ The King

Reformation Day (or last Sunday in October) is October 31 (Revised Common, Lutheran)

All Saints (or first Sunday in November) is November 1 (Revised Common, Lutheran, Roman Catholic)

US/Canadian Lectionary Comparison

The following index shows the correlation between the Sundays and special days of the church year as they are titled or labeled in the Revised Common Lectionary published by the Consultation On Common Texts and used in the United States (the reference used for this book) and the Sundays and special days of the church year as they are titled or labeled in the Revised Common Lectionary used in Canada.

Revised Common Lectionary	Canadian Revised Common Lectionary
Advent 1	Advent 1
Advent 2	Advent 2
Advent 3	Advent 3
Advent 4	Advent 4
Christmas Eve	Christmas Eve
The Nativity Of Our Lord/ Christmas Day	The Nativity Of Our Lord
Christmas 1	Christmas 1
January 1/New Year's Day	January 1/The Name Of Jesus
Christmas 2	Christmas 2
The Epiphany Of Our Lord	The Epiphany Of Our Lord
The Baptism Of Our Lord/ Epiphany 1	The Baptism Of Our Lord/ Proper 1
Epiphany 2/Ordinary Time 2	Epiphany 2/Proper 2
Epiphany 3/Ordinary Time 3	Epiphany 3/Proper 3
Epiphany 4/Ordinary Time 4	Epiphany 4/Proper 4
Epiphany 5/Ordinary Time 5	Epiphany 5/Proper 5
Epiphany 6/Ordinary Time 6	Epiphany 6/Proper 6
Epiphany 7/Ordinary Time 7	Epiphany 7/Proper 7
Epiphany 8/Ordinary Time 8	Epiphany 8/Proper 8
The Transfiguration Of Our Lord/ Last Sunday After Epiphany	The Transfiguration Of Our Lord/ Last Sunday After Epiphany
Ash Wednesday	Ash Wednesday
Lent 1	Lent 1
Lent 2	Lent 2
Lent 3	Lent 3
Lent 4	Lent 4
Lent 5	Lent 5
Passion/Palm Sunday	Passion/Palm Sunday
Maundy Thursday	Holy/Maundy Thursday
Good Friday	Good Friday

Easter Day	The Resurrection Of Our Lord
Easter 2	Easter 2
Easter 3	Easter 3
Easter 4	Easter 4
Easter 5	Easter 5
Easter 6	Easter 6
The Ascension Of Our Lord	The Ascension Of Our Lord
Easter 7	Easter 7
The Day Of Pentecost	The Day Of Pentecost
The Holy Trinity	The Holy Trinity
Proper 4/Pentecost 2/O T 9*	Proper 9
Proper 5/Pent 3/O T 10	Proper 10
Proper 6/Pent 4/O T 11	Proper 11
Proper 7/Pent 5/O T 12	Proper 12
Proper 8/Pent 6/O T 13	Proper 13
Proper 9/Pent 7/O T 14	Proper 14
Proper 10/Pent 8/O T 15	Proper 15
Proper 11/Pent 9/O T 16	Proper 16
Proper 12/Pent 10/O T 17	Proper 17
Proper 13/Pent 11/O T 18	Proper 18
Proper 14/Pent 12/O T 19	Proper 19
Proper 15/Pent 13/O T 20	Proper 20
Proper 16/Pent 14/O T 21	Proper 21
Proper 17/Pent 15/O T 22	Proper 22
Proper 18/Pent 16/O T 23	Proper 23
Proper 19/Pent 17/O T 24	Proper 24
Proper 20/Pent 18/O T 25	Proper 25
Proper 21/Pent 19/O T 26	Proper 26
Proper 22/Pent 20/O T 27	Proper 27
Proper 23/Pent 21/O T 28	Proper 28
Proper 24/Pent 22/O T 29	Proper 29
Proper 25/Pent 23/O T 30	Proper 30
Proper 26/Pent 24/O T 31	Proper 31
Proper 27/Pent 25/O T 32	Proper 32
Proper 28/Pent 26/O T 33	Proper 33
Christ The King (Proper 29/O T 34)	Proper 34/Christ The King/ Reign Of Christ
Reformation Day (October 31)	Reformation Day (October 31)
All Saints (November 1 or 1st Sunday in November)	All Saints' Day (November 1)
Thanksgiving Day (4th Thursday of November)	Thanksgiving Day (2nd Monday of October)

*O T = Ordinary Time

About The Authors

Tony S. Everett is currently the Dewey F. Beam Professor of Pastoral Care at Lutheran Theological Southern Seminary in Columbia, South Carolina, where he also consults with congregations in spiritual growth, leadership training, and conflict management. Everett previously served in the parish ministry in Ohio and Massachusetts, and during his teaching ministry he has served as an interim pastor for numerous congregations. He has also directed a community health center in Angola, New York. Everett has written pastoral care articles for *The Clergy Journal* and daily devotions for *Christ in Our Homes* (Fortress Press), and he is the author of *Where Is God in All This?* (CSS). Everett is a graduate of Youngstown State University (*summa cum laude*), Hamma School of Theology, and Boston University School of Theology.

Schuyler Rhodes is the pastor of Temple United Methodist Church in San Francisco, California. Prior to that he was the executive director of the Wesley Foundation, a broad-based campus ministry at the University of California, Berkeley. Rhodes has served as a delegate to several consultations of the World Council of Churches, secretary of the Social and International Affairs Committee of the World Methodist Council, and chair of the board of directors for Pastors for Peace and the Interreligious Foundation for Community Organizing. He has also been a consultant on Peace and Justice Ministries for the United Methodist Church's General Board of Global Ministries. A prolific writer, Rhodes is currently the "Preaching the Psalms" columnist for the preaching journal *Emphasis* (www.sermonsuite.com). He is an honors graduate of the State University of New York at Potsdam and Drew University Theological School.

Stan Purdum is the pastor of Centenary United Methodist Church in Waynesburg, Ohio. He has served as the editor for the preaching journals *Emphasis* and *Homiletics*, and has written extensively for both the religious and secular press. Purdum is the author of *New Mercies I See* (CSS) and *He Walked in Galilee* (Abingdon Press), as well as two accounts of long-distance bicycle journeys, *Roll Around Heaven All Day* and *Playing in Traffic*. Stan is a graduate of Youngstown State University, Methodist Theological School in Ohio, and Drew University Theological School.

David J. Kalas is the pastor of First United Methodist Church in Whitewater, Wisconsin. Prior to moving to Wisconsin in 1996, he served for fifteen years in youth and pastoral ministries in Virginia and Ohio. Kalas is a graduate of the University of Virginia and Union Theological Seminary of Virginia.

Timothy J. Smith is currently the senior pastor of First United Methodist Church in Millersville, Pennsylvania, and he has served several other congregations in eastern Pennsylvania during the past two decades. Over 100 of Smith's sermons have been published in the periodical *Dynamic Preaching*, and he is the author of the CSS titles *No Particular Place To Go* and *Lectionary Tales for the Pulpit* (Series II, Cycle A), as well as a contributing author to *Sermons on the First Readings* (Series I, Cycle B). Smith received his M.Div. degree with an emphasis on preaching and worship from United Theological Seminary and his B.A. degree in American history from Millersville University.